BUILDING THE TIMBER FRAME HOUSE

BUILDING THE TIMBER FRAME HOUSE

THE REVIVAL OF A FORGOTTEN CRAFT

Tedd Benson

with
James Gruber

Illustrations by Jamie Page

CHARLES SCRIBNER'S SONS
NEW YORK

Copyright © 1980 James Gruber and Tedd Benson

Library of Congress Cataloging in Publication Data

Benson, Tedd.
  Building the timber frame house.
  Bibliography: p. 210
  1. Wooden-frame houses. 2. House construction.
I. Gruber, James, joint author. II. Title.
TH4818.W6B46   694'.2   79-22535
ISBN 684-17286-0 (paper)
ISBN 684-16446-9 (cloth)

    5 7 9 11 13 15 17 19 Q/P 20 18 16 14 12 10 8 6 4

Printed in the United States of America

Book design by Elaine Golt Gongora

Specified material from *A Vanished World* by Anne G. Sneller, 1964. Reprinted by permission of Syracuse University Press, Syracuse, New York.

Specified material from "Nick Lindsay," *Working: People Talk About What They Do All Day and How They Feel About What They Do.* Copyright © 1974 by Studs Terkel. Reprinted by permission of Pantheon Books, a division of Random House, Inc., New York.

To "the boys in the beamery"—
Tim Ballantine
Tim Benson
Tom Goldschmid
Chris Madigan
Tom Page
Peter White
Their dedication, skill,
and enthusiasm
made this book possible.

ACKNOWLEDGMENTS

For their generous assistance in the preparation of this book, we are indebted to a number of people: For his sensitive and thoroughly professional editing, we thank our friend and neighbor, Mr. Fredrick E. Ulen. Photographer Tafi Brown and artist Jamie Page gave us much more than their considerable talents; we'd like to thank them for continually lifting us with their bright spirits. We are grateful to Mrs. Betty Prentiss, our typist, who never complained about the chaos; to Mary Haldane Chapman, for making her library available; to engineer John F. Kennedy, for reviewing the structural data; and to the late Caesar Parma for his computer assistance to generate the beam-design tables.

Special thanks also go to all who have employed our services. It has been a privilege to work with so many good people.

CONTENTS

PREFACE

Timber framing is as old and as full of history as the story of architecture in wood itself. As a building technique, timber framing survived through the centuries on the sound principle that it provided exceedingly durable shelter. It is being revived today because we know it does that and more: the frame can also be an effective part of the design and finish work, and is the appropriate type of framework for the application of an energy-efficient insulating skin. With these advantages, the timber-framed house, hand worked and fastened with wooden pegs, need not cost any more than homes built by conventional means.

Although the craft of joining timbers is just taking hold, there is already a widespread awareness of the subtle impact of exposed timbers in living areas of the house. Any copy of the popular home-decorating and remodeling magazines demonstrates the renewed attraction of timbers. In most instances, these timbers were applied to a completed structure only for decoration. A better understanding of the implied potential would have called for the timbers to be both the structure and the decoration. This technique also would have been cheaper.

Working with timbers offers the opportunity to be close to the material, to be challenged by the temperamental personality of wood, and to have the feeling of satisfaction that comes from having kept the mind and the hands equally busy. This kind of total involvement is the trademark of the new generation of carpenters and of many who choose to build their own homes.

This new force of home builders is possessed of considerable skill and fired with enough energy to bring the carpentry trade out of the doldrums. These carpenters will not be satisfied with attaching plywood and driving nails. They yearn to work with wood. Through timber framing, they can hope, once again, to see the building of homes as an execution of woodworking skills.

PART I: THE PAST

CHAPTER ONE
WITH BROADAXE AND ADZE
A LOOK BACK

Courtesy of Chris Madigan

This carries us back to the time of the building of our old home, now more than fifty-five years ago; though only a lad we remember the time the trees were being felled in the forest and, after a long wait for the timbers to be squared, they were hauled to the building site, and, after a time for them to season, the carpenters came and, as though but yesterday, we see them under the old apple trees astride the timbers with auger, chisel and mallet working away from morn till night. . . . Those were days of toil, days of contentment and peace.

—Radford: *Audels Carpenters and Builders Guide*, 1923

ACCORDING to Jacob Bronowski,* a turning point for man began when he developed the capacity and summoned the will to cut and to split materials to form his structures. It was the difference between aggressively probing the structure of elements and passively submitting to their raw forms. In this difference was a seed of curiosity and adventure that burst, and with it,

the mind of man expanded, for the growth of the intellect and the constructive work of the hands are the stalk and root of civilization. Before the Iron Age, homes were merely crude shelter; only slightly removed from other species, man was resigned to digging into the earth or fashioning huts with woven twigs and branches. He lived in burrows and nests, not homes. But when iron was finally wrested from stone and tools were formed, man was able to step out of his primitive past, out of the nests and pits, and into struc-

_____
* See References, page 210

1

TATEANA DWELLING,
JAPAN
C. NEOLITHIC

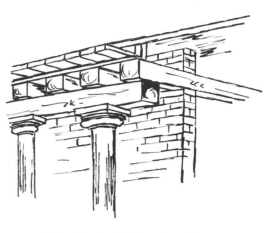

GREEK TEMPLE
C. 500 B.C.

tures that would begin to reflect and to support his bold destiny.

The first sharpened tools were probably directed toward the shaping of a most fundamental building material—wood. It was readily available, easily worked, and had already proven itself to be strong in earlier kinds of structures. So, timbers—the building unit closest to the tree itself—were the immediate choice for buildings that would now rise above the ground and start to show signs of permanence. What were built with those early tools and crudely shaped timbers were no longer just shelters but homes. They were now durable enough and functional enough to keep people settled in one area. This, in Kenneth Clark's definition, was the beginning of civilization. It was also the beginning of a building system so primal and basic that it would find its way into the development of many cultures in all parts of the world, yet so formidable and subtle that it would avoid mastery for many centuries.

If we mark the start of timber-frame construction with the fashioning of the first joints, it began around 200 B.C. Archaeological studies show that this development was simultaneous in the Far East and in Europe. And in both cases, the shapes of the first timber buildings had descended from earlier huts formed by lashing poles together over shallow pits. These huts had evolved into elongated rectangular structures with repeated central supports forming a series of bays. With a few modifications, this was a system perfectly suited to the joining of timbers, and it continues to be the fundamental design principle for timber-framed buildings today.

Right from the start, man showed an affinity to working with wood, to building with timbers. The individuality and the variety of wood maintained his curiosity; its humble acquiescence to his simple tools gave him satisfaction. Between the walls of these substantial buildings, there was security enough to release the caged and dormant portions of the mind. Therefore, greatly dependent on his construction methods, man sprinted into the future, falling many times in pursuit of an obscure goal. The development of timber framing, then, closely followed the rise and fall of numerous civilizations. There will not be an attempt here to encompass that history; it would fail and also miss the point of this book. Instead, we'll glance back and try to develop a feel for the full and sturdy past that forms the reference for our work with timbers today.

Though the origins of timber framing were early in the history of man, they were not necessarily primitive in form. Some of the greatly admired stone temples of Greece once stood as a similar network of carefully arranged and simply joined timbers. An historian in the second century A.D. wrote that

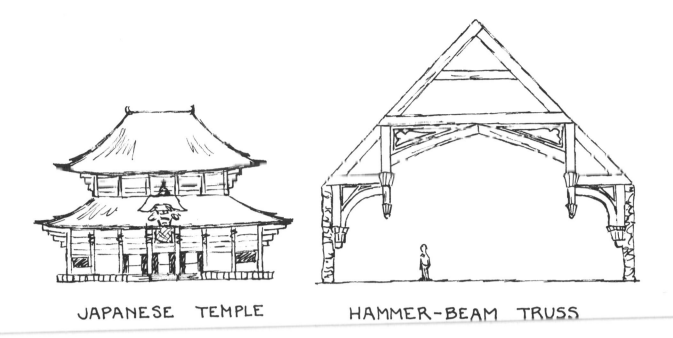

JAPANESE TEMPLE   HAMMER-BEAM TRUSS

Heraion at Olympia had one remaining wood column, the last of forty to be replaced with stone. When stone took the place of the wood that preceded it, the architecture necessarily became more massive, more monumental, in order to support the weight and reduce the spans of beams that were heavy and strong but not resilient. Because of their flexibility, wooden beams were able to make longer spans and columns didn't need to be so large. Perhaps this is why the vase painters of classical Greece depicted buildings much more airy and graceful than the stone structures that actually existed.

Farther east, in India, the same pattern was repeated—stone buildings having been the monumental duplicates of their wooden predecessors. With the help of this relationship, archaeologists have dated Indian timber-frame construction to 200 B.C. Timbers were shaped from teak and connected with simple joinery and bamboo pegs. But there was nothing primitive about the richly ornate and highly refined buildings that are believed to have been built with these simple methods.

During this same period, the craft of joining timbers was beginning to flower in another Eastern country—Japan. The Japanese, too, were putting their finest efforts toward the building of shrines and temples. But these were not destined to be replaced with stone. Japan has a history of being sub-

jected to typhoons and earthquakes, and the builders quickly discovered that there were distinct advantages to the fibrous timbers and the hingelike joints that connected them. If a building constructed from stone or brick wiggles a bit, it will crack or break; if made of timbers, it only shrugs. So the Japanese carpenters dedicated themselves to finding the answers to the mysteries of working timbers. By the sixth century, with the help of immigrant Chinese Buddhists, their achievements in wooden structures were unrivaled. In 679 the Golden Hall was built, and in 693 the Pagoda. They both still stand, the oldest surviving wooden structures in the world.

If Japanese carpentry was highly evolved, it was also fiercely competitive. The craft was developed within a family guild system that maintained tight security over construction techniques and strict authority concerning procedure among its members. Intense rivalry between the two major guilds had the positive effect of keeping the standards high; a languid or sloppy attitude could not be tolerated in the heat of contest. But in the attempt to outdo one another, these guilds often produced joints much more puzzling than they were effective. Still, they developed over four hundred joints, and many are still in use today. Japanese tradition has also given modern carpenters a special appreciation for their tools. The word that describes them, *Dōgu*, translates to "the

3

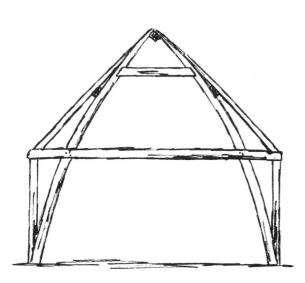

ENGLISH CRUCK   ENGLISH BOX FRAME

instruments of the way." Because Japanese carpenters are aware of all that has been accomplished with these instruments, they remain reluctant to relegate them to mere tools.

Closer to our own roots, in Europe, the evolution of timber framing was slower to mature, but when it came of age, it showed elements of sophistication and refinement previously unknown. As in Japan, there were well-organized and powerful guilds that maintained uniform high standards. But they were singular and without rivalry. Absent was the disparity from competition, and because of it there was unity and a bent toward the utilitarian. In that light, European craftsmen were able to discover the simple answers to seemingly complex problems. These were the people who built graceful roof trusses able to span sixty feet or more, entirely constructed of short timbers. And they were the ones who fashioned the vaulted ceilings so famous in the magnificent cathedrals. They found ways to use angled braces not only for stability but also for ornament. When the upper class demanded extravagance, they received ornately carved embellishments in timbers joined in complex patterns, fit even for the most fastidious of lords.

But in timber framing's humble beginnings, there was no adornment; there was only a naturally curved tree, split length-wise, with the halves inclined toward each other and joined at the peak. That was a "cruck" (see Glossary). When two or more of these crucks were connected, they formed a primitive frame. In a later refinement, a crossbeam was used to brace them and walls were built from the ends of the crossbeams to the base of the cruck. Finally, for lack of suitably bent trees, vertical posts were added and the cruck was reduced to simple rafters. Since it was no longer curved like a cruck (from *crook*), this new refinement was called a box frame. The simple elements of this box frame have been the basis for almost all the timber-framed structures that have followed.

The Norsemen, from northern Europe, were among those influenced by these developments. During the Viking era, they brought home some knowledge of the construction work being done by the English and French. When they combined this knowledge with their own ingenious shipbuilding skills, they were soon building lofty timber-framed sanctuaries—monumental and difficult. In building these famous "stave churches," which numbered over seven hundred at one time, many construction problems were solved. From the twenty-five still standing, we can see how they rise in a tier effect, with a central roof surrounded by narrower, lean-to roof surfaces and topped with towers. The result is impressive.

4

Courtesy of Chris Mulligan

EARLY COLONIAL BENT
c. 1600-1700

To make the open frames livable buildings, carpenters and masons in other European countries and the British Isles commonly filled in between the timbers with bricks, plaster, or a plaster-and-stick composite called wattle and daub. This system would seem to offer almost no merit: the infilling was heavy, putting undue stresses on the frame; and brick and plaster have almost no insulation value. With every sigh or sag in a constantly shifting and breathing frame, there would be a new crack to fill; furthermore, the posts and beams of the structure itself were subjected daily to the ravages of the weather. Despite these shortcomings, the English Tudor buildings and the French manor houses, so constructed, are revered around the world as models of architectural elegance. And, truly, the white filling behind the dark frame produces clean lines and appealing contrast.

When the first European colonists set foot in the New World, they took a step backward in time. The wealth of virgin resources was spread resplendent before their eyes, but the fruitful rewards lay beyond the walls created by their lack of tools and skill and the bitter reality of a harsh New England winter. Immediate shelter was desperately needed; those who struggled through the ravages of the first few winters made their stand from crude pits covered with thatch and turf. Therefore, the history of timber framing in this country repeated the entire history of the craft from its Iron Age origins.

The experience of the first few winters was costly and cruel for many settlers, but through it they learned important lessons about the New World; more important, they learned to appreciate their own ability to adapt and experiment. In a sense, it helped them to sever their bonds with the Old World. Therefore, as timber framing developed in this country, those who practiced it naturally reached back to the mother countries for the age-old guidelines, but they took only what was needed and then moved in separate directions.

From humble origins, and with no kings or lords to please, the colonists first cleaned from the frames most of the embellishments, of which they had no need. Before they left England, they might have witnessed the impasse of the master joiners, who had so completely mastered the wooden joining methods that the only challenges that remained were those of adornment. In this, the joiners were in a frustrating and losing battle with those who molded plaster. The pragmatic American craftsmen turned from that and sought instead the subtle beauty of simple shapes and lines.

Although the first colonists came from England, others followed from France, Germany, Holland, and Scandinavia. With them they brought traditions, opinions, and infor-

5

OLD SHIP MEETING HOUSE
HINGHAM, MASS.
1681

mation about building methods that were tossed into the melting pot and gently affected the state of the whole. Most of the timber framing done here could not be said to have originated from this or that country. It was a blend, and peculiarly American.

Mainly, American timber framing achieved its own form because North American conditions were so different from those in Europe. In the virgin forests of New England, trees of great length and breadth were commonplace. There was hardly a timber for any building that could not be hewn from a single tree; the need for the sophisticated joining methods to splice timbers lengthwise had almost been eliminated. Another factor was that the temperature variation in America was so great (110° F. average between high and low readings in Plymouth, Massachusetts, as opposed to 63° F. in Plymouth, England) that filling between the timbers with masonry produced very drafty

results; sheathing skins had to be attached over the frames to protect both the timbers and the inhabitants.

The emerging new country enjoyed another special attribute that was a significant, if subtle, factor in the development of timber framing. There was a spirit of cooperation and neighborliness that would bring whole communities together for the purpose of helping one family raise their building. The timber-framing system was quickly modified so that large units could be preassembled, and the building could be easily erected in a day.

The spirit of community and goodwill was the ultimate variable. Massive frames could now be built by the average man for common purposes. Barns and houses sprouted in the towns and in the country; wherever men and women were willing to work toward dreams, there was vigor enough in the land, in the forests, and in the people to make them real.

6

CHAPTER TWO
STRUCTURES for TODAY
Timbers and Frames

The massive framing of our early houses is a thing to delight anyone possessed of the smallest amount of architectural sense. A feeling of boundless strength, of security and steadfastness, as well as a notable kind of dignity, is inseparable from the ponderous timbers which go to make up these mighty frames.

—J. Frederick Kelly: *Early Domestic Architecture of Connecticut*, 1963

THE loss of timber framing as the dominant building system in this country was simultaneous with the loss of the human element in almost everything. The swiftness of the movement westward and the pace of industrialization seemed to demand a different attitude toward work. At the same time that the needs of a quickly changing world were being provided with ever greater efficiency, a distance began to develop between us and our environment. We flexed our muscles, and like the working of some miracle drug, this new technology made us feel powerful, no longer a part of nature, but above it.

With this new knowledge, fancy machines, and heavy equipment, we would subdue the elements in our environment, conquer them. Our relationship to the stuff of our world became that of master to slave. Materials not shaped by human beings working with a

sense of partnership and respect were forced to submit to the power and to the limitations of machines. In this context, shoes were no longer made by the cobbler, the fires in the smithy's forge slowly died, and houses were not built by the hands of craftsmen, but with the assembly of various manufactured materials. And so, in our race to enter the promised land at the other end of the assembly line, we left behind vast stores of knowledge that for centuries had been passed through generations. Whole crafts were lost. Among these was timber framing, the joiner's craft.

In particular, it was the development of stud construction that was the hare that left the tortoise of timber framing in the dust. Indeed, it was a significant development. Without the stud-framing method (also known as "platform" and "balloon" framing),

7

Courtesy of Tafi Brown

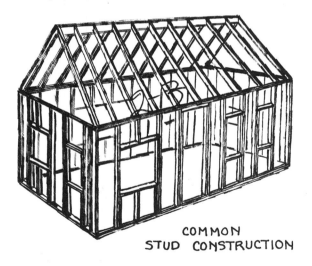
COMMON
STUD CONSTRUCTION

other improvements in our society would have been severely crippled. Whole towns and cities that were built practically overnight depended on this simplified building system. (For instance, in eight years Cripple Creek, Colorado, grew from a population of fifteen to fifty thousand.)

Certainly the use of stud construction has continued to provide housing needs effectively for a growing and increasingly mobile population for the past hundred years. But

today we have fewer illusions about the promises of technology. We have come to recognize that there is often a price to pay for this kind of efficiency. In this case, it is perhaps not entirely the fault of the building system. It also has to do with the attitude the builder and the purchaser bring to a method that offers many tempting opportunities for shortcuts. This deficiency was seen as early as 1923 by the author of *Audels Carpenters and Builders Guide* in his introduction to balloon framing: "This is a cheap and as usually put together a more or less objectionable construction. A well built balloon frame is satisfactory for a moderate sized house, but how often is one well built?" The situation has not changed. Houses today can easily be built in thirty days. But the inherent probability is that, both architecturally and structurally, they will not last.

Much of the meaning behind the word *home* has been lost in the last century. No longer are homes permanent habitations for our families, built with great-grandchildren in mind. Today our homes tend to be built for temporary shelter and for resale. We seem to have assumed that anything that can be produced easily can be replaced easily. Like many other products of our age, houses, too, quickly deteriorate. However, rising building costs and mortgage rates have helped us become acutely aware of the cost of replacing buildings that are of poor quality. And people have tired of living in homes whose shapes and lines and spaces are as predictable as the materials that produce them. Some of us are beginning to demand something not only more durable but also more personal.

It's ironic that one of the best ways that this demand can be met in our modern age is in the revival of an ancient building system. The craft of timber framing was predominant in the days when people could not afford to have expendable items. Everything was done by hand. Each building project demanded a huge labor effort, often spanning many years. There was no time for shoddy construction. Building with timbers is returning today as both labor and materials become increasingly expensive. Again people are becoming very concerned that neither should be squandered on poor quality buildings.

It's ironic, too, that it is as a result of space-age inventions that timber framing is again

Above: This house, designed and built by architect Bill D'Antonio, demonstrates that the timber frame can become the predominant theme in the living environment. The frame was constructed by Ed Levin.
Photo by Robert Gere

Below: Living spaces can be defined by the wooden timbers. The house belongs to Dimitri and Mary Gerakaris; the frame is by Ed Levin.
Photo by Richard Starr

practical and desirable. We can use electric power tools to help reduce the labor effort needed to prepare the timbers. There is also the advantage of various kinds of lifting and moving equipment to make working with timbers easier and safer.

Perhaps the most important difference is in the way we can use new insulations in combination with our timber frames. The development of rigid foam has been the most important improvement of insulation in this century. It has comparatively high thermal-resistance values and doesn't permit moisture or air penetration nearly as much as other types of insulation. With the use of rigid foam panels, we can now completely wrap our framework with a blanket of insulation, instead of interrupting the insulation with the frame as we do in stud construction. By separating a rigid frame from the insulating skin, each becomes as effective as it can be without needing to compensate for the other.

Another advantage of placing a weather-resistant skin over the structural skeleton is that the frame of the building can be com-

INSULATION SKIN APPLIED
TO OUTSIDE OF STRUCTURE
IN TIMBER FRAME

INSULATION INTERRUPTED
BY FRAMING IN
STUD CONSTRUCTION

pletely protected from the elements and from condensation. With this kind of protection, the frame can be expected to last indefinitely. It is as warm and as dry as the people who live in the building and will neither deteriorate nor rot as long as the skin is intact. Should this outer covering deteriorate or if remodeling is desired, the skin can easily be replaced without changing the frame. This combination of high-insulation value and the complete protection of the frame is unprecedented in home construction.

With the timbers of the frame completely exposed to the interior of the house, they not only support the structure but also become a predominant theme in the living environment. The interior spaces are defined by the edges, angles, and shapes of wooden timbers instead of by the surfaces and openings of sheathed walls. With this unobtrusive definition of living areas, they can be open to each other for an easier flow of traffic and heat, yet there exists a feeling of natural separation, as suggested by the timbers.

There is something in the look and feel of timbers that appeals to people. Try to find a copy of *House Beautiful* or *House and Garden* that doesn't show houses that reveal timbers. Fine restaurants and fast-food restaurants, shopping centers, and churches all have found the effect of timbers to be beneficial to their decor. But the craft of timber joinery has been nearly lost for many years, and most of the current applications demonstrate this ignorance by nailing or bolting false timbers to structures that already exist. Sophisticated techniques have even been developed to make fake plastic timbers that can be glued to ceilings and walls.

But just the effect of timbers is not enough. Timbers are more aesthetically pleasing when they demonstrate that beauty is enhanced by function. The fact that the timbers are a part of the structure of the building and that each piece helps to support loads and resist forces gives them meaning. This continuity of purpose supports the inherent dignity of wood. It deserves to be more than a decoration or an afterthought.

Wood is a great resource. The attributes it contains as a building material put it into a class by itself. Wood is symbiotic with natural forces, responding to them with strength characterized by tremendous resilience. Unadorned, it embellishes both cathedrals and cabins. The properties in wood that make a

The old timbers add a special charm to this kitchen.
Courtesy of Robert H. Brown

Reusing old timbers in a recently constructed house.
Courtesy of Robert H. Brown

chair sturdy and attractive can do the same thing for a building. To build with a stud-frame system, which simply by its linear arrangement loses the beauty of wood, poses an aesthetic dilemma. Studs are used for expediency, but ultimately they will be sandwiched between sheathing layers that tend to be plain, unattractive, and expensive. If we are drawn to the qualities in wood, why not build with a system that enhances its strengths and reveals its beauty, and be done with it?

We are finding, again, that basic needs are very often best satisfied with basic elements. Food, clothing, and shelter—these are critical to our existence. To the extent that we can satisfy these needs, the level of our civilization and the quality of our lives is determined. We tend to be conservative about these basic and primal concerns and are reluctant to accept substitutes. Many of the modern substitutes and alternatives have been found to be unsatisfactory. We would rather not have chemicals in our food, synthetics in our clothes, or the sterility of manufactured, imitation materials in our homes. We look for garden-fresh food, cotton or wool, and we look for wood. The way in which posts, beams, and braces of the timber structure bring wood into the home is natural, and the effect is easy to live with.

I have found it a privilege to be a carpenter in New England. To have learned the trade in the shadow of some of the most finely constructed buildings in the country, among people who still appreciate craftsmanship, has made the honing of skills exciting. The evidence of the old buildings that have defied the harsh Northeast weather for centuries has been an effective education. These houses, barns, churches, and town halls all seem to reflect the practicality of people who lived close to the earth. The shapes are simple and classic; the construction methods are simple and durable. Neither seems very affected by time. The architecture has been emulated repeatedly, but the building system has been largely ignored.

I was forced to pay very close attention to the strength of a timber frame when I bought an old barn to be dismantled so that the pieces could be used to build my workshop. It was convincing evidence that old-fashioned building methods might yet be the most advanced. After all the sheathing on the building had been removed, we decided to pull the building down so that the timbers could be taken out more easily. It was a three-sided foundation, so we pulled the supports out from beneath the structure, thinking it would simply cave in. That fifty-by-eighty-foot, three-story barn hardly sagged! It was an incredible demonstration of the truss effect given by the braces in the frame.

We were impressed. But we were also running out of time. So, not to be thwarted, we replaced some of the supports and cut all of the braces out of the frame with a chain saw. (It was starting to get crude.) When we pulled the supports out again, it sagged a little more, but not much. Angry now, we hooked a cable to one of the corner posts and to my four-wheel-drive pickup and proceeded to dig substantial little holes for each of my wheels. Finally, with the aid of a wrecker truck, we were able to get the timbers to hinge in their pinned joints. After pulling with the wrecker for several hours, the frame leaned over—but didn't come apart. With a great deal of effort, the timbers eventually had to be removed from the frame one at a time. When I recovered from the frustration, I resolved that one day I would build using this system.

It was disappointing to discover that there is practically nothing written on the subject. What the masters of the trade did leave with us, though, are frames—plenty of them. So anywhere possible, I would study timber frames, noting joinery at various locations, taking measurements, and doing the best I could to ascertain techniques. Books couldn't have done better.

With first-hand observation, I was able to notice small things: how marks were made, variations in lumber dimension, wood species used, and so on. Studying frames on the site has also given me the advantage of being able to discover why some joints obviously worked better than others, getting to understand how the frames went together, and learning to recognize the work of a particular carpenter. In all the frames that have been studied, there are many more similarities than differences. One would have to conclude that, despite the lack of written information, this was a refined and ordered trade. The early carpenters were taking advantage of the whole evolution that preceded them. Passing down through the generations were some general guidelines and rules that were as specific as if they were etched on the

Traditional saltbox with an overhang along the front.
Courtesy of Tafi Brown

surface of the timbers that were being worked.

This sense of historical precedent must not be lost. As we begin to learn the craft, the single most important responsibility we have is to pay attention to the lessons of the past. The development of any trade is full of those things that failed as well as those that worked. In general, the joints and structural design practices that survived did so because they were historically successful. In the course of refining timber frames for two thousand years, most of the imaginable variations have already been attempted. (See References, Hewett and Seike). For instance, there is no reason to try to invent new joints. We will describe in this book some of the best joints that are found in American and European homes and barns. To frame with timbers, one must learn how to fashion these basic joints and learn where and how to use them. In order to bring timber framing into the modern era, it is important that we begin by emulating the masters of old.

The framed overhang is a New England construction tradition dating from the 1600s. *Courtesy of Tafi Brown*

13

TIMBER FRAMING TODAY

MASSIVE TIMBERS, SOME WEIGHING AS MUCH AS 500 POUNDS, ARE CUT AND FRAMED TOGETHER USING TIME-TESTED MORTISE AND TENON JOINTS. THESE TIMBERS, ONCE RAISED AND PEGGED INTO POSITION, FORM WHAT WE CALL A TIMBER FRAME. FOLLOWING ANCIENT TRADITION, NO NAILS OR METAL FASTENERS OF ANY TYPE ARE USED.

PLANNING

CAREFUL AND THOROUGH PLANNING IS VITAL FOR BUILDING WITH TIMBERS. THE ENTIRE FRAME, INCLUDING ALL JOINTS, MUST BE DESIGNED BEFORE ONE TIMBER IS CUT.

SHOULDERED
MORTISE AND TENON

FRAMES PREPARED IN THE SHOP

THE KEY TO SUCCESSFUL TIMBER FRAMING IS IN THE PRECUTTING OF THE TIMBERS. THE POSTS, BEAMS, AND BRACES ARE SAWED TO LENGTH AND THE MORTISES AND TENONS ARE DRILLED AND CUT. WHEN ALL THE TIMBERS ARE CUT, PLANED, SANDED, AND MARKED, THE FRAME IS READY FOR ASSEMBLY AT THE SITE.

HOW THE FRAMES ARE RAISED

AT THE BUILDING SITE, THE POSTS AND BEAMS ARE FITTED TOGETHER IN BENTS ON THE GROUND AND PEGGED. WHERE OUR FOREFATHERS USED MANY MEN, ROPES, POLES, AND PULLEYS, TODAY WE CAN USE A CRANE TO LIFT ONE ENTIRE BENT INTO PLACE AT A TIME. THESE ARE JOINED WITH CONNECTING TIMBERS, THEN PEGGED, AND THE FRAME IS COMPLETED.

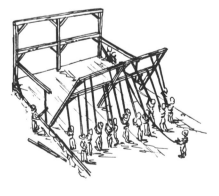

BARN RAISING
BY HAND

FRAME
RAISING
BY CRANE

CONT....

TIMBER FRAMING TODAY.... CONT.

WHAT IS A BENT?

A BENT IS THE STRUCTURAL NETWORK OF TIMBERS THAT MAKE UP ONE CROSS-SECTIONAL PIECE OF THE FRAME. IT DETERMINES THE SHAPE OF THE HOUSE, FIXING ITS HEIGHT AND WIDTH.

HOW BENTS ARE TIED TOGETHER

EVERY FRAME HAS AT LEAST TWO, AND USUALLY THREE OR MORE, BENTS WHICH ARE TIED TOGETHER BY CONNECTING BEAMS, THUS FORMING BAYS. THE SPAN OF THESE CONNECTING TIMBERS FIXES THE DISTANCE BETWEEN BENTS.

INTERIOR SPACE DIVISION
(THE FLOOR PLAN)

THE BENT SHAPE AND THE LENGTHS OF THE BAYS ARE ADJUSTED TO ACCOMMODATE SIZES AND LOCATIONS OF INTERIOR SPACES FOR CHIMNEYS, STAIRWAYS, BATHROOMS, BEDROOMS, AND OTHER LIVING QUARTERS.

ENCLOSING THE FRAME

UNLIKE CONVENTIONAL STUD FRAMING, THE TIMBER FRAME DOES NOT RELY ON SHEATHING FOR RIGIDITY. THE INTERIOR FINISH MATERIAL AND THE INSULATION ARE APPLIED TO THE OUTSIDE OF THE TIMBERS. THE FRAMEWORK IS WELL PROTECTED FROM WEATHER CHANGES AND IS COMPLETELY REVEALED TO THE INTERIOR OF THE HOUSE.

TIMBERS of the FRAME

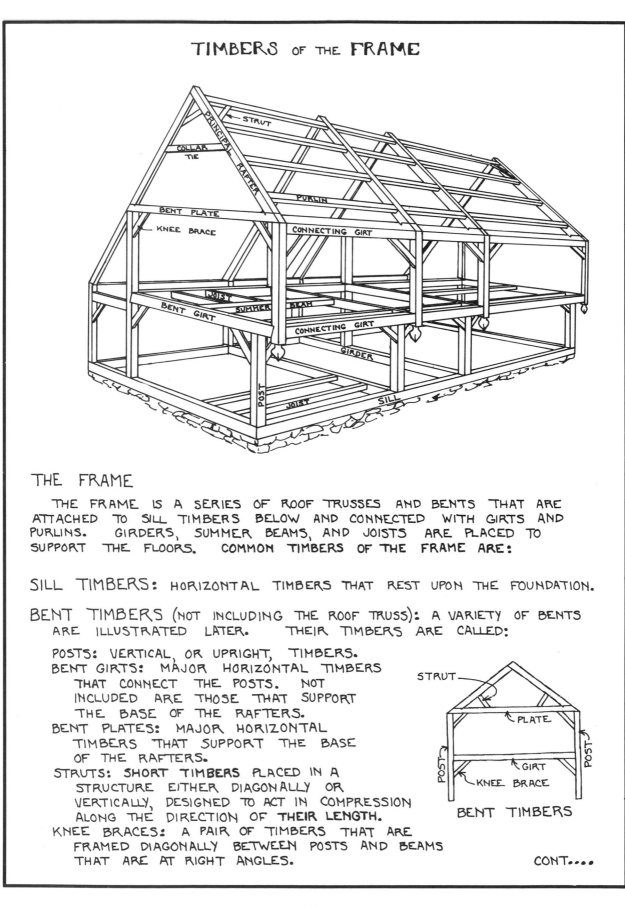

THE FRAME

THE FRAME IS A SERIES OF ROOF TRUSSES AND BENTS THAT ARE ATTACHED TO SILL TIMBERS BELOW AND CONNECTED WITH GIRTS AND PURLINS. GIRDERS, SUMMER BEAMS, AND JOISTS ARE PLACED TO SUPPORT THE FLOORS. COMMON TIMBERS OF THE FRAME ARE:

SILL TIMBERS: HORIZONTAL TIMBERS THAT REST UPON THE FOUNDATION.

BENT TIMBERS (NOT INCLUDING THE ROOF TRUSS): A VARIETY OF BENTS ARE ILLUSTRATED LATER. THEIR TIMBERS ARE CALLED:

POSTS: VERTICAL, OR UPRIGHT, TIMBERS.

BENT GIRTS: MAJOR HORIZONTAL TIMBERS THAT CONNECT THE POSTS. NOT INCLUDED ARE THOSE THAT SUPPORT THE BASE OF THE RAFTERS.

BENT PLATES: MAJOR HORIZONTAL TIMBERS THAT SUPPORT THE BASE OF THE RAFTERS.

STRUTS: SHORT TIMBERS PLACED IN A STRUCTURE EITHER DIAGONALLY OR VERTICALLY, DESIGNED TO ACT IN COMPRESSION ALONG THE DIRECTION OF **THEIR LENGTH.**

KNEE BRACES: A PAIR OF TIMBERS THAT ARE FRAMED DIAGONALLY BETWEEN POSTS AND BEAMS THAT ARE AT RIGHT ANGLES.

BENT TIMBERS

CONT....

TIMBERS of the FRAME.... cont.

TIMBERS THAT CONNECT BENTS: THESE TIMBERS CONNECT PAIRS OF BENTS TO FORM RIGID BAYS. THEIR DEFINITIONS ARE ANALOGOUS TO THOSE ABOVE.

   CONNECTING GIRTS: SEE DEFINITION PREVIOUS PAGE AND DRAWING (RIGHT).
   KNEE BRACES: DEFINED PREVIOUS PAGE.

TIMBERS FOR FRAMING FLOORS:

   GIRDERS: MAJOR TIMBERS THAT SPAN BETWEEN SILLS.
   SUMMER BEAMS: MAJOR TIMBERS THAT SPAN BETWEEN GIRTS OR PLATES.
   JOISTS: SMALL, PARALLEL RUNNING TIMBERS THAT COMPLETE THE FLOOR FRAME.

TIMBERS FOR FRAMING ROOFS: A VARIETY OF ROOF TRUSSES WILL BE ILLUSTRATED. THE TIMBERS THAT FORM THESE TRUSSES ARE:

   PRINCIPAL RAFTERS: SLOPING TIMBERS OF THE ROOF FRAME JOINED TOGETHER AT THE PEAK AND FRAMED AT THEIR BASE INTO A BENT PLATE.
   COMMON RAFTERS: SECONDARY RAFTERS, USUALLY SMALLER THAN PRINCIPAL RAFTERS, LOCATED BETWEEN BENTS.
   COLLAR TIE: HORIZONTAL CONNECTOR AT APPROXIMATELY MID-SPAN OF A PAIR OF RAFTERS. IT REDUCES RAFTER SAGGING OR SPREADING.
   KING POST: SINGLE VERTICAL TIMBER FRAMED INTO A ROOF TRUSS TO ADD RIGIDITY. RUNS FROM PLATE TO RAFTER PEAK.
   QUEEN POSTS: PAIR OF VERTICAL TIMBERS FRAMED INTO A ROOF TRUSS TO ADD RIGIDITY.
   PURLINS: HORIZONTAL TIMBERS THAT CONNECT RAFTER TRUSSES.
   RIDGE POLE: A HORIZONTAL TIMBER AT THE PEAK OF THE ROOF TO WHICH THE RAFTERS ARE ATTACHED.
   KNEE BRACES AND STRUTS: SEE DEFINITIONS, PREVIOUS PAGE.

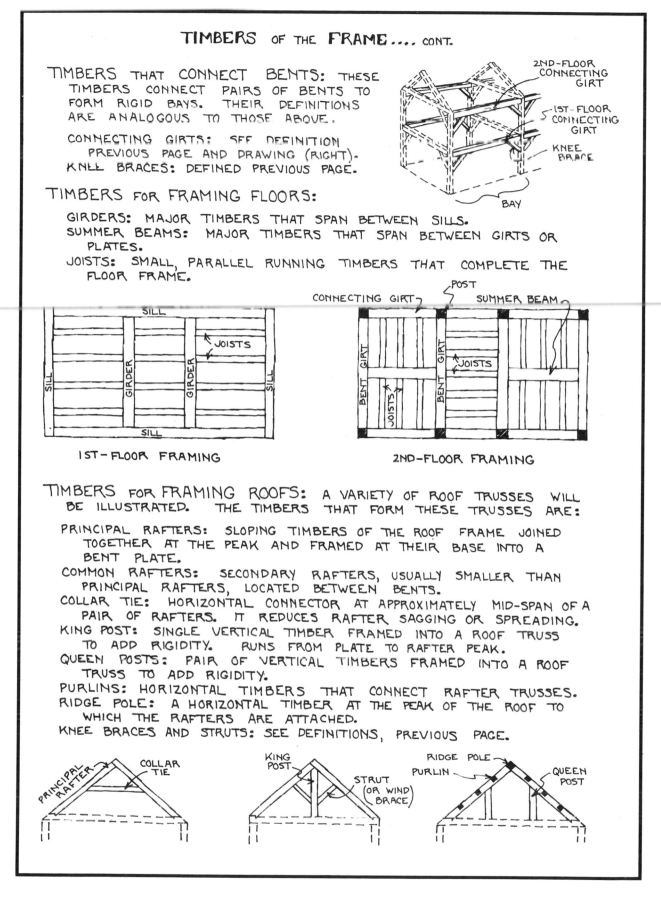

BENTS

THERE ARE SEVERAL METHODS FOR PUTTING TIMBER-FRAMED HOUSES TOGETHER. WE ARE CONVINCED THAT THE BEST SYSTEM IS THE PREASSEMBLY AND RAISING OF BENTS. A BENT IS A COMBINATION OF INTERLOCKING TIMBERS THAT FORMS A TRUSS. THIS TRUSS, OR RIGID FRAMEWORK, DEFINES THE CROSS-SECTION OF A BUILDING.

THE BENT PIECES ARE FITTED AND PEGGED ON THE GROUND AND THEN RAISED AS UNITS. GIRTS, SUMMER BEAMS, AND PURLINS ARE THE CONNECTING PIECES THAT TIE THESE UNITS TOGETHER. BENT CONSTRUCTION REDUCES THE CRANE TIME BECAUSE MANY PIECES ARE ALREADY CONNECTED AND IT ALLOWS THE MOST COMPLICATED JOINERY TO BE FITTED ON THE DECK INSTEAD OF TWO STORIES UP.

WE ILLUSTRATE HERE A SERIES OF BENTS THAT SHOULD GIVE AN IDEA OF THE ALMOST INFINITE VARIATIONS THAT ARE POSSIBLE.

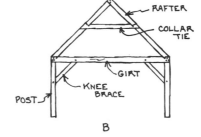

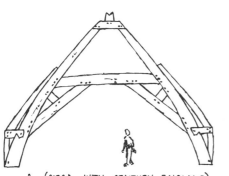

A (CIRCA - 14TH CENTURY, ENGLAND)

ONE OF THE EARLIEST BENTS USED IN ENGLAND WAS THE CRUCK "A-FRAME." A BOWED TREE WAS SPLIT DOWN THE MIDDLE AND THE TWO HALVES WERE JOINED AT THE PEAK TO FORM A PRIMITIVE TRUSS REFERRED TO AS A "CRUCK" FRAME.

B

THE SIMPLEST BENT CONSISTS OF TWO POSTS, A GIRT, AND A PAIR OF RAFTERS STRENGTHENED WITH KNEE BRACES AND A COLLAR TIE.

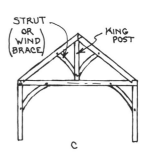

C

A VARIATION ON THE LAST BENT IS TO USE CURVED BRACES AND A KING POST.

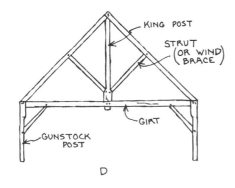

D

THE KING POST SYSTEM SHOWN HERE ALLOWS A GREATER SPAN WITH ONLY TWO POSTS.

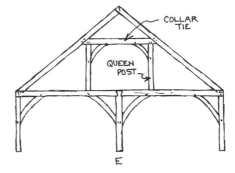

E

ADDING A THIRD POST INCREASES THE SPAN OF THE BENT. THE RAFTERS ARE SUPPORTED WITH QUEEN POSTS AND A COLLAR TIE. THIS MIGHT BE CONSIDERED A TRADITIONAL CAPE COD FRAME.

CONT....

BENTS.... CONT.

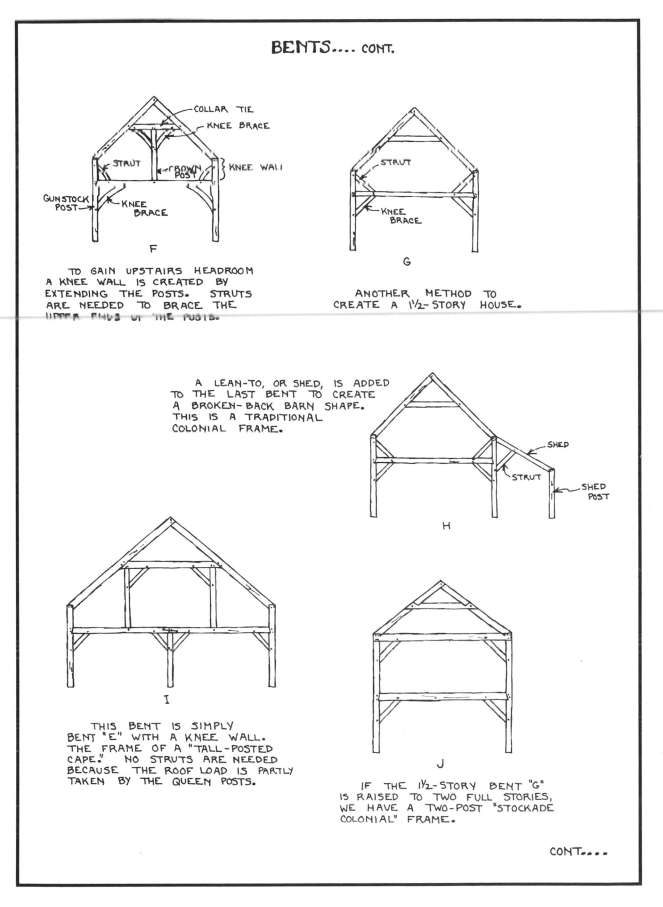

COLLAR TIE

KNEE BRACE

STRUT

CROWN POST

KNEE WALL

GUNSTOCK POST

KNEE BRACE

F

TO GAIN UPSTAIRS HEADROOM
A KNEE WALL IS CREATED BY
EXTENDING THE POSTS. STRUTS
ARE NEEDED TO BRACE THE
UPPER ENDS OF THE POSTS.

STRUT

KNEE BRACE

G

ANOTHER METHOD TO
CREATE A 1½-STORY HOUSE.

A LEAN-TO, OR SHED, IS ADDED
TO THE LAST BENT TO CREATE
A BROKEN-BACK BARN SHAPE.
THIS IS A TRADITIONAL
COLONIAL FRAME.

SHED

STRUT

SHED POST

H

I

THIS BENT IS SIMPLY
BENT "E" WITH A KNEE WALL.
THE FRAME OF A "TALL-POSTED
CAPE." NO STRUTS ARE NEEDED
BECAUSE THE ROOF LOAD IS PARTLY
TAKEN BY THE QUEEN POSTS.

J

IF THE 1½-STORY BENT "G"
IS RAISED TO TWO FULL STORIES,
WE HAVE A TWO-POST "STOCKADE
COLONIAL" FRAME.

CONT....

19

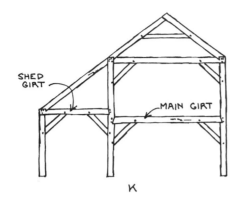

K

ADDING A LEAN-TO OR SHED
TO THE LAST BENT GIVES A
TWO-STORY "SALTBOX" FRAME.
THE SHED GIRT IS OFFSET
FROM THE MAIN GIRT TO PERMIT
PEGGING OF CONNECTING GIRTS.

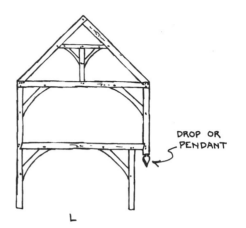

L

ADDING A FRAMED
OVERHANG AND A CROWN-POST
ROOF TRUSS TO BENT "J"
GIVES THIS BENT. THE
OVERHANG WAS AN EARLY
AMERICAN TRADITION.

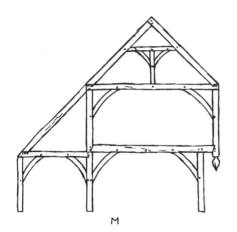

M

A SHED ADDED TO THE
LAST BENT CREATES THIS
BENT. A SALTBOX WITH
A FRAMED OVERHANG.

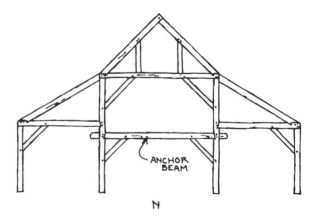

N

ADDING TWO SHEDS TO A
TWO-STORY COLONIAL GIVES A
BARN FRAME. NOTE THE
ANCHOR BEAM, A CHARACTERISTIC
PENNSYLVANIA DUTCH STYLE.

CONT....

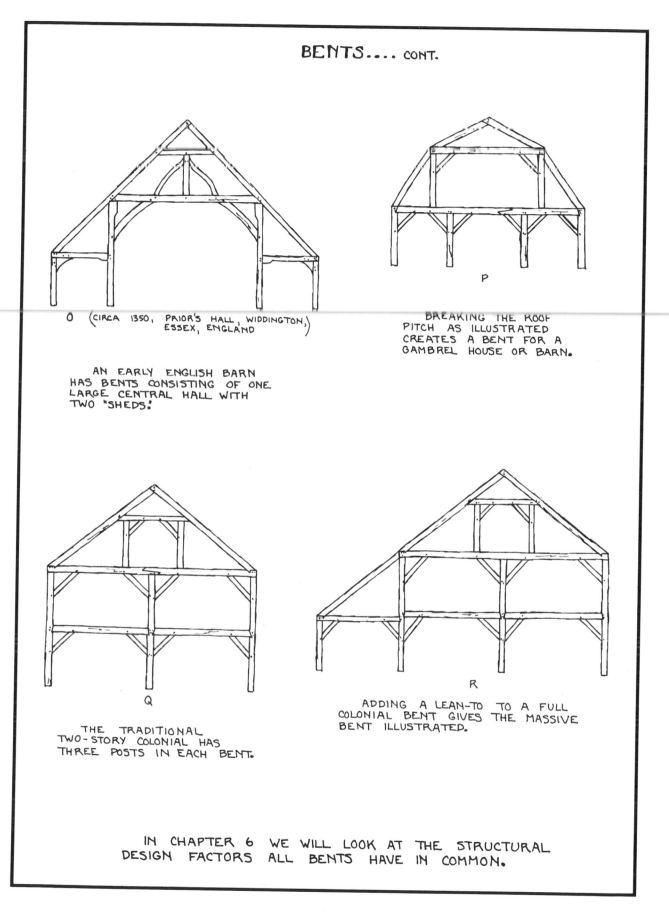

O (CIRCA 1350, PRIOR'S HALL, WIDDINGTON, ESSEX, ENGLAND)

BREAKING THE ROOF
PITCH AS ILLUSTRATED
CREATES A BENT FOR A
GAMBREL HOUSE OR BARN.

AN EARLY ENGLISH BARN
HAS BENTS CONSISTING OF ONE
LARGE CENTRAL HALL WITH
TWO "SHEDS."

P

Q

THE TRADITIONAL
TWO-STORY COLONIAL HAS
THREE POSTS IN EACH BENT.

R

ADDING A LEAN-TO TO A FULL
COLONIAL BENT GIVES THE MASSIVE
BENT ILLUSTRATED.

IN CHAPTER 6 WE WILL LOOK AT THE STRUCTURAL
DESIGN FACTORS ALL BENTS HAVE IN COMMON.

"A great spirit of cooperation among people. . . . (Arthur and Dudley, *The Barn*)

There is also no reason to invent new methods of assembly. Among those things that would seem to fall into the category of an historical rule is that frames should be built as a series of rigid trusses. The use of these cross-sectional trusses or "bents" is so prevalent that any other method of assembly would have to be considered an exception. Even the early cruck buildings were a form of bent construction. The reason for using this method is founded in common sense. In timber framing the full weight of the building and the forces on the building are directed through the posts. (Typically, there are only eight to twelve posts in a frame.) The formation of the bent directs the forces of the roof, walls, and floor toward the posts and also increases their rigidity with bracing and high quality joinery. Once the bents are assembled and raised into position, they need only be connected with beams and braces to complete the structure of the building.

It was in America that the use of the bent was perfected. There was a great spirit of cooperation among people who shared in the struggle for survival. When buildings were being raised, it was common for many people in the area to come together to lend a hand. The master carpenter would construct complete bents of massive buildings on the ground prior to the raising. The bents were then raised into position by the large number of people gathered for the occasion.

Obviously, this method allows for greater control in fitting joints. It also has the advantage of reducing the time of the actual raising of the frame to a single day. For these reasons, we have adopted this method as being the most beneficial to our interests. The only significant difference between the meth-

22

We prefer to use a crane to raise the bents. *Courtesy of Tafi Brown*

ods described in this book and the ones perfected in early America is that—for reasons of economy and safety—we prefer the use of a crane to lift large bents. In other respects, we defer to the historical success of the bent system.

The best moments in my not very scholastic study of old timber frames are when I recognize enough similarities among buildings to be able to identify the builder. Unfortunately, I haven't dug into town or family records and therefore don't know one particular person, who comes to mind, by name. But he and I have something in common—a language we both understand—through which a recognition of his work seems undeniable. The marks he scribed in the timbers, the numbering system, the type of wood he preferred, the way certain pieces are joined; these kinds of things not only help to

identify the man but also tell something about what he was like.

It doesn't take too long to be able to recognize the difference between a frame put together by a master joiner and one built by a farmer simply trying to take care of his needs. Not all old frames are good frames. Along with so many examples demonstrating sophistication of knowledge and technique, there have been some that weren't worth the time it took to put them together. I saw one in upper New York State constructed completely of white birch timbers, which do not weather well; furthermore, the joinery in the frame was just as poor as the choice of wood. The only redeeming value of this type of frame is that, as it crumbles into the earth, it gives many fine lessons in "how not to."

On the other hand, there are a few frames

23

Ed Levin of Canaan, New Hampshire, after studying the ancient methods of European framing, constructed this inspiring hammer-beam truss roof for Dimitri Gerakaris's blacksmith shop. *Courtesy of Richard Starr*

near Concord, New Hampshire, that are put together with chestnut, patience, and skill. The pride this master joiner took in his work is seen in the condition of the building after two hundred years of use. Viewing the work of this man makes me feel like the proverbial kid in a candy store — not knowing what will be the most important bit of information I can take away with me.

The overall response to the work of the old masters tends to be one of tremendous respect. I can't help feeling that the acquired knowledge of those early carpenters, coupled with their instinctive understanding of the nature of wood, was somehow deeper than the data generated by our mathematicians and engineers. With computers at his fingertips, wouldn't some latter-day engineer love to take credit for the development of the hammer-beam truss or for designing some of the sophisticated interlocking joinery common to twelfth- or thirteenth-century England or Japan? Wouldn't any twentieth-century architect feel compelled to celebrate his good fortune if his was the first pencil to sketch the outline of the classic cape or salt-box? Yet these were the developments of men who were simply responding to their environment, creating simple, durable structures with the materials at hand to protect themselves from the weather.

It is important, I think, to try to learn this kind of response. Instead of blindly following the standards and procedures presented to us by mail order plans and then building with materials like the plywood that is made from wood harvested in the United States, trucked to lumberyards, trucked to the building site, and applied to the building, there to delaminate in the first rainstorm; instead of that, all of us need to develop discrimination about "customary practice" to ensure that house construction is more sensible and more satisfactory.

Nevertheless, in this century there have been a great many developments in the home-building industry that are as desirable to our current life-style as they are beneficial to sound construction. Stronger foundations, effective drainage systems, tighter windows, better heating and ventilating techniques, and insulation are all significant modern improvements. Marrying timber framing with these kinds of things brings together some of the best offerings of the Old World and the New. If by doing this we are also able to bring old-fashioned values to contemporary home construction, then timber framing will be as sought after as low mortgage rates.

In the interim, timber-frame construction is often sought after simply for the value it can give for the same dollar. Almost as if there were a miserly spell cast upon the construction process, the consequence of a finely joined and finished timber frame is generally to eliminate the need for many other expensive installations. The result is that despite the extra expense of fashioning good joints in timbers, the completed timber-frame house generally does not cost any more per square foot than houses built by conventional means.

Timber framing has other advantages.

Practically any shape or style of building can be adapted to the joints and procedures that put timbers together. Its limitations come more in size than in design. (For instance, I don't believe the walls should be taller than what can be spanned by a single timber.) But it works most easily in the simple lines and shapes that are classic the world over: steeply pitched roofs over rectilinear living areas. As it happens, these shapes are coming back into architecture because the pitch of the roof and its large surface area make it naturally suited to solar collection panels. Steeply pitched roofs also have a tendency to shed the elements rapidly, and consequently do not wear out so quickly.

These classic shapes have survived because they stand on promises, not dreams. Consider the cape style home. With primary living areas on the first floor and bedrooms between the rafters, it continues to provide the greatest amount of living space for the least amount of money. In building, there

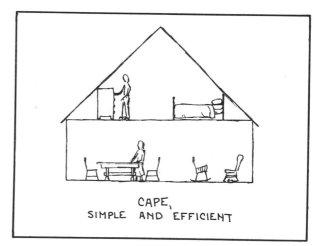

CAPE,
SIMPLE AND EFFICIENT

DESIGNING a FLOOR PLAN

IF SIMPLICITY AND COMMON SENSE GOVERN THE DESIGNING OF A FLOOR PLAN, THE PIECES OF THE PUZZLE WILL FALL INTO PLACE.

A METHOD of APPROACH

DETERMINE THE BASIC OVERALL SIZE OF YOUR HOUSE. THE NUMBER OF BEDROOMS, BATHS, AND THE SIZE OF THE LIVING AREAS REQUIRED WILL GIVE A GOOD IDEA OF THE SQUARE FOOTAGE NEEDED.

DECIDE ON THE BASIC SHAPE OF THE STRUCTURE: SALTBOX, CAPE, GAMBREL, COLONIAL, GABLE ROOF, SHED ROOF, OR CONTEMPORARY DESIGN.

DETERMINE THE BENTS REQUIRED. THE SHAPE OF THE GABLE END OF THE PROPOSED HOUSE WILL BE THE SHAPE OF THE REQUIRED BENTS. THE HOUSE WILL THEN BE A SERIES OF THE SAME OR SIMILAR BENTS CONNECTED TO FORM A SERIES OF BAYS. ADDITIONS OR ELLS CAN BE INCORPORATED BY USING DIFFERENT BENT PLANS.

DRAW A PLAN VIEW OF THE FRAME AND SKETCH A FLOOR PLAN. POSTS ARE SHOWN AS SOLID SQUARES AND OVERHEAD BEAMS AS DOTTED LINES. SINCE THE FRAME IS SELF-SUPPORTING WITHOUT WALLS, THE PARTITIONS CAN BE PLACED ANYWHERE. A MORE NATURAL FEELING WILL PREVAIL, HOWEVER, IF MAJOR PARTITIONS OR ROOM DIVISIONS ARE LOCATED AT POSTS OR UNDER MAJOR BEAMS. THIS USUALLY SUGGESTS THAT THE FIRST- AND SECOND-FLOOR PLANS SHOULD BE QUITE CLOSELY RELATED. TRY TO MAKE A FLOOR PLAN WORK IN A SYMBIOTIC RELATIONSHIP WITH THE FRAME.

ON THE NEXT FEW PAGES ARE THREE EXAMPLES OF FLOOR PLANS DESIGNED TO CORRELATE WITH THEIR FRAMES.

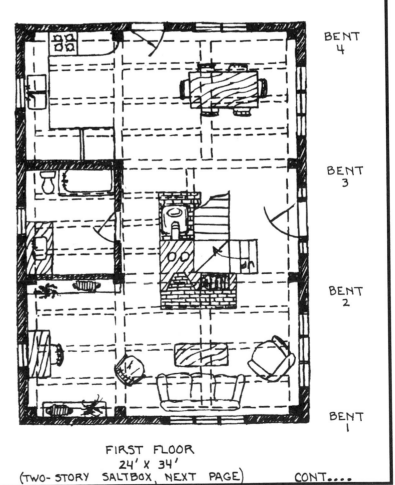

BENT 4

BENT 3

BENT 2

BENT 1

FIRST FLOOR
24' X 34'
(TWO-STORY SALTBOX, NEXT PAGE)

CONT....

TWO-STORY SALTBOX

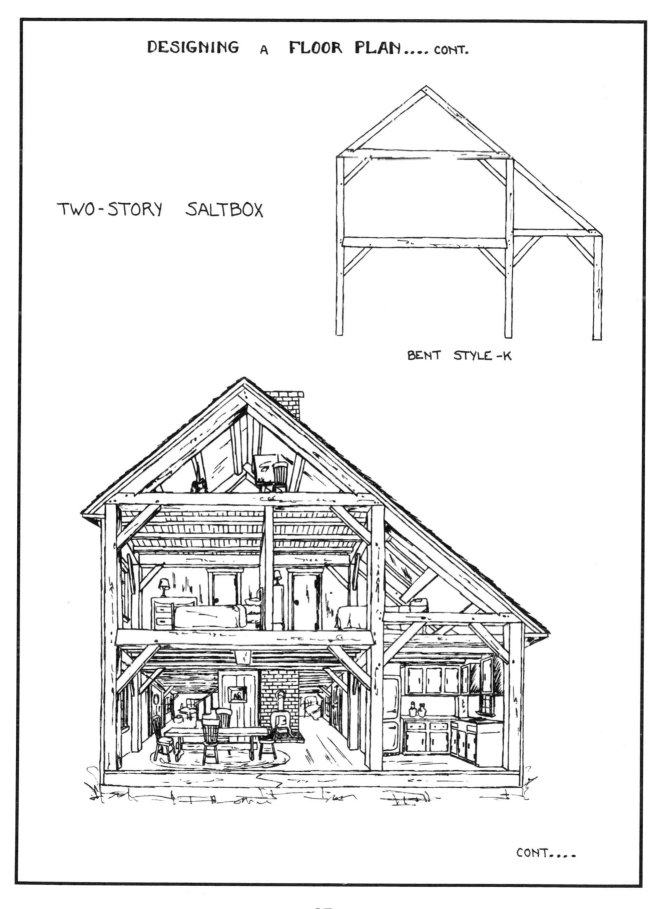

BENT STYLE -K

CONT....

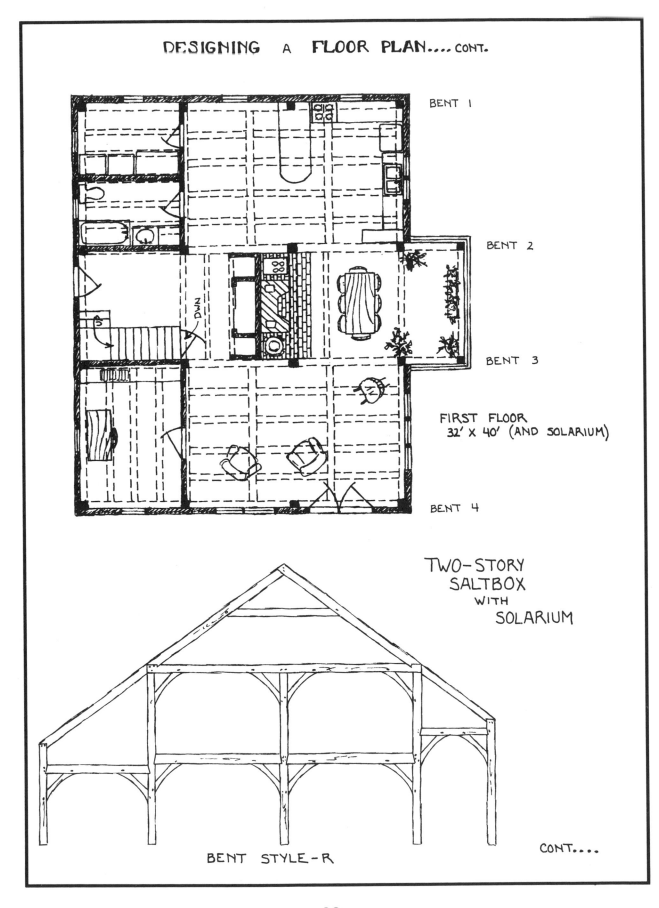

BENT 1

BENT 2

BENT 3

FIRST FLOOR
32' X 40' (AND SOLARIUM)

BENT 4

TWO-STORY
SALTBOX
WITH
SOLARIUM

DWN

BENT STYLE-R

CONT....

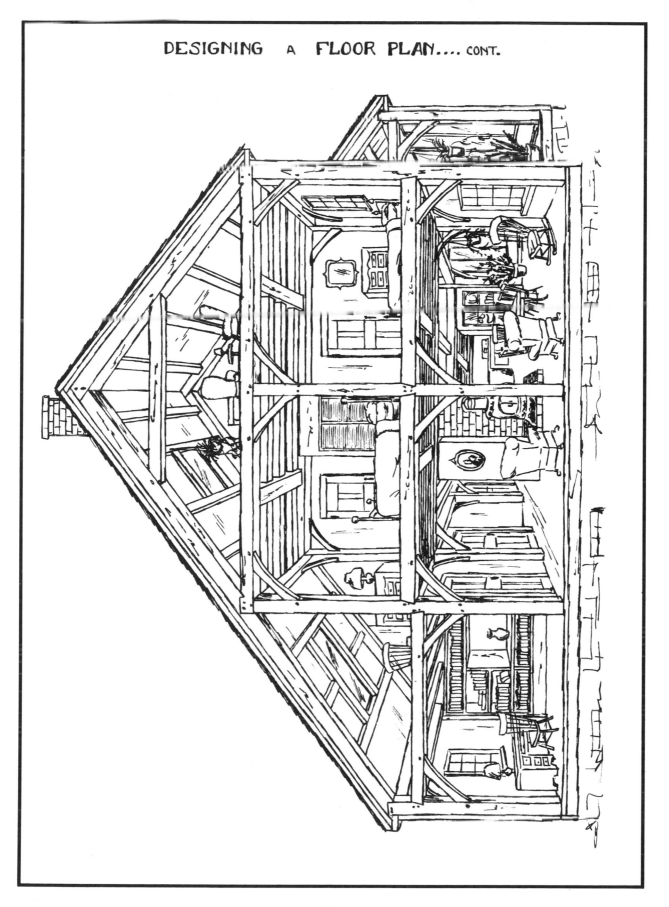

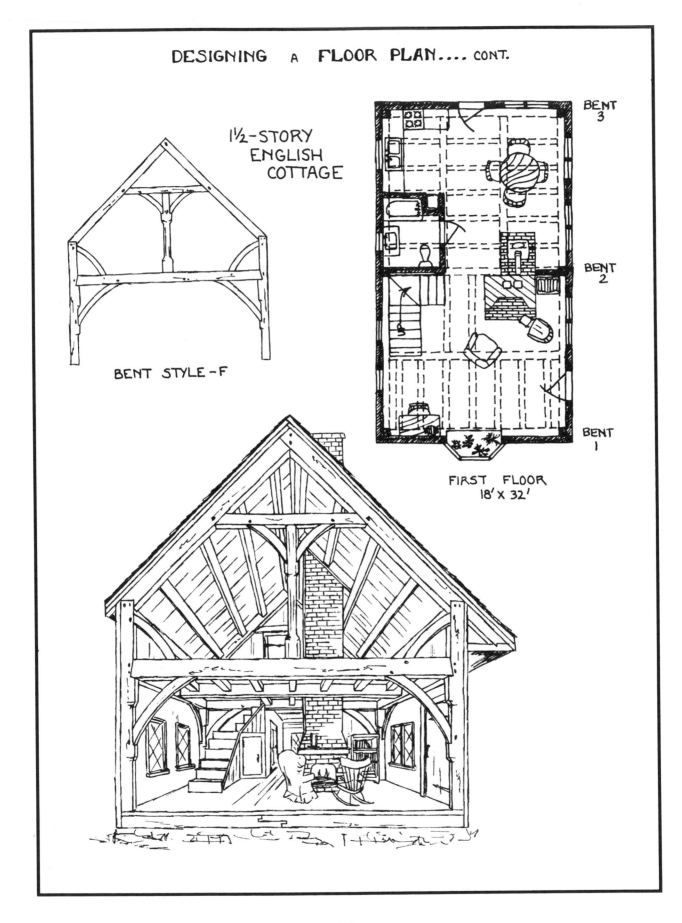

1½-STORY
ENGLISH
COTTAGE

BENT STYLE-F

BENT 3

BENT 2

BENT 1

FIRST FLOOR
18' X 32'

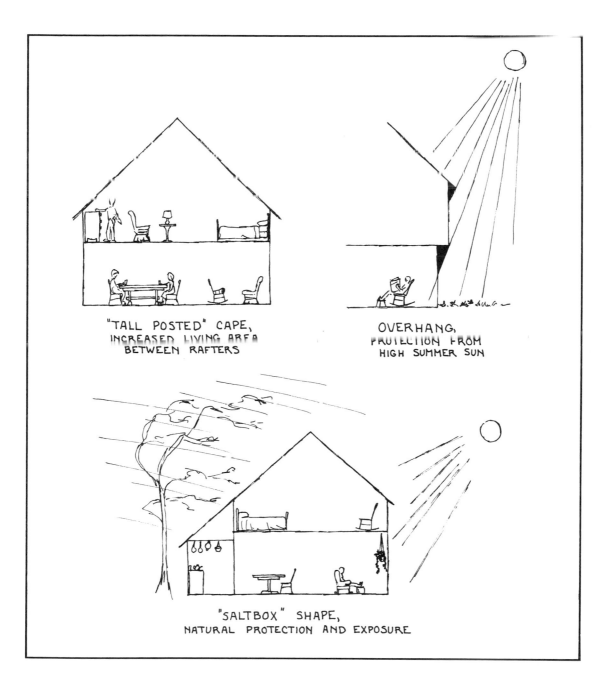

"TALL POSTED" CAPE,
INCREASED LIVING AREA
BETWEEN RAFTERS

OVERHANG,
PROTECTION FROM
HIGH SUMMER SUN

"SALTBOX" SHAPE,
NATURAL PROTECTION AND EXPOSURE

isn't anything quite as simple as putting up four single-story walls and a gable roof. That's why the cape and variations of the cape are so common, regardless of the building technique. The "tall-posted cape" gives a knee-wall effect on the second floor that simply raises the roof and provides even more square footage very efficiently.

The style that is called a saltbox has a low wall and roofline on the north side for protection from harsh weather and maintains a tall wall on the south for natural exposure to the sun's warmth. It's as simple as turning your

back to the wind and your face to the sun. The saltbox is an easy way to use the shape of the building to provide natural light, heat, and protection.

Another classic feature of ancient construction is the overhang. The effect of having the second floor cantilevered beyond the first is that it stiffens the floor framing and also provides good protection from the sun during the summer months. What all the traditional building styles have in common is that they are still relatively easy and economical to build, are well suited to the needs

The interior can be finished after moving in. *Courtesy of Robert H. Brown*

of today's world as well as yesterday's, and have a built-in affinity for timber framing.

Since the timbers act as the dominant part of the decor, they tend to replace some of the finish work that might otherwise have had to be done. The beauty of the wood, the quality of the joinery, and the design of the framework can give the frame itself a sculptured, furniturelike appearance. It *is* the finish work. When the building is closed in, just a little taping of sheetrock or some window trim is all that is needed to complete the exterior walls. The building is already insulated, weathertight, and, although very little has been done to the interior, there is a finished quality about it. Many people feel that with some plumbing to a bathroom and the kitchen, it is quite livable in this condition. They can stop borrowing money, move in, and work on the house one room at a time.

The effect of describing the living areas with timbers instead of solid walls means that fewer partitions and doors are needed. Opening the living areas up in this manner is also helpful for natural circulation of passive solar or wood heat. The space between the large supporting posts allows large non-structural wall areas to be fitted with the expanses of glass that are suitable for solar collection.

What all this adds up to is that the building that incorporates timber framing can be the most sensible building of all in the twentieth century. Even with the extra expense of a finely constructed framework, it can compete in cost with conventional construction. All the while, a stronger and a more durable house has been built. This house has better insulation and is naturally suited to large areas of glass and to the circulation of heat. It was energy-efficient to build and is energy-efficient to live in. The fact that building with timbers addresses the concerns and accommodates the technology of our era makes such building as practical today as it was two hundred years ago.

It is most practical and efficient when it is practiced on a small scale: by individuals

Space between posts allows large expanses of glass. *Courtesy of Tafi Brown*

building for themselves or by small com panies whose concerns are with high quality instead of misplaced technology and exorbitant profits. There aren't machines made that can duplicate efficiently and accurately the joining techniques described in the following chapters. Shortcuts and compromises to the time-proven joints and assembly techniques can seriously affect the soundness of the structure. So building with frameworks of timbers that are connected only with joints and wooden pegs is not so much a business as a craft. This craft can readily be learned by people who are willing to bring to it hard labor and the sensitive understanding of their hands.

CHAPTER THREE
THE JOINER'S VISION
DESCRIPTION AND LAYOUT

Courtesy of Robert H. Brown

To blow in the flute is not to play it. It is necessary to move the fingers.

—Goethe

THOSE of us who practice timber joinery today have a difficult role. We are students without a teacher. The evolution of the craft passed gracefully through two thousand years, its products emerging as steadfast monuments to many civilizations on many continents. Clearly, the practice of timber joinery had many masters who produced buildings of unarguable strength. But in the late nineteenth century the skill itself largely disappeared, having fallen victim to the burgeoning industrial era.

It was the task of wooden joinery that caused timber framing to fall out of favor. For the needs of people on the run, making joints in the large pieces of wood was considered too tedious, too time-consuming. Some of us are reconsidering. We turn in one direction and see that the houses constructed by modern techniques just a few years ago are today's deteriorating slums. Looking the other way, we see timber-framed buildings that are still standing proud, although they are two, three, five hundred, and even a thousand years old. It leads us to believe that carefully joining timbers to make frameworks for houses can be an extremely eco-

nomical effort. So we are trying to reach back to relearn and to rekindle this craft.

We must begin with a change in attitude. With so much prefabricated today, the carpenter's work is often reduced to a simple assembly process. The studs are precut, the windows and doors are prehung, and the trusses are prebuilt. There are carpenters who have practiced their trade for many years who have no idea how to cut a rafter or build stairs and who have never made a mortise-and-tenon joint. For these people, the day's work is often drudgery. There is neither tough challenge nor thrilling reward. Their most active tool is the hammer they swing with ferocity, as if in revenge for all that's lost. The need for human skill has been slowly sifted from the task of house building; working wood in the modern building trades most often means driving a nail through it. And somewhere within himself, the modern builder knows it is not just the knowledge and the skills that are lost—gone with them is some sense of personal dignity. If I shuddered a bit when the tenth-year high school reunion book identified me only as "a carpenter living in New Hampshire," it was because I knew that carpentry today is not a respected trade.

There was a time when years as an apprentice were followed by years as a journeyman, and one became a master of the trade, finally, because his knowledge of the craft was complete. His close association with his mentor not only taught him many things that could never have been put on paper, but also a thorough understanding of techniques, tools, building arithmetic, and rather sophisticated geometry. His knowledge of wood and woodworking accumulated over many years, along with the dust and shavings from a well-used workbench. When this man received the title "master" it was deserved, and for achieving it he was respected. When he built, it was with a feeling of confidence and responsibility. His buildings were not just jointed and pegged; they were also held together with a chain of knowledge tempered by time. And he was well aware that each of his products would help to define the strength of his own link in that chain. He built to last.

Achieving the difficult goal of making wooden connections sufficient to tie the structure of a building together is no simple matter. The concept is simple, but the task is significant and should not be taken for granted. If we plan to practice joinery in timbers, and if we hope one day to master it, then our work begins at the benches of those who built with mallet and chisel because there was no other way. We must serve our apprenticeship. Although we don't have the voices of these ancient masters to help us along, they left plenty of hints and thoughtful advice in the joints that silently persist. When our work is done in response to the work of the accomplished carpenters who preceded us, then we, too, can build with confidence. When we look at our work as the continuation of an ancient tradition, not the beginning of a new concept, then the maintenance of high standards will be implicit. And when we have fully accepted the notion that we are the apprentices and the journeymen of this craft, only then will the buildings we construct begin to show the touches of a master.

Good timber joinery is a marvel—wood tightly fitted into wood held together with a wooden pin; a simple formula that has proven it will respond to the forces by hinging and bending instead of breaking or tearing. An introduction of iron would only decrease the resilience and increase the wearing action. So, wooden joinery is primal and basic, but the strength that is imparted to the structure when it is done with expertise will forever be a fascination.

On the other hand, bad joinery in timbers is a mockery. When it is poorly executed, demonstrating either an ignorance of, or a resistance to, the standards of the past, then it stumbles clumsily in the dark, and should not have been done at all. (See "Building for Strength," Chapter Six, for inherent dangers of bad joinery.)

Building with timbers is gaining renewed popularity. In some circles it is even fashionable. When something becomes fashionable, there are plenty of people willing to leap into the parade without asking where it came from or where it's going. But tools in the back of a pickup don't make a carpenter; mortises and tenons don't make a timber frame. The tools must be used with knowledge and skill and the joints must be designed for strength and be cut to fit.

Joinery is the heart of timber framing. The work of making a frame is inextricably bound to that of making joints. Shaping and fitting joints are what the craft is all about. Until there are well-worked joints that can connect the pieces into a meaningful structure, there are only scattered piles of timbers. The timbers can be hand-hewn or they can be ordered from a sawmill; either way, the joints must be carefully shaped.

The joints described in this chapter are fundamental. They were gleaned from the best and the most consistent found in old buildings. The notion that these are strong joints doesn't come from theory or conjecture; it comes from staring at their amazing results. Don't be tempted by simplified joinery. The old-timers had no reason to waste time; if they could have simplified without sacrificing strength, they would have done so. Don't attempt to invent new joints. Somebody, somewhere, in the long history of this craft, beat you to it. If you can't find them, they maybe weren't strong enough to survive.

JOINERY: an INTRODUCTION

TO HELP DESCRIBE THE JOINERY OF A TIMBER FRAME, WE ILLUSTRATE HERE A SMALL TRADITIONAL NEW ENGLAND COTTAGE. THIS COTTAGE IS DELIBERATELY A POTPOURRI OF FRAMING TO ILLUSTRATE THE TYPICAL LOCATIONS OF AS MANY JOINTS AS POSSIBLE. EACH OF THE JOINTS NAMED IS DEMONSTRATED IN THIS CHAPTER.

HOW TO KEEP ALL THOSE JOINTS ORGANIZED

THIS COTTAGE CONSISTS OF NEARLY 200 TIMBERS AND 400 JOINTS. IMAGINE THE CONFUSION ON THE DAY THAT THE FRAME IS TO BE ASSEMBLED IF THE TIMBERS HAVE NOT BEEN LABELED. THE LABELING SYSTEM WE USE IS QUITE SIMPLE:

- NUMBER THE BENTS 1, 2, 3, ETC. FROM LEFT TO RIGHT. THE FLOOR PLAN (NEXT PAGE) IS ACCOMPANIED BY ARROWS SHOWING THE DIRECTION FROM WHICH THE BENT DRAWING IS VIEWED.
- LABEL POSTS A, B, C, ETC. FROM FRONT TO BACK.
- GIVE BAY NUMBERS (SPACE BETWEEN TWO BENTS) IN ROMAN NUMERALS, AS I, II, III, ETC.
- GIRTS, SUMMER BEAMS, AND JOISTS ARE ALSO LABELED WITH THE FLOOR NUMBER.
- IN ADDITION TO LABELING A TIMBER WITH ITS LOCATION WITHIN THE FRAME, ITS ORIENTATION MUST ALSO BE GIVEN. THIS INCLUDES "TOP", "BOTTOM", "OUTSIDE FACE", AND "INSIDE FACE". LABELING THE SIDES OF TIMBERS, PARTICULARLY POSTS, WITH NORTH, SOUTH, EAST, AND WEST IS HELPFUL FOR ORIENTATION.

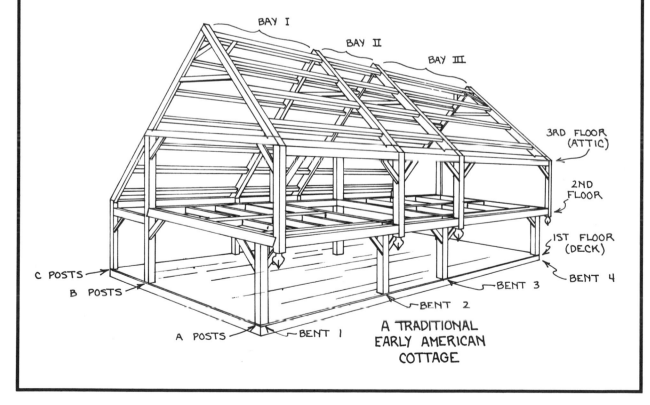

A TRADITIONAL EARLY AMERICAN COTTAGE

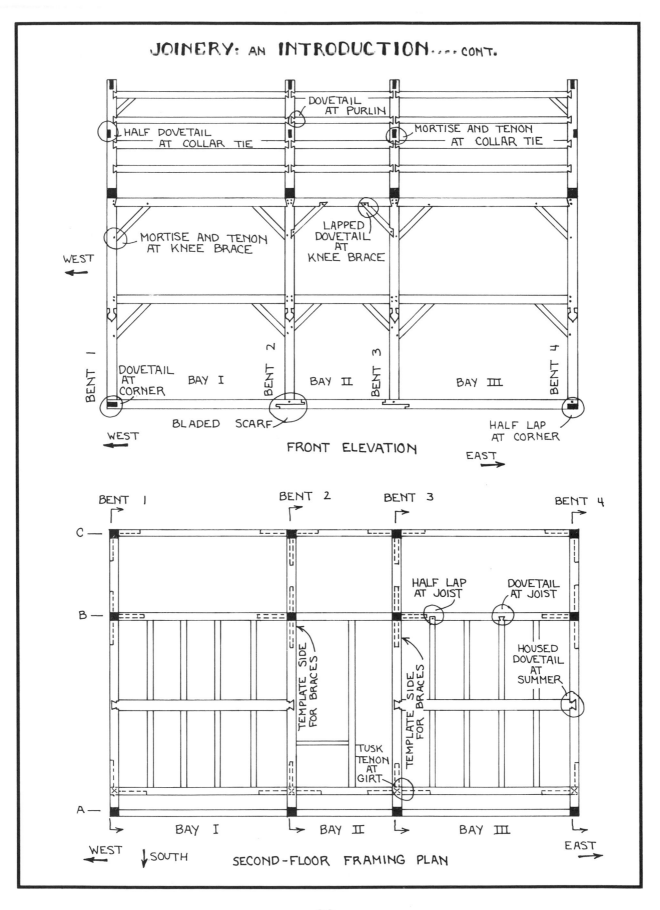

DOVETAIL AT PURLIN

HALF DOVETAIL AT COLLAR TIE

MORTISE AND TENON AT COLLAR TIE

MORTISE AND TENON AT KNEE BRACE

LAPPED DOVETAIL AT KNEE BRACE

WEST

BENT 1

BENT 2

BENT 3

BENT 4

BAY I

BAY II

BAY III

DOVETAIL AT CORNER

BLADED SCARF

HALF LAP AT CORNER

WEST

EAST

FRONT ELEVATION

BENT 1

BENT 2

BENT 3

BENT 4

C —

B —

A —

HALF LAP AT JOIST

DOVETAIL AT JOIST

HOUSED DOVETAIL AT SUMMER

TEMPLATE SIDE FOR BRACES

TEMPLATE SIDE FOR BRACES

TUSK TENON AT GIRT

BAY I

BAY II

BAY III

WEST

SOUTH

EAST

SECOND-FLOOR FRAMING PLAN

JOINERY: AN INTRODUCTION....CONT.

MARKING TIMBERS

A LUMBER CRAYON IS EASY TO USE FOR LABELING. AFTER A TIMBER IS CUT AND BEFORE IT IS PLANED AND SANDED, TRANSFER THIS INFORMATION TO THE ENDS. IF THE BEAMS ARE TO BE LEFT ROUGH, USE PENCIL INSTEAD.

SOME DEFINITIONS AND SYMBOLS

IN THE FOLLOWING PAGES, THESE TERMS AND SYMBOLS ARE USED TO DESCRIBE LAYING OUT JOINERY:

TEMPLATE: A PATTERN OF A JOINT CUT OUT OF A THIN SHEET SUCH AS PLYWOOD, USED FOR LAYING OUT AND TESTING THE ACCURACY OF A JOINT.

FRAMING SQUARE: VITAL TO LAYING OUT JOINTS. IT IS USED FOR SQUARING OFF TIMBERS, DRAWING PERPENDICULAR LINES ON A TIMBER, AND AS $1\frac{1}{2}$-INCH AND 2-INCH TEMPLATES.

SHADED AREA: AREA OF WOOD THAT IS TO BE REMOVED WHEN JOINT IS CUT.

W_G, W_S, ETC: LARGE LETTER, W= WIDTH OF TIMBER, D= DEPTH OF TIMBER. SUBSCRIPT INDICATES NAME OF TIMBER.

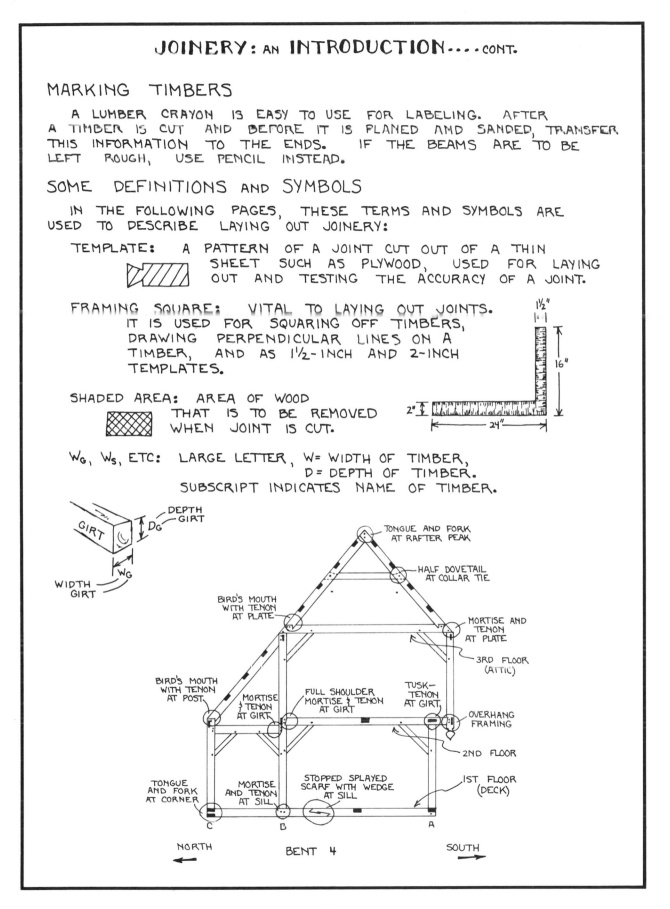

BENT 4

NORTH

SOUTH

MORTISE AND TENON

The most basic timber-framing joint is the mortise and tenon. It's a simple, straight projection from one timber received by a slot in another. When it is joined and pinned, it's a good way to tie timbers or to lock them, but the joint itself should be designed to carry only a light load. Its most common uses are for nonload-bearing girts and to lock posts to a plate and a sill.

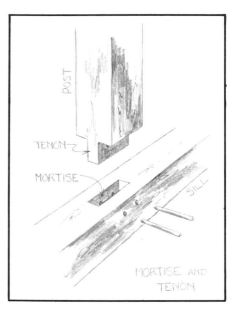

SHOULDERED MORTISE AND TENON

Adding a shoulder to the mortise and tenon gives it entirely different load-support qualities. It's a simple variation, but it makes a great difference in strength. By having the lower surface of the beam project into the post, the full width of the beam supports the load rather than just the width of the tenon. This allows the joint to bear three to four times more weight than the simple mortise and tenon.

Courtesy of Tafi Brown

Courtesy of Tafi Brown

ANCHOR-BEAM JOINT

The Pennsylvania Dutch used a variation of the shouldered mortise and tenon in their barns. They let the tenon of a massive girt pass through the post and extend over a foot beyond. The tenon was then not only pegged through the post but was also wedged from the opposite side. The tying strength of this joint was so great and so important to the over-all rigidity of the frame that the timber came to be known as an anchor beam.

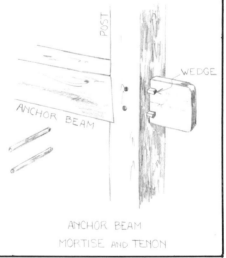

KNEE-BRACE JOINT

The rigidity of the frame is greatly dependent upon the effect of properly fitted knee braces. They stiffen the posts and beams within the framework by connecting them diagonally. Because of the triangulation created by this piece, all the layouts and cuts must be extremely accurate or the brace will not fit. The braces are deceptively difficult to join, but it's worth doing well.

In thirteenth-century England, buildings were raised practically timber by timber, making it far easier to join the braces after the major timbers had been raised. These braces were lap jointed, as they traversed several timbers.

By the fourteenth century, the braces were smaller, and larger sections of the frame were assembled on the ground. This led to the more frequent use of the mortise-and-tenon joint. When timber framing was practiced in this country, the mortise-and-tenon brace was practically universal. Since the tenon is fully surrounded by wood, this type of connection helps the brace to resist buckling and rotation and is therefore better.

Courtesy of Tafi Brown

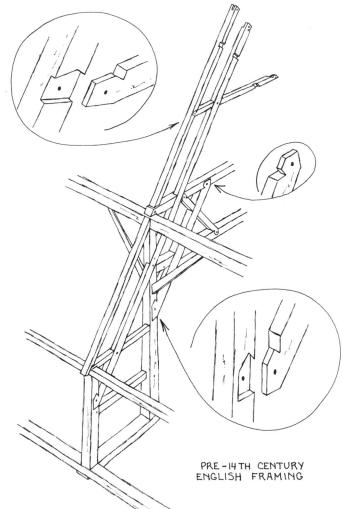

PRE-14TH CENTURY
ENGLISH FRAMING

SCARF JOINT

The scarf joint is used to splice two timbers end-to-end to make one longer timber. The complicated timber scarfs are some of the most sophisticated and difficult joints in the whole woodworking field. Their use can be dated back to A.D. 1200. They developed so quickly that by A.D. 1400 scarfing timbers was general practice. Research has revealed at least twenty-four different scarf joints in the evolution of timber framing in Tudor England.

It was necessity that caused the development of the scarf. When long timbers were no longer available, it didn't mean that buildings became shorter. It meant that the joiners had to solve their problems with what they had; therefore, the need for scarfing. The colonists enjoyed a brief period of "join-

42

Courtesy of Tafi Brown

er's bliss" when they were able to hew a timber to practically any normal building's length from the virgin forests in the new country. But that era is gone and those of us who work with timbers today must learn again the art of scarfing.

The most important principle to remember is that the joint itself is a compromise. One would rather have a longer timber. Realizing this fact, respect the joint for what it is and don't ask it to do the work of a complete timber. The scarf is primarily a tying joint and should have support underneath or nearby.

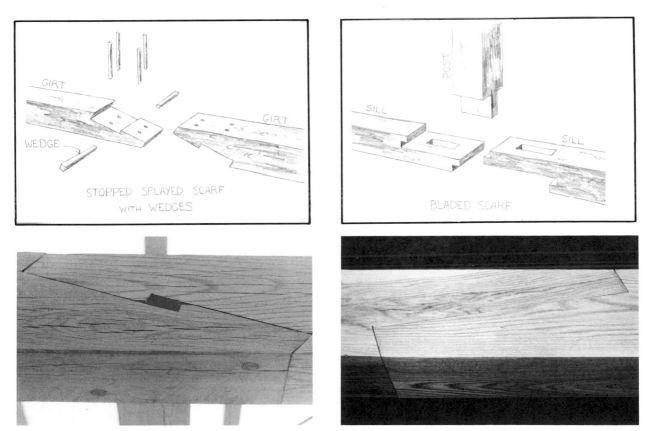

Courtesy of Tafi Brown

Courtesy of Robert H. Brown

43

Courtesy of Robert H. Brown

Courtesy of Robert H. Brown

HOUSED DOVETAIL

The housed dovetail is unique in that it is the only major timber connection that does not use a peg. The joint is designed so that the timber can be placed in the structure after the bents have been raised. The wedging effect of the dovetail and the weight of the timber lock this joint into place. The "housing" helps the timber to retain its strength at the connection. This ingenious joint, drawing its strength from precise cutting of the two connections, seems to have been developed by American settlers.

Courtesy of Robert H. Brown

44

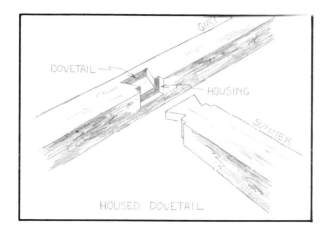

TUSK TENON

The tusk tenon can be used in place of the housed-dovetail joint. When pegged, the tenon holds the joint together. The tusk is the lower housed area that allows a major cross section of the beam to bear the weight at the joint. There is some dispute as to the name of this joint, but tusk tenon is the term most commonly used in this country.

DOVETAIL

The simple dovetail is commonly used to join the smaller members, such as joists and purlins. The joint is designed to support a load and also serves as a tie between larger timbers.

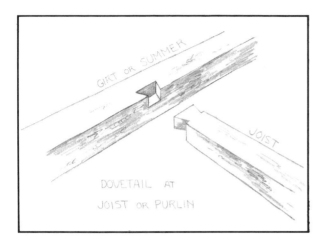

Courtesy of Robert H. Brown

CORNER JOINTS AT SILL

The goal at the corner of the sills is to make a locking connection and maintain full support for the post. The simple solution is to use the tenon from the post as a pin to lock the corner timbers together. One of the best possibilities for this joint is the dovetail, which adds some internal geometric tying strength. These joints require support under the sills.

Courtesy of Robert H. Brown

46

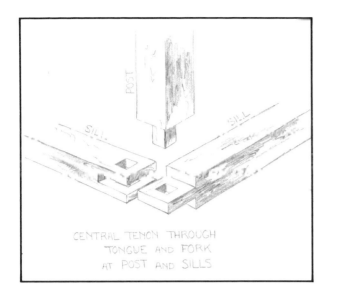

CENTRAL TENON THROUGH
TONGUE AND FORK
AT POST AND SILLS

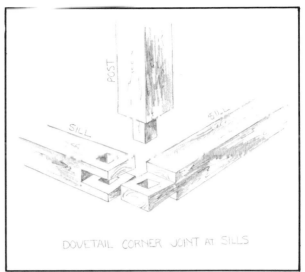

DOVETAIL CORNER JOINT AT SILLS

JOINTS AT RAFTER FEET

Rafters are attached to the frame on the plate or directly to the post. Each of the methods described here has a notch that is cut into the rafter that looks something like the open beak of a bird, or "bird's mouth." This notch helps to keep the rafter from spreading and is an important part of the joint. Either a pegged tenon or a trunnel (a peg at least one and one-half inches in diameter) should position the rafter securely.

Courtesy of Tafi Brown

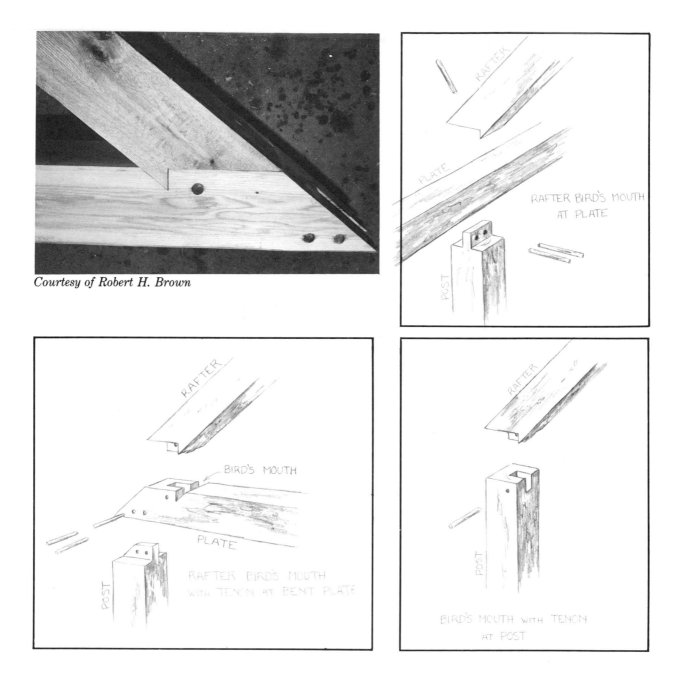

Courtesy of Robert H. Brown

RAFTER

PLATE

POST

RAFTER BIRD'S MOUTH
AT PLATE

RAFTER

BIRD'S MOUTH

PLATE

POST

RAFTER BIRD'S MOUTH
WITH TENON AT BENT PLATE

RAFTER

POST

BIRD'S MOUTH WITH TENON
AT POST

TONGUE AND FORK

The tongue and fork, an ancient joint, ties the rafters at their peak. This is a method for securely locking the rafters together without the use of a ridgepole. Traditionally, the ridgepole would run the full length of the building, with individual rafters mortised into it. It is not uncommon to find a ridgepole in an old building to be more than fifty feet long. Today, because timbers of this length are not generally available, we use the tongue-and-fork joint.

RAFTER

RAFTER

TONGUE AND FORK
AT RAFTER PEAK

Courtesy of Tafi Brown

Courtesy of Robert H. Brown

COLLAR-TIE JOINT

This drawing shows a half-lapped dovetail as the collar tie to rafter connection. Another common way to join them is with a central mortise and tenon. Since the purpose of the collar tie is to resist rafter spreading and sagging, the type of joint to use is determined by how the rafters fit into the framework. If a pair of rafters join a plate that spans the width of the building, there is little chance of spreading. In this case, the purpose of the collar tie would be only to resist sagging, and for that the central mortise and tenon would be adequate. If the rafter is framed to a post or plate that is not securely connected, the half-lapped dovetail would be better, because its interlocking geometry gives intrinsic resistance to rafter spreading.

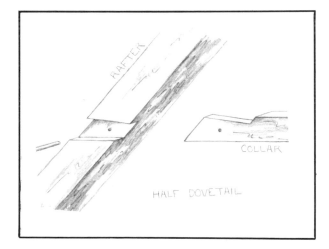

49

FRAMED OVERHANG

The framing of an overhang is a composite of joinery. The drawing illustrates how several types of joints can work together to form a strong unit. In the complete frame, the intersection of timbers becomes a major design consideration. As a general rule, more than three beams should not meet at the same elevation on a post.

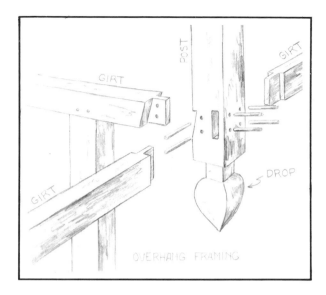

Courtesy of Tafi Brown

The best allies to the timber joiner are his imagination and his respect for the wood. He must be able to picture the timber with the wood removed, revealing the joints, and envision that timber attached to the rest of the framework in the position for which it is best suited. The joiner should realize the significance of the timber itself. As each line is drawn, he is illustrating the destiny of a tree whose history probably predates his own, whose rhythm of life was as real as his own. He knows, too, that when his job is properly done the life of the timber will continue. It will shrink, swell, move, breathe, bear loads, and resist winds, essentially doing the same work that it did when it stood in the forest. Only its location will have changed.

With this understanding, these layout lines take on new importance. Behind the lines etched into this timber are decisions: about a position in a living framework, about joints that will be strong, and about wood that will be seen in a house that was built to last.

TIMBER LAYOUT
THE FIRST STEPS

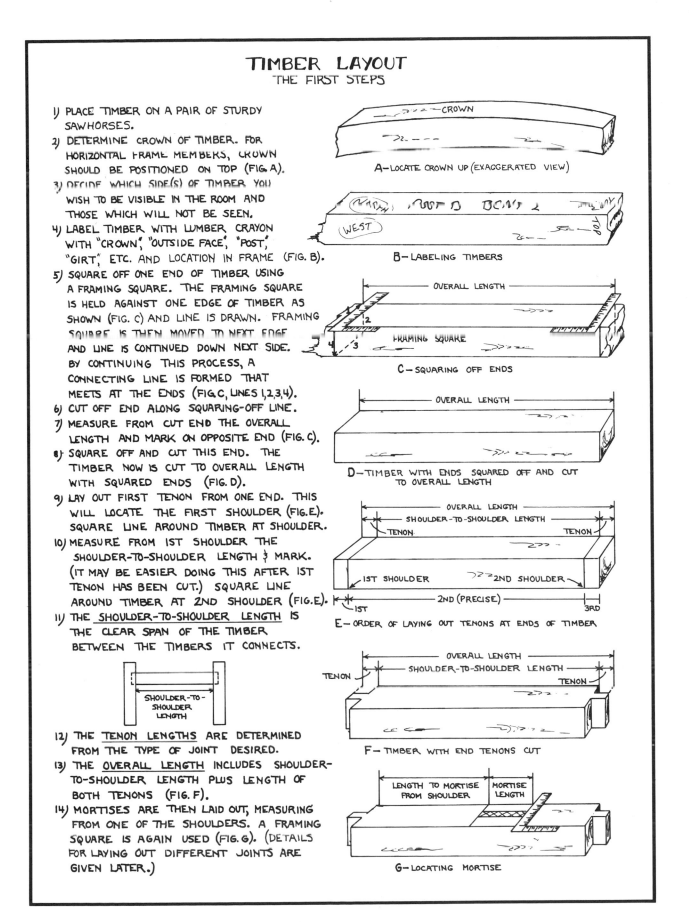

1) PLACE TIMBER ON A PAIR OF STURDY SAWHORSES.

2) DETERMINE CROWN OF TIMBER. FOR HORIZONTAL FRAME MEMBERS, CROWN SHOULD BE POSITIONED ON TOP (FIG. A).

A—LOCATE CROWN UP (EXAGGERATED VIEW)

3) DECIDE WHICH SIDE(S) OF TIMBER YOU WISH TO BE VISIBLE IN THE ROOM AND THOSE WHICH WILL NOT BE SEEN.

4) LABEL TIMBER WITH LUMBER CRAYON WITH "CROWN", "OUTSIDE FACE", "POST", "GIRT", ETC. AND LOCATION IN FRAME (FIG. B).

B—LABELING TIMBERS

5) SQUARE OFF ONE END OF TIMBER USING A FRAMING SQUARE. THE FRAMING SQUARE IS HELD AGAINST ONE EDGE OF TIMBER AS SHOWN (FIG. C) AND LINE IS DRAWN. FRAMING SQUARE IS THEN MOVED TO NEXT EDGE AND LINE IS CONTINUED DOWN NEXT SIDE. BY CONTINUING THIS PROCESS, A CONNECTING LINE IS FORMED THAT MEETS AT THE ENDS (FIG C, LINES 1,2,3,4).

C—SQUARING OFF ENDS

6) CUT OFF END ALONG SQUARING-OFF LINE.

7) MEASURE FROM CUT END THE OVERALL LENGTH AND MARK ON OPPOSITE END (FIG. C).

8) SQUARE OFF AND CUT THIS END. THE TIMBER NOW IS CUT TO OVERALL LENGTH WITH SQUARED ENDS (FIG. D).

D—TIMBER WITH ENDS SQUARED OFF AND CUT TO OVERALL LENGTH

9) LAY OUT FIRST TENON FROM ONE END. THIS WILL LOCATE THE FIRST SHOULDER (FIG. E). SQUARE LINE AROUND TIMBER AT SHOULDER.

10) MEASURE FROM 1ST SHOULDER THE SHOULDER-TO-SHOULDER LENGTH & MARK. (IT MAY BE EASIER DOING THIS AFTER 1ST TENON HAS BEEN CUT.) SQUARE LINE AROUND TIMBER AT 2ND SHOULDER (FIG. E).

E—ORDER OF LAYING OUT TENONS AT ENDS OF TIMBER

11) THE SHOULDER-TO-SHOULDER LENGTH IS THE CLEAR SPAN OF THE TIMBER BETWEEN THE TIMBERS IT CONNECTS.

SHOULDER-TO-SHOULDER LENGTH

12) THE TENON LENGTHS ARE DETERMINED FROM THE TYPE OF JOINT DESIRED.

13) THE OVERALL LENGTH INCLUDES SHOULDER-TO-SHOULDER LENGTH PLUS LENGTH OF BOTH TENONS (FIG. F).

F—TIMBER WITH END TENONS CUT

14) MORTISES ARE THEN LAID OUT, MEASURING FROM ONE OF THE SHOULDERS. A FRAMING SQUARE IS AGAIN USED (FIG. G). (DETAILS FOR LAYING OUT DIFFERENT JOINTS ARE GIVEN LATER.)

G—LOCATING MORTISE

THE MORTISE AND TENON

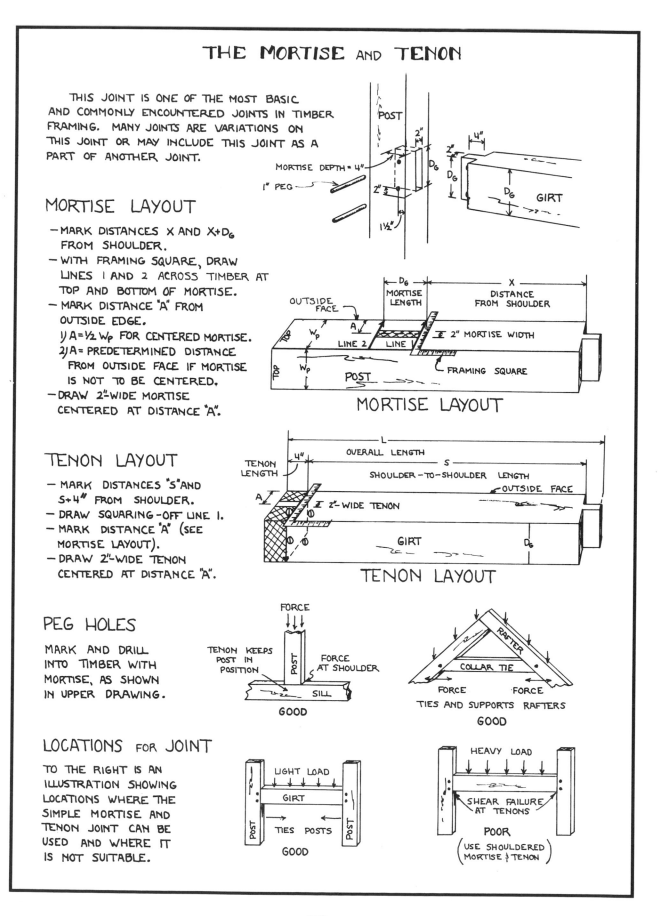

THIS JOINT IS ONE OF THE MOST BASIC AND COMMONLY ENCOUNTERED JOINTS IN TIMBER FRAMING. MANY JOINTS ARE VARIATIONS ON THIS JOINT OR MAY INCLUDE THIS JOINT AS A PART OF ANOTHER JOINT.

POST

MORTISE DEPTH = 4"

1" PEG

2"

D_G

2"

1½"

4"

2"

D_G

D_G

GIRT

MORTISE LAYOUT

- MARK DISTANCES X AND X+D_G FROM SHOULDER.
- WITH FRAMING SQUARE, DRAW LINES 1 AND 2 ACROSS TIMBER AT TOP AND BOTTOM OF MORTISE.
- MARK DISTANCE "A" FROM OUTSIDE EDGE.
  1) A=½ W_P FOR CENTERED MORTISE.
  2) A= PREDETERMINED DISTANCE FROM OUTSIDE FACE IF MORTISE IS NOT TO BE CENTERED.
- DRAW 2"-WIDE MORTISE CENTERED AT DISTANCE "A".

OUTSIDE FACE

D_G MORTISE LENGTH

X DISTANCE FROM SHOULDER

TOP

W_P

A

LINE 2   LINE 1

2" MORTISE WIDTH

W_P

TOP

POST

FRAMING SQUARE

MORTISE LAYOUT

TENON LAYOUT

- MARK DISTANCES "S" AND S+4" FROM SHOULDER.
- DRAW SQUARING-OFF LINE 1.
- MARK DISTANCE "A" (SEE MORTISE LAYOUT).
- DRAW 2"-WIDE TENON CENTERED AT DISTANCE "A".

L OVERALL LENGTH

TENON LENGTH   4"

S SHOULDER-TO-SHOULDER LENGTH

OUTSIDE FACE

A

2"-WIDE TENON

GIRT

D_G

TENON LAYOUT

PEG HOLES

MARK AND DRILL INTO TIMBER WITH MORTISE, AS SHOWN IN UPPER DRAWING.

FORCE

TENON KEEPS POST IN POSITION

POST

FORCE AT SHOULDER

SILL

GOOD

RAFTER

COLLAR TIE

FORCE   FORCE

TIES AND SUPPORTS RAFTERS

GOOD

LOCATIONS FOR JOINT

TO THE RIGHT IS AN ILLUSTRATION SHOWING LOCATIONS WHERE THE SIMPLE MORTISE AND TENON JOINT CAN BE USED AND WHERE IT IS NOT SUITABLE.

LIGHT LOAD

GIRT

POST   POST

TIES POSTS

GOOD

HEAVY LOAD

SHEAR FAILURE AT TENONS

POOR

(USE SHOULDERED MORTISE & TENON)

THE SHOULDERED MORTISE AND TENON

THE SHOULDERED MORTISE AND TENON JOINT SHOULD BE USED IN PLACE OF A SIMPLE MORTISE AND TENON WHEN THE GIRT IS BEARING A FULL FLOOR LOAD. THE SHOULDER BEARS MOST OF THE VERTICAL WEIGHT OF THE GIRT AND THE PEGGED TENON HOLDS THE JOINT TOGETHER.

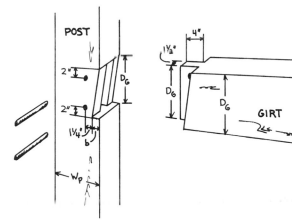

MORTISE LAYOUT

- LAY OUT 1½"-WIDE MORTISE EITHER CENTERED OR PREDETERMINED DISTANCE FROM OUTSIDE.
- MAKE TEMPLATE AS SHOWN.
- PLACE TEMPLATE WITH "MARK" LINING UP WITH EDGE OF TIMBER. BE CERTAIN THAT TEMPLATE IS SQUARE WITH TIMBER.
- MARK SHOULDER LAYOUT LINE.
- PLACE TEMPLATE ON OPPOSITE SIDE OF TIMBER AND REPEAT.
- LOCATE PEG HOLES AS SHOWN ABOVE.

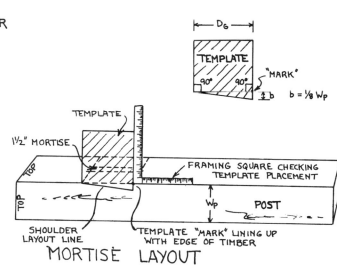

MORTISE LAYOUT

TENON LAYOUT

- LAY OUT 1½"-WIDE TENON EITHER CENTERED OR PREDETERMINED DISTANCE FROM THE OUTSIDE.
- PLACE TEMPLATE ON GIRT.
- DRAW SHOULDER LAYOUT LINE.
- PLACE ON OPPOSITE SIDE AND REPEAT.

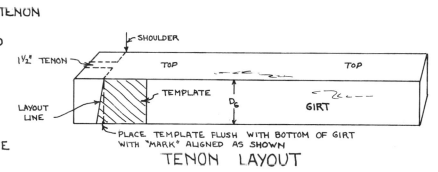

TENON LAYOUT

KNEE BRACE JOINTS

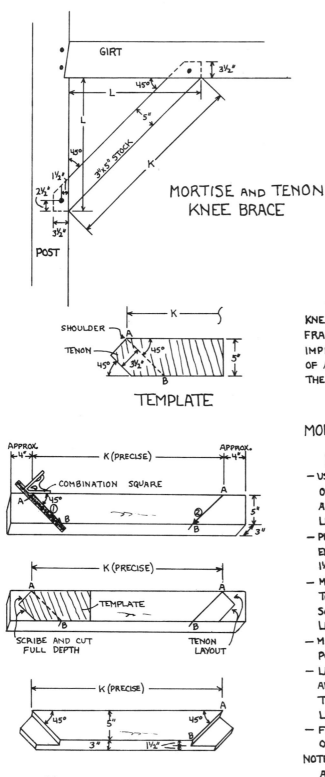

MORTISE AND TENON
KNEE BRACE

GIRT

3½"

45°

L

L

45°

5"

3"x5" STOCK

K

1½"

2½"

3½"

POST

TEMPLATE

SHOULDER

TENON

A

45°

45°

3½"

B

K

5"

SIZES OF BRACES $L^2 + L^2 = K^2$	
L	K
24"	33 15/16"
30"	42 7/16"
36"	50 15/16"
42"	59 7/16"
48"	67 7/8"

DETERMINATION OF
KNEE BRACE LENGTHS
USING PYTHAGOREAN
THEOREM

THE PRECISE LAYING OUT AND CUTTING OF KNEE BRACES IS ONE OF THE MOST IMPORTANT FRAMING PROCEDURES. KNEE BRACES IMPROPERLY MEASURED BY ONLY A FRACTION OF AN INCH, WHEN ASSEMBLED, WILL THROW THE ENTIRE FRAME OUT OF SQUARE.

MORTISE AND TENON KNEE BRACE

KNEE BRACE LAYOUT

- USING 3"x5" STOCK, DETERMINE ROUGH OVERALL LENGTH OF KNEE BRACE FROM ABOVE TABLE OF SIZES (ROUGH OVERALL LENGTH = K+8").
- PLACE COMBINATION SQUARE 4" FROM ONE END. SCRIBE 45° ANGLE (LINE 1). CUT LINE 1½" DEEP (½ DEPTH OF KNEE BRACE).
- MEASURE VERY PRECISELY DISTANCE K TO SECOND SHOULDER. PLACE COMBINATION SQUARE AND SCRIBE 45° LINE 2. CUT LINE 1½" DEEP.
- MAKE TEMPLATE AS SHOWN ABOVE WITH POINTS A AND B MARKING OUT SHOULDER.
- LAY TEMPLATE ON CUT LINE 1 (POINTS A AND B ON TEMPLATE LINING UP). SCRIBE TENON LAYOUT AND CUT ON LAYOUT LINE FULL DEPTH.
- FLIP TEMPLATE AND REPEAT ON OPPOSITE END
- NOTE: 3 OR 4 CUTS 1½" DEEP OVER TENON AREA WILL MAKE WOOD REMOVAL EASIER

APPROX. 4"

K (PRECISE)

APPROX. 4"

COMBINATION SQUARE

A

45°

B

1

A

2

B

5"

3"

K (PRECISE)

A

A

TEMPLATE

B

B

TENON LAYOUT

SCRIBE AND CUT
FULL DEPTH

K (PRECISE)

45°

5"

45°

A

3"

1½"

B

KNEE BRACE LAYOUT

CONT....

MORTISE LAYOUT

— MEASURE FROM SHOULDER OF POST OR BEAM DISTANCE L (SEE TABLE, "SIZES OF BRACES"). MARK AND SQUARE ACROSS TIMBER.

— MEASURE BACK DISTANCE OF $7\frac{1}{8}$". MARK AND SQUARE ACROSS TIMBER. THIS LAYS OUT ENDS OF MORTISE.

— LAY OUT $1\frac{1}{2}$" MORTISE. NOTE DIFFERENT LOCATIONS OF MORTISES FOR CENTERED AND FLUSH-TO-THE-OUTSIDE KNEE BRACES.

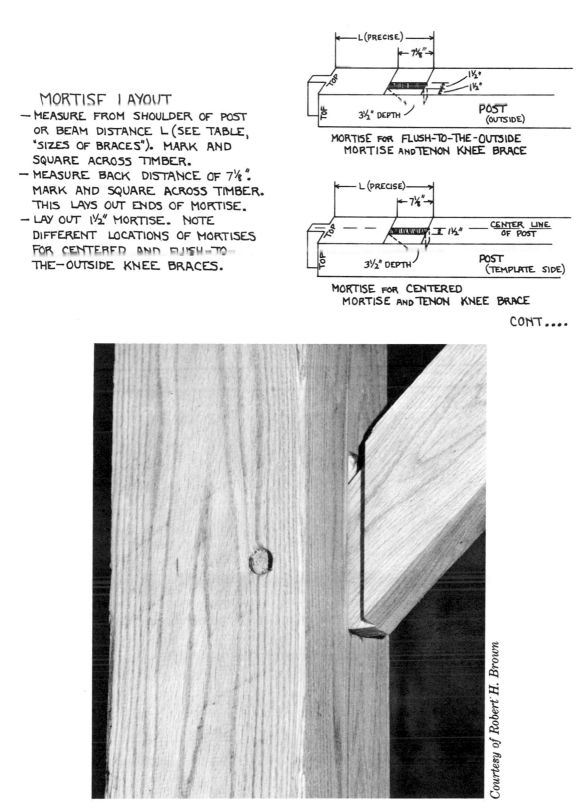

L (PRECISE)

$7\frac{1}{8}$"

$1\frac{1}{2}$"

$1\frac{1}{2}$"

TOP

TOP

$3\frac{1}{2}$" DEPTH

POST (OUTSIDE)

MORTISE FOR FLUSH-TO-THE-OUTSIDE MORTISE AND TENON KNEE BRACE

L (PRECISE)

$7\frac{1}{8}$"

$1\frac{1}{2}$"

CENTER LINE OF POST

TOP

TOP

$3\frac{1}{2}$" DEPTH

POST (TEMPLATE SIDE)

MORTISE FOR CENTERED MORTISE AND TENON KNEE BRACE

CONT....

Courtesy of Robert H. Brown

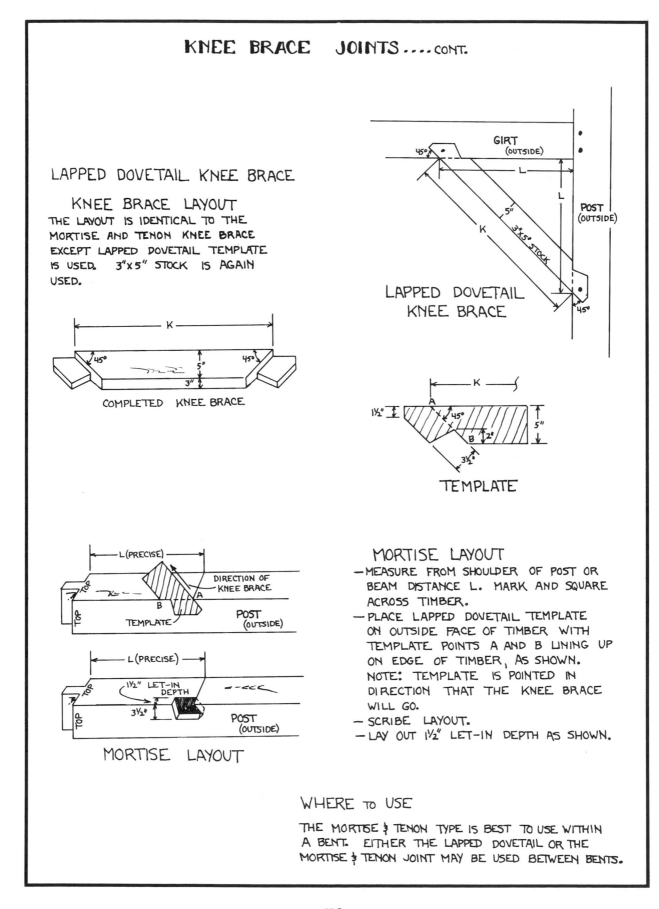

LAPPED DOVETAIL KNEE BRACE

KNEE BRACE LAYOUT

THE LAYOUT IS IDENTICAL TO THE MORTISE AND TENON KNEE BRACE EXCEPT LAPPED DOVETAIL TEMPLATE IS USED. 3"x 5" STOCK IS AGAIN USED.

COMPLETED KNEE BRACE

GIRT (OUTSIDE)

POST (OUTSIDE)

3"x 5" STOCK

LAPPED DOVETAIL KNEE BRACE

TEMPLATE

L (PRECISE)

DIRECTION OF KNEE BRACE

TEMPLATE

POST (OUTSIDE)

L (PRECISE)

1½" LET-IN DEPTH

POST (OUTSIDE)

MORTISE LAYOUT

MORTISE LAYOUT

—MEASURE FROM SHOULDER OF POST OR BEAM DISTANCE L. MARK AND SQUARE ACROSS TIMBER.

—PLACE LAPPED DOVETAIL TEMPLATE ON OUTSIDE FACE OF TIMBER WITH TEMPLATE POINTS A AND B LINING UP ON EDGE OF TIMBER, AS SHOWN. NOTE: TEMPLATE IS POINTED IN DIRECTION THAT THE KNEE BRACE WILL GO.

—SCRIBE LAYOUT.

—LAY OUT 1½" LET-IN DEPTH AS SHOWN.

WHERE TO USE

THE MORTISE & TENON TYPE IS BEST TO USE WITHIN A BENT. EITHER THE LAPPED DOVETAIL OR THE MORTISE & TENON JOINT MAY BE USED BETWEEN BENTS.

SCARF JOINTS

THE SCARF JOINT IS A METHOD OF JOINING, OR SPLICING, TWO TIMBERS END TO END TO MAKE A LONGER TIMBER. THREE BASIC TYPES ARE ILLUSTRATED.

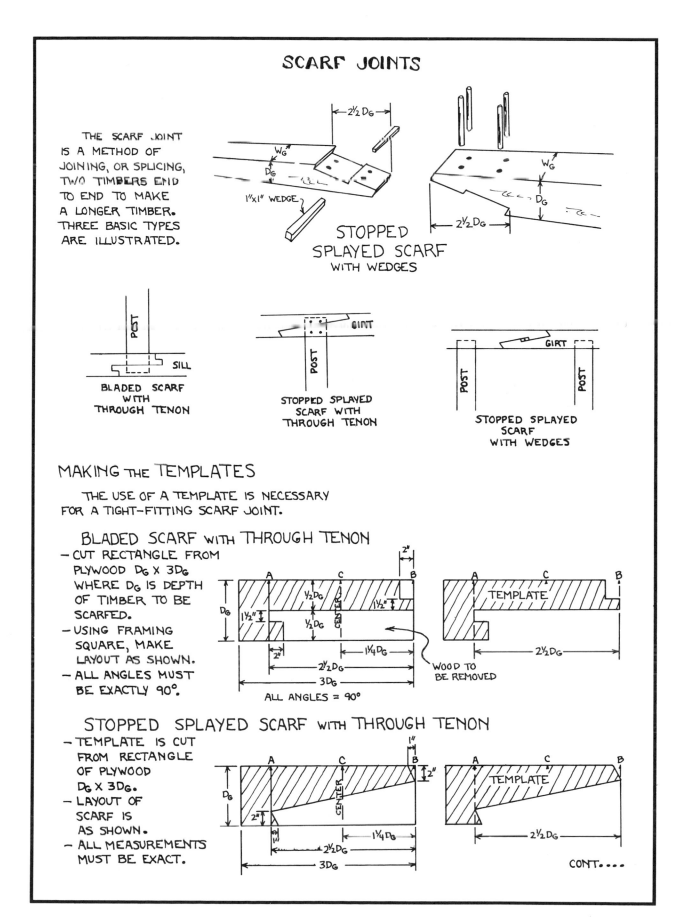

STOPPED SPLAYED SCARF WITH WEDGES

BLADED SCARF WITH THROUGH TENON

STOPPED SPLAYED SCARF WITH THROUGH TENON

STOPPED SPLAYED SCARF WITH WEDGES

MAKING the TEMPLATES

THE USE OF A TEMPLATE IS NECESSARY FOR A TIGHT-FITTING SCARF JOINT.

BLADED SCARF with THROUGH TENON

- CUT RECTANGLE FROM PLYWOOD D_G X $3D_G$ WHERE D_G IS DEPTH OF TIMBER TO BE SCARFED.
- USING FRAMING SQUARE, MAKE LAYOUT AS SHOWN.
- ALL ANGLES MUST BE EXACTLY 90°.

ALL ANGLES = 90°

WOOD TO BE REMOVED

TEMPLATE

STOPPED SPLAYED SCARF with THROUGH TENON

- TEMPLATE IS CUT FROM RECTANGLE OF PLYWOOD D_G X $3D_G$.
- LAYOUT OF SCARF IS AS SHOWN.
- ALL MEASUREMENTS MUST BE EXACT.

TEMPLATE

CONT....

STOPPED SPLAYED SCARF WITH WEDGES

- CUT RECTANGLE FROM PLYWOOD D_G X $3D_G$.
- MARK OFF LENGTH $2\frac{1}{2}D_G$.
- MARK POINTS W, X, Y AND Z AS SHOWN.
- USE COMBINATION SQUARE TO DRAW 45° LINE THROUGH POINTS W AND Z.
- DRAW LINES CONNECTING POINTS W $\frac{1}{2}$ Y AND POINTS X $\frac{1}{2}$ Z.
- DRAW CENTER LINE THROUGH POINT C USING FRAMING SQUARE.
- MARK OUT AREA 1" BOTH SIDES OF CENTER LINE, AS SHOWN, FOR WEDGE AREA.
- CUT OUT TEMPLATE.

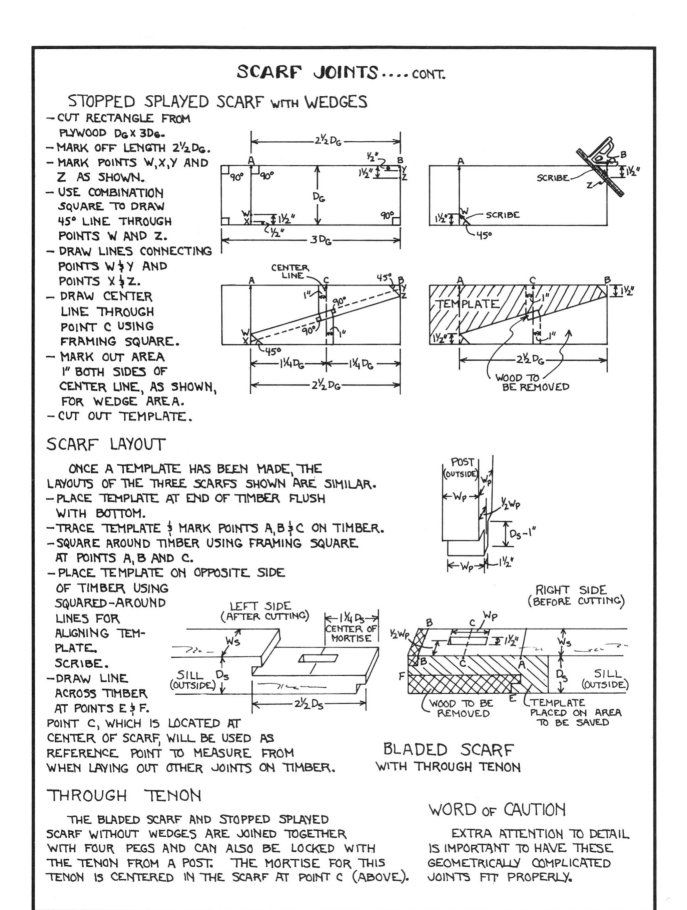

SCARF LAYOUT

ONCE A TEMPLATE HAS BEEN MADE, THE LAYOUTS OF THE THREE SCARFS SHOWN ARE SIMILAR.
- PLACE TEMPLATE AT END OF TIMBER FLUSH WITH BOTTOM.
- TRACE TEMPLATE $\frac{1}{2}$ MARK POINTS A, B $\frac{1}{2}$ C ON TIMBER.
- SQUARE AROUND TIMBER USING FRAMING SQUARE AT POINTS A, B AND C.
- PLACE TEMPLATE ON OPPOSITE SIDE OF TIMBER USING SQUARED-AROUND LINES FOR ALIGNING TEMPLATE. SCRIBE.
- DRAW LINE ACROSS TIMBER AT POINTS E $\frac{1}{2}$ F.
POINT C, WHICH IS LOCATED AT CENTER OF SCARF, WILL BE USED AS REFERENCE POINT TO MEASURE FROM WHEN LAYING OUT OTHER JOINTS ON TIMBER.

BLADED SCARF
WITH THROUGH TENON

THROUGH TENON

THE BLADED SCARF AND STOPPED SPLAYED SCARF WITHOUT WEDGES ARE JOINED TOGETHER WITH FOUR PEGS AND CAN ALSO BE LOCKED WITH THE TENON FROM A POST. THE MORTISE FOR THIS TENON IS CENTERED IN THE SCARF AT POINT C (ABOVE).

WORD OF CAUTION

EXTRA ATTENTION TO DETAIL IS IMPORTANT TO HAVE THESE GEOMETRICALLY COMPLICATED JOINTS FIT PROPERLY.

THE HOUSED DOVETAIL
AT SUMMER BEAM

THE HOUSED DOVETAIL WILL BE PRINCIPALLY USED WHEN FRAMING THE ENDS OF THE SUMMER BEAM INTO A GIRT OR PLATE. THE DOVETAIL IS THE FLARED END OF THE TENON THAT LOOKS LIKE A DOVE'S TAIL. THE "HOUSED" SECTION IS THE EXTENSION OF THE MAJOR PART OF THE SUMMER INTO THE GIRT.

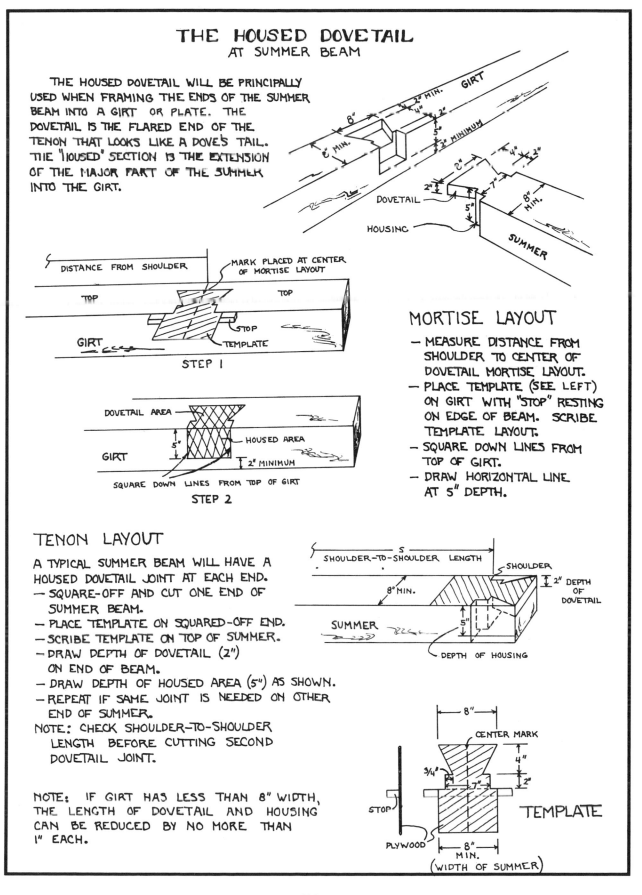

STEP 1

STEP 2

MORTISE LAYOUT

- MEASURE DISTANCE FROM SHOULDER TO CENTER OF DOVETAIL MORTISE LAYOUT.
- PLACE TEMPLATE (SEE LEFT) ON GIRT WITH "STOP" RESTING ON EDGE OF BEAM. SCRIBE TEMPLATE LAYOUT.
- SQUARE DOWN LINES FROM TOP OF GIRT.
- DRAW HORIZONTAL LINE AT 5" DEPTH.

TENON LAYOUT

A TYPICAL SUMMER BEAM WILL HAVE A HOUSED DOVETAIL JOINT AT EACH END.
- SQUARE-OFF AND CUT ONE END OF SUMMER BEAM.
- PLACE TEMPLATE ON SQUARED-OFF END.
- SCRIBE TEMPLATE ON TOP OF SUMMER.
- DRAW DEPTH OF DOVETAIL (2") ON END OF BEAM.
- DRAW DEPTH OF HOUSED AREA (5") AS SHOWN.
- REPEAT IF SAME JOINT IS NEEDED ON OTHER END OF SUMMER.

NOTE: CHECK SHOULDER-TO-SHOULDER LENGTH BEFORE CUTTING SECOND DOVETAIL JOINT.

NOTE: IF GIRT HAS LESS THAN 8" WIDTH, THE LENGTH OF DOVETAIL AND HOUSING CAN BE REDUCED BY NO MORE THAN 1" EACH.

TEMPLATE

59

TUSK TENON JOINT

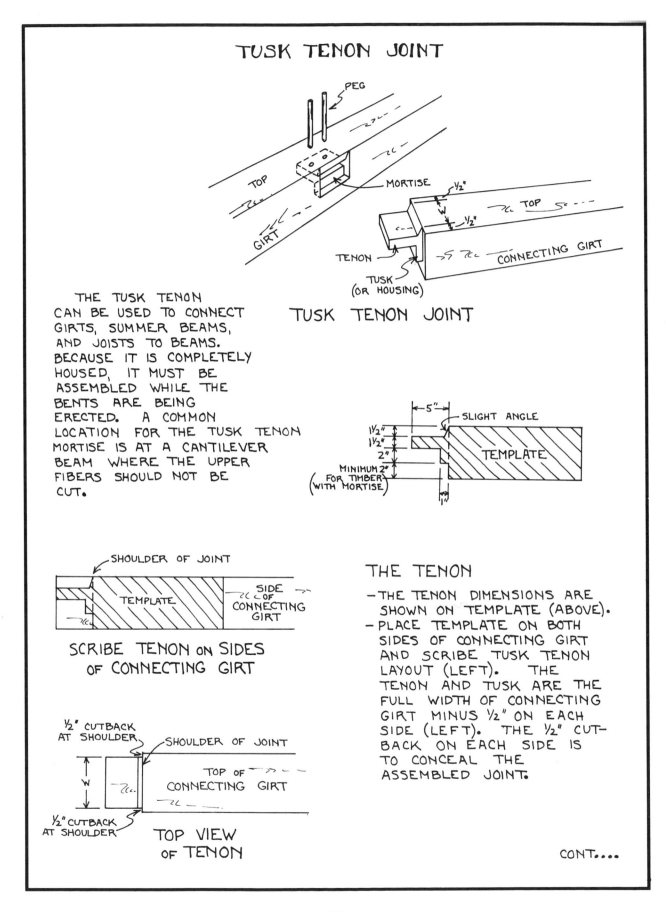

PEG

TOP

GIRT

MORTISE

½"

½"

TOP

TENON

CONNECTING GIRT

TUSK
(OR HOUSING)

TUSK TENON JOINT

THE TUSK TENON CAN BE USED TO CONNECT GIRTS, SUMMER BEAMS, AND JOISTS TO BEAMS. BECAUSE IT IS COMPLETELY HOUSED, IT MUST BE ASSEMBLED WHILE THE BENTS ARE BEING ERECTED. A COMMON LOCATION FOR THE TUSK TENON MORTISE IS AT A CANTILEVER BEAM WHERE THE UPPER FIBERS SHOULD NOT BE CUT.

5"

SLIGHT ANGLE

1½"
1½"
2"

TEMPLATE

MINIMUM 2"
FOR TIMBER
(WITH MORTISE)

1"

SHOULDER OF JOINT

TEMPLATE

SIDE OF CONNECTING GIRT

SCRIBE TENON ON SIDES OF CONNECTING GIRT

THE TENON

- THE TENON DIMENSIONS ARE SHOWN ON TEMPLATE (ABOVE).
- PLACE TEMPLATE ON BOTH SIDES OF CONNECTING GIRT AND SCRIBE TUSK TENON LAYOUT (LEFT). THE TENON AND TUSK ARE THE FULL WIDTH OF CONNECTING GIRT MINUS ½" ON EACH SIDE (LEFT). THE ½" CUTBACK ON EACH SIDE IS TO CONCEAL THE ASSEMBLED JOINT.

½" CUTBACK AT SHOULDER

SHOULDER OF JOINT

W

TOP OF CONNECTING GIRT

½" CUTBACK AT SHOULDER

TOP VIEW OF TENON

CONT....

TUSK TENON JOINT.... CONT.

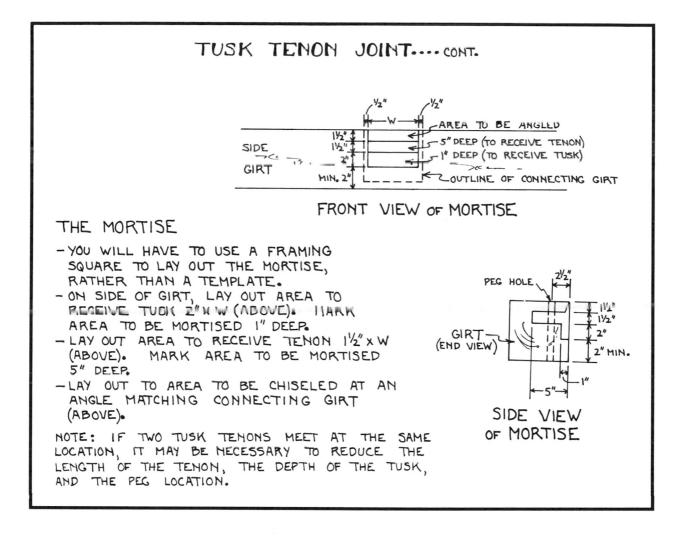

FRONT VIEW of MORTISE

THE MORTISE

- YOU WILL HAVE TO USE A FRAMING SQUARE TO LAY OUT THE MORTISE, RATHER THAN A TEMPLATE.
- ON SIDE OF GIRT, LAY OUT AREA TO RECEIVE TUSK 2" x W (ABOVE). MARK AREA TO BE MORTISED 1" DEEP.
- LAY OUT AREA TO RECEIVE TENON 1½" x W (ABOVE). MARK AREA TO BE MORTISED 5" DEEP.
- LAY OUT TO AREA TO BE CHISELED AT AN ANGLE MATCHING CONNECTING GIRT (ABOVE).

NOTE: IF TWO TUSK TENONS MEET AT THE SAME LOCATION, IT MAY BE NECESSARY TO REDUCE THE LENGTH OF THE TENON, THE DEPTH OF THE TUSK, AND THE PEG LOCATION.

SIDE VIEW OF MORTISE

DOVETAIL AND HALF LAP
FOR JOISTS AND PURLINS

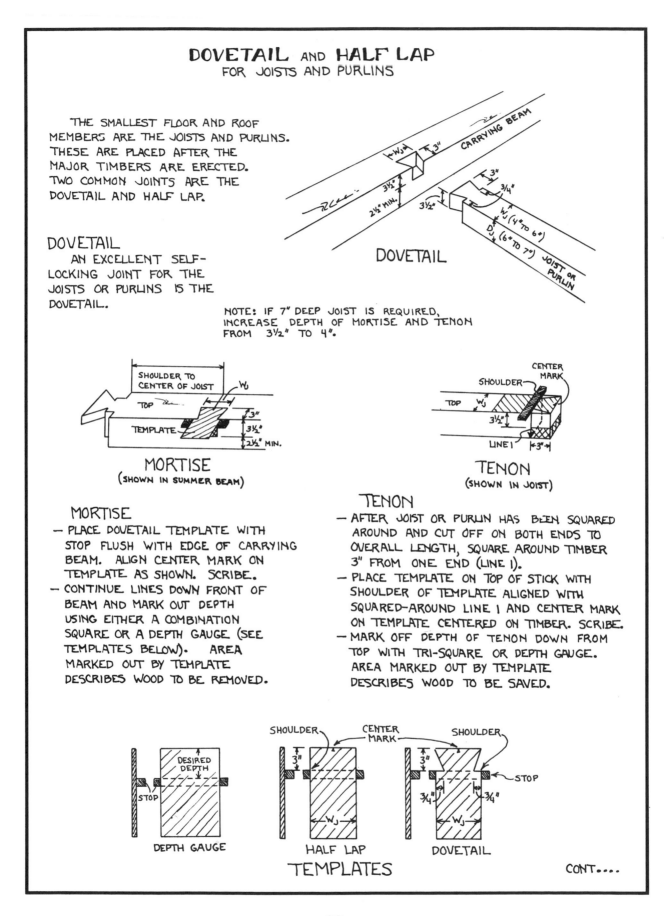

THE SMALLEST FLOOR AND ROOF MEMBERS ARE THE JOISTS AND PURLINS. THESE ARE PLACED AFTER THE MAJOR TIMBERS ARE ERECTED. TWO COMMON JOINTS ARE THE DOVETAIL AND HALF LAP.

DOVETAIL

AN EXCELLENT SELF-LOCKING JOINT FOR THE JOISTS OR PURLINS IS THE DOVETAIL.

NOTE: IF 7" DEEP JOIST IS REQUIRED, INCREASE DEPTH OF MORTISE AND TENON FROM 3½" TO 4".

DOVETAIL

MORTISE
(SHOWN IN SUMMER BEAM)

TENON
(SHOWN IN JOIST)

MORTISE

- PLACE DOVETAIL TEMPLATE WITH STOP FLUSH WITH EDGE OF CARRYING BEAM. ALIGN CENTER MARK ON TEMPLATE AS SHOWN. SCRIBE.
- CONTINUE LINES DOWN FRONT OF BEAM AND MARK OUT DEPTH USING EITHER A COMBINATION SQUARE OR A DEPTH GAUGE (SEE TEMPLATES BELOW). AREA MARKED OUT BY TEMPLATE DESCRIBES WOOD TO BE REMOVED.

TENON

- AFTER JOIST OR PURLIN HAS BEEN SQUARED AROUND AND CUT OFF ON BOTH ENDS TO OVERALL LENGTH, SQUARE AROUND TIMBER 3" FROM ONE END (LINE 1).
- PLACE TEMPLATE ON TOP OF STICK WITH SHOULDER OF TEMPLATE ALIGNED WITH SQUARED-AROUND LINE 1 AND CENTER MARK ON TEMPLATE CENTERED ON TIMBER. SCRIBE.
- MARK OFF DEPTH OF TENON DOWN FROM TOP WITH TRI-SQUARE OR DEPTH GAUGE. AREA MARKED OUT BY TEMPLATE DESCRIBES WOOD TO BE SAVED.

DEPTH GAUGE

HALF LAP

DOVETAIL

TEMPLATES

CONT....

62

DOVETAIL AND HALF LAP.... CONT.
FOR JOISTS AND PURLINS

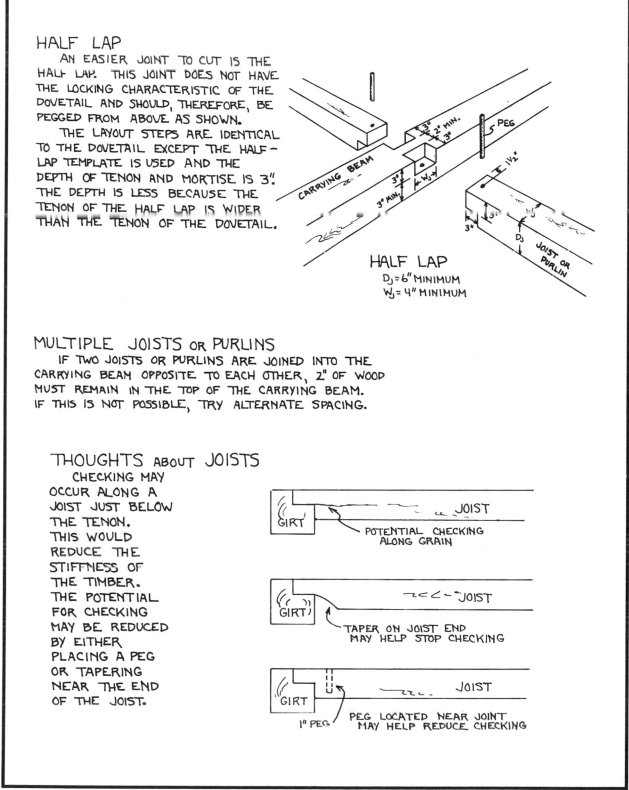

HALF LAP
AN EASIER JOINT TO CUT IS THE
HALF LAP. THIS JOINT DOES NOT HAVE
THE LOCKING CHARACTERISTIC OF THE
DOVETAIL AND SHOULD, THEREFORE, BE
PEGGED FROM ABOVE AS SHOWN.

THE LAYOUT STEPS ARE IDENTICAL
TO THE DOVETAIL EXCEPT THE HALF-
LAP TEMPLATE IS USED AND THE
DEPTH OF TENON AND MORTISE IS 3".
THE DEPTH IS LESS BECAUSE THE
TENON OF THE HALF LAP IS WIDER
THAN THE TENON OF THE DOVETAIL.

HALF LAP
D_J = 6" MINIMUM
W_J = 4" MINIMUM

MULTIPLE JOISTS OR PURLINS
IF TWO JOISTS OR PURLINS ARE JOINED INTO THE
CARRYING BEAM OPPOSITE TO EACH OTHER, 2" OF WOOD
MUST REMAIN IN THE TOP OF THE CARRYING BEAM.
IF THIS IS NOT POSSIBLE, TRY ALTERNATE SPACING.

THOUGHTS ABOUT JOISTS
CHECKING MAY
OCCUR ALONG A
JOIST JUST BELOW
THE TENON.
THIS WOULD
REDUCE THE
STIFFNESS OF
THE TIMBER.
THE POTENTIAL
FOR CHECKING
MAY BE REDUCED
BY EITHER
PLACING A PEG
OR TAPERING
NEAR THE END
OF THE JOIST.

63

CORNER JOINTS AT SILL

    THE REQUIREMENTS OF THESE JOINTS ARE TO CONNECT AND LOCK SILL TIMBERS AT RIGHT ANGLES AND TO PROVIDE A MORTISE TO RECEIVE A TENON FROM THE CORNER POST.

    THE TENON IS LOCATED IN THE POST SO THAT THE OUTSIDE FACES OF THE POST ARE FLUSH WITH THE OUTSIDE FACES OF THE SILLS. TO MAKE CERTAIN THAT THE BOTTOMS OF THE TIMBERS ARE FLUSH WITH THE FOUNDATION, LAYOUT MEASUREMENTS ARE TAKEN FROM THE BOTTOM EDGE. USE A FRAMING SQUARE TO LAY OUT THESE JOINTS.

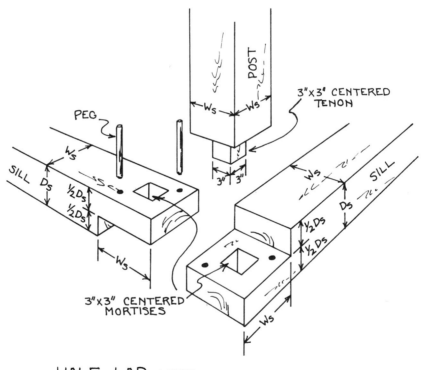

HALF LAP WITH THROUGH-POST TENON

    THE HALF-LAP JOINT (ABOVE) IS THE EASIEST TO CUT. THE THROUGH TENON FROM THE POST AND THE PEGS LOCK THE JOINT TOGETHER.

CONT....

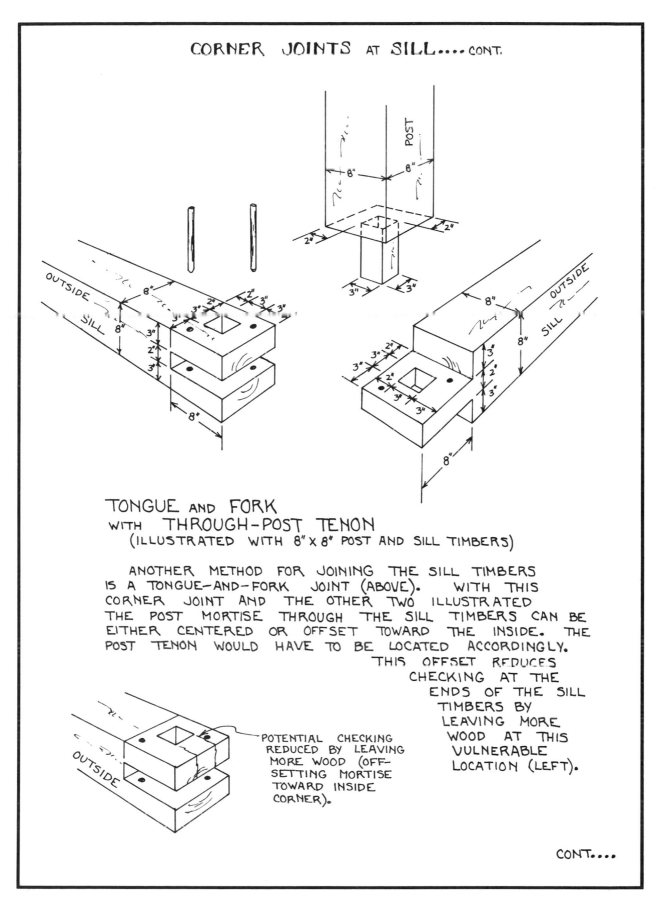

TONGUE AND FORK
WITH THROUGH-POST TENON
(ILLUSTRATED WITH 8" X 8" POST AND SILL TIMBERS)

ANOTHER METHOD FOR JOINING THE SILL TIMBERS IS A TONGUE-AND-FORK JOINT (ABOVE). WITH THIS CORNER JOINT AND THE OTHER TWO ILLUSTRATED THE POST MORTISE THROUGH THE SILL TIMBERS CAN BE EITHER CENTERED OR OFFSET TOWARD THE INSIDE. THE POST TENON WOULD HAVE TO BE LOCATED ACCORDINGLY. THIS OFFSET REDUCES CHECKING AT THE ENDS OF THE SILL TIMBERS BY LEAVING MORE WOOD AT THIS VULNERABLE LOCATION (LEFT).

POTENTIAL CHECKING REDUCED BY LEAVING MORE WOOD (OFF-SETTING MORTISE TOWARD INSIDE CORNER).

CONT....

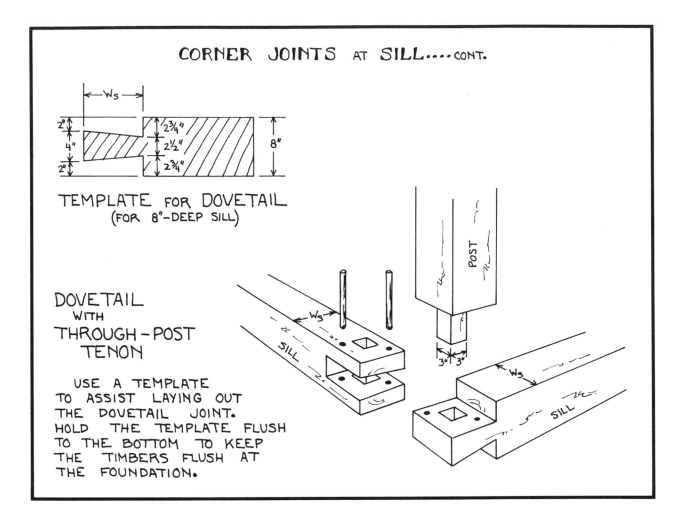

TEMPLATE FOR DOVETAIL
(FOR 8"-DEEP SILL)

DOVETAIL
WITH
THROUGH-POST
TENON

USE A TEMPLATE
TO ASSIST LAYING OUT
THE DOVETAIL JOINT.
HOLD THE TEMPLATE FLUSH
TO THE BOTTOM TO KEEP
THE TIMBERS FLUSH AT
THE FOUNDATION.

RAFTER FEET BIRD'S-MOUTH JOINT
THE TENONS

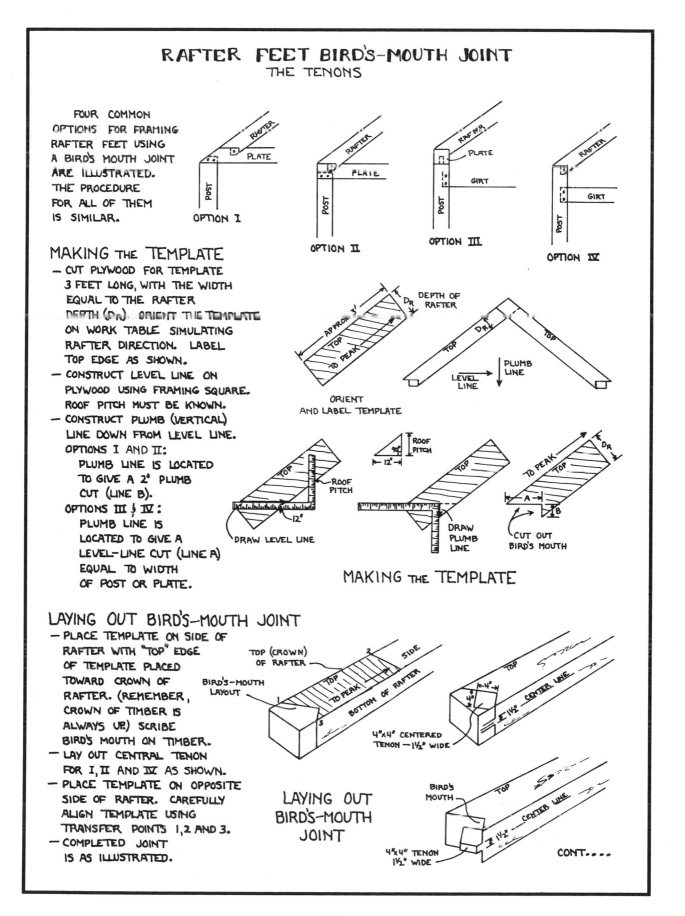

FOUR COMMON OPTIONS FOR FRAMING RAFTER FEET USING A BIRD'S MOUTH JOINT ARE ILLUSTRATED. THE PROCEDURE FOR ALL OF THEM IS SIMILAR.

OPTION I

OPTION II

OPTION III

OPTION IV

MAKING THE TEMPLATE

- CUT PLYWOOD FOR TEMPLATE 3 FEET LONG, WITH THE WIDTH EQUAL TO THE RAFTER DEPTH (D_R). ORIENT THE TEMPLATE ON WORK TABLE SIMULATING RAFTER DIRECTION. LABEL TOP EDGE AS SHOWN.
- CONSTRUCT LEVEL LINE ON PLYWOOD USING FRAMING SQUARE. ROOF PITCH MUST BE KNOWN.
- CONSTRUCT PLUMB (VERTICAL) LINE DOWN FROM LEVEL LINE.
  OPTIONS I AND II:
  PLUMB LINE IS LOCATED TO GIVE A 2" PLUMB CUT (LINE B).
  OPTIONS III & IV:
  PLUMB LINE IS LOCATED TO GIVE A LEVEL-LINE CUT (LINE A) EQUAL TO WIDTH OF POST OR PLATE.

DEPTH OF RAFTER

ORIENT AND LABEL TEMPLATE

MAKING THE TEMPLATE

LAYING OUT BIRD'S-MOUTH JOINT

- PLACE TEMPLATE ON SIDE OF RAFTER WITH "TOP" EDGE OF TEMPLATE PLACED TOWARD CROWN OF RAFTER. (REMEMBER, CROWN OF TIMBER IS ALWAYS UP.) SCRIBE BIRD'S MOUTH ON TIMBER.
- LAY OUT CENTRAL TENON FOR I, II AND IV AS SHOWN.
- PLACE TEMPLATE ON OPPOSITE SIDE OF RAFTER. CAREFULLY ALIGN TEMPLATE USING TRANSFER POINTS 1, 2 AND 3.
- COMPLETED JOINT IS AS ILLUSTRATED.

LAYING OUT BIRD'S-MOUTH JOINT

RAFTER FEET BIRD'S MOUTH JOINT.... CONT.
THE MORTISES

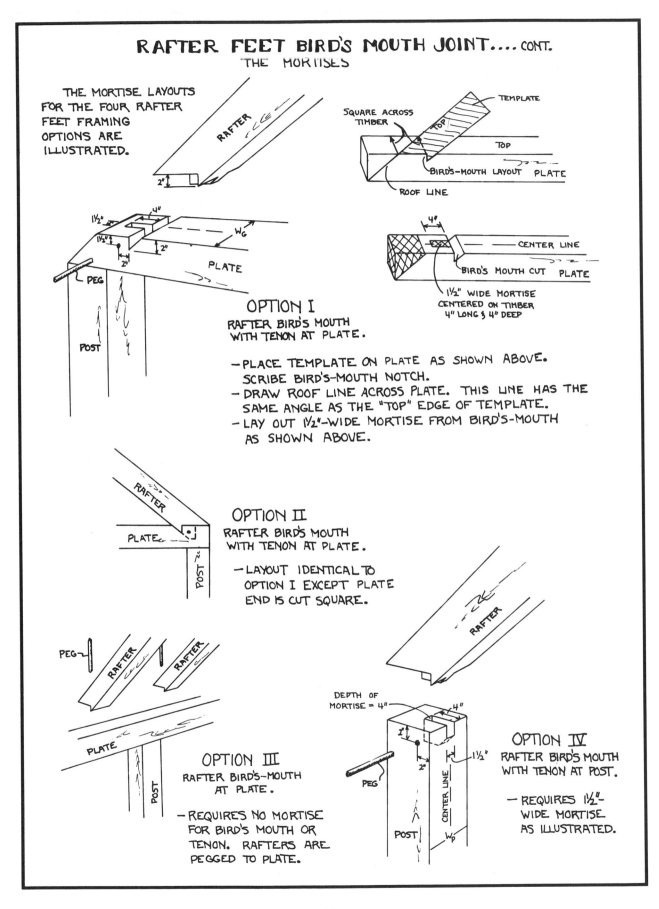

THE MORTISE LAYOUTS FOR THE FOUR RAFTER FEET FRAMING OPTIONS ARE ILLUSTRATED.

SQUARE ACROSS TIMBER

TEMPLATE

TOP

TOP

BIRD'S-MOUTH LAYOUT   PLATE

ROOF LINE

CENTER LINE

BIRD'S MOUTH CUT   PLATE

1½" WIDE MORTISE CENTERED ON TIMBER 4" LONG & 4" DEEP

OPTION I
RAFTER BIRD'S MOUTH WITH TENON AT PLATE.

- PLACE TEMPLATE ON PLATE AS SHOWN ABOVE. SCRIBE BIRD'S-MOUTH NOTCH.
- DRAW ROOF LINE ACROSS PLATE. THIS LINE HAS THE SAME ANGLE AS THE "TOP" EDGE OF TEMPLATE.
- LAY OUT 1½"-WIDE MORTISE FROM BIRD'S-MOUTH AS SHOWN ABOVE.

OPTION II
RAFTER BIRD'S MOUTH WITH TENON AT PLATE.

- LAYOUT IDENTICAL TO OPTION I EXCEPT PLATE END IS CUT SQUARE.

OPTION III
RAFTER BIRD'S-MOUTH AT PLATE.

- REQUIRES NO MORTISE FOR BIRD'S MOUTH OR TENON. RAFTERS ARE PEGGED TO PLATE.

OPTION IV
RAFTER BIRD'S MOUTH WITH TENON AT POST.

- REQUIRES 1½"- WIDE MORTISE AS ILLUSTRATED.

DEPTH OF MORTISE = 4"

TONGUE AND FORK AT RAFTER PEAK

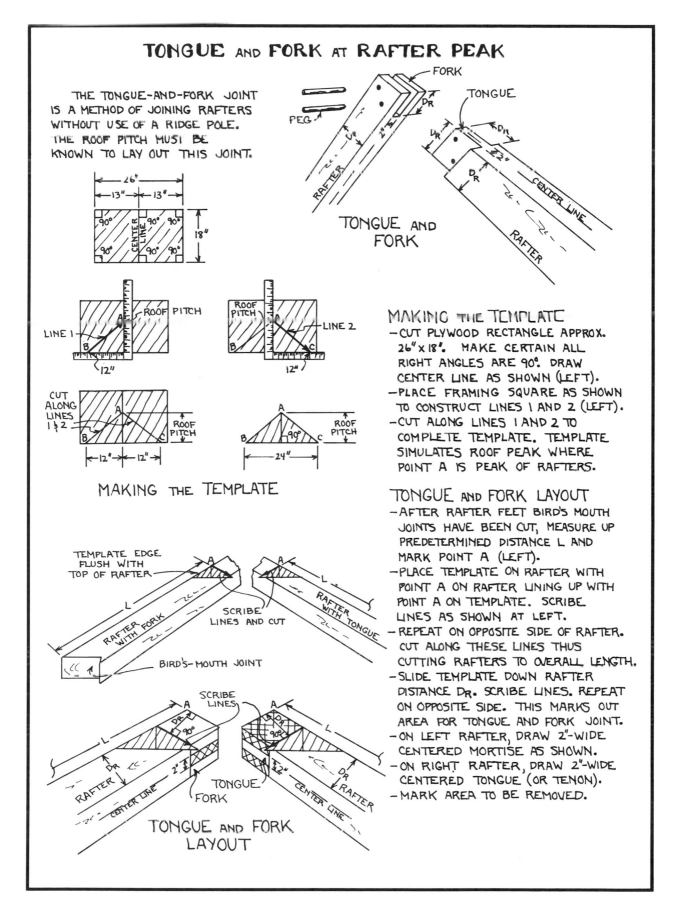

THE TONGUE-AND-FORK JOINT IS A METHOD OF JOINING RAFTERS WITHOUT USE OF A RIDGE POLE. THE ROOF PITCH MUST BE KNOWN TO LAY OUT THIS JOINT.

TONGUE AND FORK

MAKING THE TEMPLATE

TONGUE AND FORK LAYOUT

MAKING THE TEMPLATE

- CUT PLYWOOD RECTANGLE APPROX. 26" x 18". MAKE CERTAIN ALL RIGHT ANGLES ARE 90°. DRAW CENTER LINE AS SHOWN (LEFT).
- PLACE FRAMING SQUARE AS SHOWN TO CONSTRUCT LINES 1 AND 2 (LEFT).
- CUT ALONG LINES 1 AND 2 TO COMPLETE TEMPLATE. TEMPLATE SIMULATES ROOF PEAK WHERE POINT A IS PEAK OF RAFTERS.

TONGUE AND FORK LAYOUT

- AFTER RAFTER FEET BIRD'S MOUTH JOINTS HAVE BEEN CUT, MEASURE UP PREDETERMINED DISTANCE L AND MARK POINT A (LEFT).
- PLACE TEMPLATE ON RAFTER WITH POINT A ON RAFTER LINING UP WITH POINT A ON TEMPLATE. SCRIBE LINES AS SHOWN AT LEFT.
- REPEAT ON OPPOSITE SIDE OF RAFTER. CUT ALONG THESE LINES THUS CUTTING RAFTERS TO OVERALL LENGTH.
- SLIDE TEMPLATE DOWN RAFTER DISTANCE D_R. SCRIBE LINES. REPEAT ON OPPOSITE SIDE. THIS MARKS OUT AREA FOR TONGUE AND FORK JOINT.
- ON LEFT RAFTER, DRAW 2"-WIDE CENTERED MORTISE AS SHOWN.
- ON RIGHT RAFTER, DRAW 2"-WIDE CENTERED TONGUE (OR TENON).
- MARK AREA TO BE REMOVED.

COLLAR TIE HALF DOVETAIL

THE COLLAR TIE HELPS RESIST RAFTER SAGGING OR SPREADING. THE HALF DOVETAIL JOINT CAN RESIST BOTH TYPES OF FORCES. THIS JOINT IS SIMILAR TO THE DOVETAIL KNEE BRACE JOINT EXCEPT THAT THE ANGLE AT WHICH THE COLLAR TIE MEETS THE RAFTERS IS NOT NECESSARILY 45°. RATHER, THE ANGLE DEPENDS ON THE PITCH OF THE ROOF.

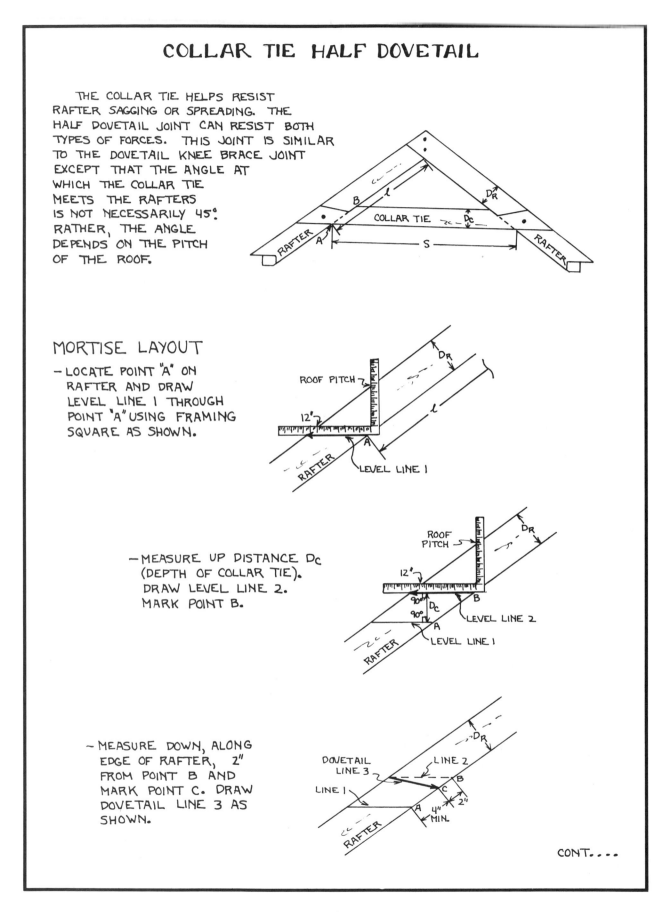

MORTISE LAYOUT

- LOCATE POINT "A" ON RAFTER AND DRAW LEVEL LINE 1 THROUGH POINT "A" USING FRAMING SQUARE AS SHOWN.

- MEASURE UP DISTANCE D_C (DEPTH OF COLLAR TIE). DRAW LEVEL LINE 2. MARK POINT B.

- MEASURE DOWN, ALONG EDGE OF RAFTER, 2" FROM POINT B AND MARK POINT C. DRAW DOVETAIL LINE 3 AS SHOWN.

CONT....

70

COLLAR TIE HALF DOVETAIL.... CONT.

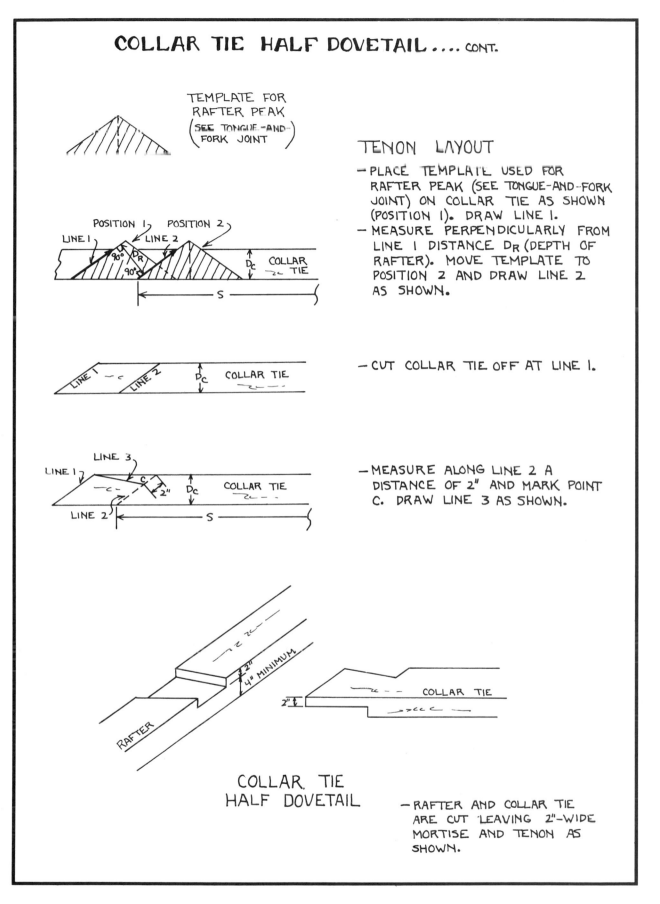

TEMPLATE FOR
RAFTER PEAK
(SEE TONGUE-AND-
FORK JOINT)

POSITION 1   POSITION 2

LINE 1   LINE 2

80°
90°

D_R

D_C COLLAR
TIE

S

LINE 1   LINE 2 D_C COLLAR TIE

LINE 3

LINE 1   c   2" D_C COLLAR TIE

LINE 2   S

2"
4" MINIMUM

RAFTER

2"   COLLAR TIE

COLLAR TIE
HALF DOVETAIL

TENON LAYOUT

- PLACE TEMPLATE USED FOR RAFTER PEAK (SEE TONGUE-AND-FORK JOINT) ON COLLAR TIE AS SHOWN (POSITION 1). DRAW LINE 1.
- MEASURE PERPENDICULARLY FROM LINE 1 DISTANCE D_R (DEPTH OF RAFTER). MOVE TEMPLATE TO POSITION 2 AND DRAW LINE 2 AS SHOWN.

- CUT COLLAR TIE OFF AT LINE 1.

- MEASURE ALONG LINE 2 A DISTANCE OF 2" AND MARK POINT C. DRAW LINE 3 AS SHOWN.

- RAFTER AND COLLAR TIE ARE CUT LEAVING 2"-WIDE MORTISE AND TENON AS SHOWN.

JOINERS' NOTES

ACCURACY

ACCURACY CANNOT BE OVEREMPHASIZED DURING THE LAYING OUT OF JOINTS. BECAUSE THE TIMBERS ARE HEAVY AND CUMBERSOME, TRIAL FITTING IN THE SHOP IS IMPRACTICAL FOR ALL BUT A FEW JOINTS. AN EXCELLENT METHOD TO AVOID COSTLY ERRORS IS TO HAVE A SECOND PERSON CHECK OUT ALL JOINT LAYOUTS BEFORE THEY ARE CUT. REMEMBER THE OLD ADAGE "MEASURE TWICE, CUT ONCE".

TRY TO WORK THE TIMBERS IN THE ORDER THAT THEY WILL BE ASSEMBLED. DOING SO WILL ALLOW YOU TO CHECK EASILY WHETHER OR NOT THE JOINTS WILL CORRESPOND. CUTTING THE POSTS FIRST WILL ALLOW YOU TO MAKE FINE ADJUSTMENTS IN GIRT LENGTHS TO COMPENSATE FOR SLIGHTLY OVER- OR UNDERSIZED POSTS.

WOOD SHRINKAGE

IT'S A GOOD IDEA TO MAKE EACH TENON APPROXIMATELY 1/8" SHORTER THAN ITS CORRESPONDING MORTISE. THIS ALLOWS FOR WOOD SHRINKAGE FROM DRYING.

LEAVE 1/8" SPACE FOR SHRINKAGE

NO SIGNIFICANT SHRINKAGE ALONG GRAIN

SHRINKAGE ACROSS GRAIN

TIMBERS NOT TRUE TO STATED DIMENSIONS

HYPOTHETICALLY, A 6" X 8" TIMBER SHOULD BE EXACTLY 6" X 8". DO NOT USE "DIMENSIONAL LUMBER", WHICH IS TYPICALLY 1/2 OR MORE INCHES SMALLER THAN ITS NOMINAL SIZE. THE TIMBERS THAT YOU PURCHASE OR HAVE CUT FOR YOU SHOULD BE FROM A QUALITY SAWMILL THAT WILL PROVIDE TIMBERS CUT SQUARE AND NEARLY TRUE TO STATED DIMENSIONS (± 1/8 INCH). TRY AS YOU MIGHT, YOU WILL PROBABLY STILL HAVE TO WORK WITH SOME TIMBERS THAT MAY VARY UP TO 3/8". MORE THAN THIS VARIATION AND THE TIMBER WILL EITHER HAVE TO BE PLANED OR CAREFULLY USED IN A LOCATION IN WHICH THE VARIATION'S EFFECT WILL BE SMALL.

CONT....

LAYING OUT JOINTS ON UNDER- OR OVERSIZED TIMBERS

ERRORS IN TIMBER WIDTH

GABLE-END BENTS (BENTS 1 AND 4 IN "JOINERY: GETTING STARTED") AND OUTSIDE CONNECTING GIRTS ARE LAID OUT WITH ALL MEASUREMENTS FOR THE MORTISES AND TENONS MADE FROM THE OUTSIDE FACE. THE ASSEMBLED TIMBERS WILL THEN BE FLUSH ON THE OUTSIDE OF THE FRAME. THIS IS EXTREMELY HELPFUL WHEN APPLYING THE EXTERIOR WALLS.

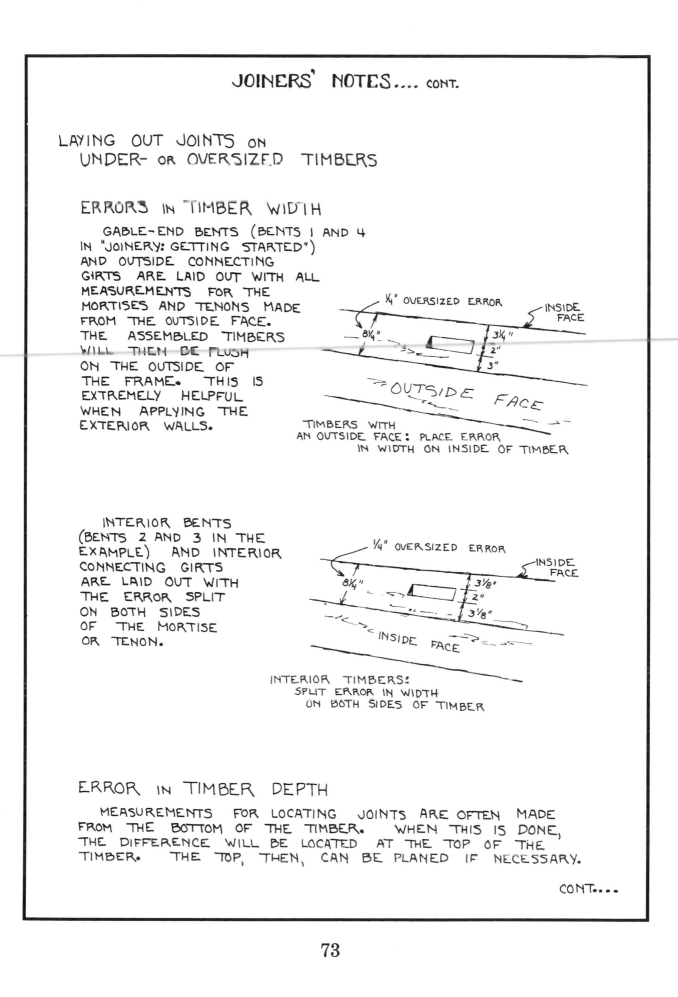

1/4" OVERSIZED ERROR

INSIDE FACE

8 1/4"

3 1/4"
2"
3"

OUTSIDE FACE

TIMBERS WITH AN OUTSIDE FACE: PLACE ERROR IN WIDTH ON INSIDE OF TIMBER

INTERIOR BENTS (BENTS 2 AND 3 IN THE EXAMPLE) AND INTERIOR CONNECTING GIRTS ARE LAID OUT WITH THE ERROR SPLIT ON BOTH SIDES OF THE MORTISE OR TENON.

1/4" OVERSIZED ERROR

INSIDE FACE

8 1/4"

3 1/8"
2"
3 1/8"

INSIDE FACE

INTERIOR TIMBERS: SPLIT ERROR IN WIDTH ON BOTH SIDES OF TIMBER

ERROR IN TIMBER DEPTH

MEASUREMENTS FOR LOCATING JOINTS ARE OFTEN MADE FROM THE BOTTOM OF THE TIMBER. WHEN THIS IS DONE, THE DIFFERENCE WILL BE LOCATED AT THE TOP OF THE TIMBER. THE TOP, THEN, CAN BE PLANED IF NECESSARY.

CONT....

JOINERS' NOTES.... CONT.

A NOTE ON JOIST AND PURLIN LENGTHS

A FEW MOMENTS OF THOUGHT WILL REVEAL THAT THE MAJOR TIMBERS WHICH ARE UNDER- OR OVERSIZED WILL AFFECT THE REQUIRED LENGTHS OF JOISTS AND PURLINS. EITHER THE ERROR IN THE WIDTH OF MAJOR TIMBERS IS ACCOUNTED FOR PRIOR TO CUTTING PURLINS AND JOISTS, OR THE SECOND ENDS OF THESE TIMBERS ARE CUT ON THE DAY OF THE RAISING AFTER THE ACTUAL SPAN MEASUREMENTS HAVE BEEN MADE.

PLANNING

PLANNING FOR A HOUSE ENCOMPASSES MANY ASPECTS. HERE WE FOCUS ON JOINTS, TRYING TO ANSWER THE QUESTION, HOW WILL EACH TIMBER BE JOINED INTO THE FRAME AND, CONSEQUENTLY, WHAT JOINTS WILL EACH TIMBER CONTAIN? WE MUST CONSIDER:

- THE STRENGTHS AND ATTRIBUTES OF A NUMBER OF POSSIBLE JOINTS THAT COULD BE USED IN A LOCATION.

- WHAT TYPES OF FORCES EACH JOINT WILL HAVE TO BEAR (SEE CHAPTER 6).

- MULTIPLE MORTISES AT ONE LOCATION THAT WOULD STRUCTURALLY WEAKEN THE TIMBER. AS AN EXAMPLE, THREE IS USUALLY THE MAXIMUM NUMBER OF GIRTS THAT SHOULD BE RECEIVED BY A POST AT ONE LOCATION (RIGHT). AT ANY CROSS-SECTIONAL PLANE, AT LEAST 50% OF THE WOOD SHOULD REMAIN AFTER ALL MORTISES HAVE BEEN CUT.

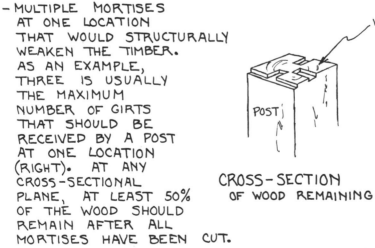

WOOD REMAINING AFTER ALL MORTISES HAVE BEEN REMOVED

POST

CROSS-SECTION OF WOOD REMAINING

- HOW EACH TIMBER WILL BE ASSEMBLED AND RAISED (SEE CHAPTER 5). ANALOGOUS TO A CHINESE PUZZLE, THE METHOD OF ASSEMBLING DICTATES THE TYPES OF INTERLOCKING JOINTS. ASK YOURSELF WHILE PLANNING YOUR JOINERY, CAN THESE JOINTS BE ASSEMBLED IN THE ORDER I WILL BE RAISING THE FRAME?

CHAPTER FOUR
THE JOINER'S WORK
REMOVING WOOD

Fine wooden structures seem to speak with
the heart of the master carpenters who
constructed them with obvious respect for the
soul of their timber.

—Kiyosi Seike: *The Art of Japanese Joinery*

IN our shop there are some fine people. Because I have worked closely with them for several years, I am convinced that working wood is only partially the mastery of the techniques of cutting, shaping, and mortising—the removal of wood. It's a delicate operation. The tools for the task also include those stored on the inside: feelings and emotions and values. If they are not also maintained with a sharp edge, the result can be a hacking of the timber and boredom in the individual. On the other hand, I have observed in the people here that quality work is interwoven with quality in the individual, and that one brings a sense of richness and clarity to the other.

Because these people bring so much of their lives to their work, they are craftsmen. Things that are made by craftsmen share a common element: whether the product is made of silver, glass, clay, cloth, or wood, a close look will show that it also contains the spirit of the individual. Indeed, the significant difference between something that has been worked by the hand of man and a production-line item is the existence of that human spirit. Computers and assembly lines can create with abundance, but only men and women with their hands and tools and love can create with feeling. We fail in so many ways if we refuse to allow the workmen attributes like romance and vision and wisdom. In their own vernacular, through their chosen element, sensitive people might well become poets, prophets, or philosophers.

The key, I think, is sensitivity. The relationship one establishes between himself and his work is personal. One person doesn't teach another how to feel. But it seems to me that if an individual feels nothing at all in response to his work—no meaning, no magic, no romance—then he is in sad condition. In a kind of job that to some people might seem dull and mundane, the sensitive individual finds meaning and purpose. In so doing, he elevates both himself and his craft. Look at the understanding that Nick Lindsey, a carpenter in Studs Terkel's *Working*, has about driving a nail:

> But every once in a while there's stuff that comes in on you. All of a sudden something falls into place. Suppose you're driving an eight-penny galvanized finishing nail into this siding. Your whole universe is rolled onto the head of that nail. Each lick is sufficient to justify your life. You say "Okay, I'm not trying to get this nail out of the way so I can get onto something important. There's nothing more important. It's right there." And it goes—pow! It's not getting that nail in that's on your mind. It's hitting it—hitting it square, hitting it straight. Getting it now. That one lick.

Somehow, both the nail and Nick become more dignified because of his perception of the significance of the moment. When you open up to your work, submit to it, allow it to move you and change you, then you will begin to notice that boredom is something that happens to other people.

I came to the building trades from educational experiences I found vague and esoteric. I lost my patience for philosophy that couldn't agree about the existence of man, for discussions of literature that wouldn't leave Melville's whale alone, and for boring scientific monologues that seemed to become ever more erudite in direct ratio to the simplicity of the matter. My first carpentry project was building a pair of sawhorses, and they weren't particularly good. But I recall being very excited by them. The conciseness of the response to my work was eloquent in ways I had never known. The immediate lessons I learned about myself and about wood in those two sawhorses assured me that never again would I allow the dimensions of my classroom to be so limited.

Working with wooden timbers is, in fact, really more like an intense personal discussion than a classroom. You must learn how to listen as well as how to speak. Wood is a natural element and holds laws and relationships that are universal as well as unique individual traits. When your communication with it is complete, you will learn things that go far beyond woodworking. Wood is alive and must be treated with the same kind of dignity and respect given to other living things. With that, a conversation can begin as you bring the stuff of your own life into

contact with the rich life of this beautiful natural element.

You don't just walk up to a timber and hack away at it obliviously. Instead, you learn to approach it with a sense of curiosity. The idea is to look it over; observe what you can. The story of the timber's life is told in part by the growth rings. Interpreting this tale will give some valuable clues about its mysterious eccentricities. Is the tree old or young? (I have found the older wood to be more difficult to work, as if it gets more tenacious with age, but it often seems more stable as well.) Did the tree grow quickly or slowly? There are indications here about where and how this tree grew, and you will learn to become responsive to these subtle differences. The tight grain of the slow-growing tree seems more reliable, less likely to crush; there is a sense of maturity in this wood.

An observation of the growth rings will also tell you whether the timber is the heart of the tree or perhaps one of the quarters. (This information will help you to understand how that wood will "move" and where to expect the most shrinkage.) A glance at the rings will reveal whether your work is being done parallel or tangential with them. As it is driven with the mallet, the chisel seems to cut better tangential to the rings, while paring can be very precise when you are pushing parallel with the direction of the rings. A simple examination of one element of the timber—the annual growth rings—and a sense of understanding is starting to develop.

As a tree struggles for life, it finds a way to respond to the nature of its surroundings: whether the land is flat or hilly, has thick growth or sparse; whether rocky, sandy, swampy, or loamy; whether windy or calm, on the north side of the hill or the south. All these things make a difference, and you begin to notice them in the straight or twisted grain or in the size and location of the knots. When you develop an awareness of these characteristics and become sensitive to how they should change your working habits and how best to utilize that piece of wood in the framework, then somehow your response to its individuality allows that tree to continue its struggle for life.

When you have admitted that the timber too has a sense of purpose, a natural will to live, then your dialogue will be one of mutual respect. If there is too much ego or a stubborn and inflexible will, then the nature of

You don't just hack away obliviously. *Courtesy of Robert H. Brown*

Wood will never lie to you. *Courtesy of Tafi Brown*

wood is to fight back, to find a way to foil the plan. If there is timidity and lack of understanding, then the nature of wood is to overwhelm and to confuse. So in order to draw from that timber a spirit of cooperation, you must possess not only the sharp tools and the clever hands, but also confidence tempered with humility.

What you give to wood is exactly what you get in return: joints either fit or they don't; the work was either a fight or a delightful collaboration of wills. The accuracy of hands, tools, and spirit cannot be falsified. In the torn and broken fibers on a poorly cut tenon, one can see anger and frustration. In the extreme excess of wood that was removed from the sides and bottom of a sloppy mortise (as if this were the way to assure a fit), one sees a total lack of confidence. For the work to possess a feeling of unity and durability, it must be done with clarity and poise. If it is going to possess a sense of lightness that allows it to flow and float in its surroundings, then it was born of a dance that was swung between an agile mind and limber hands.

These timbers will not fail to respond in equal measure to the depth of your involvement. When the warmth of the human spirit is brought to the work, then the product will exude that warmth and be more comfortable to live with.

A natural outgrowth of maintaining an elevated dialogue with wood is to purchase and maintain excellent tools. The needs of your task and the aspirations of your spirit are communicated through tools. To beat a timber with a dull or second-rate chisel is somehow merciless and shows lack of respect. To attempt high quality work with poor quality tools demonstrates a lack of concern for your own time and energy.

The tool returns to you in performance what you give to it in care and attention. You are crisp and concise in your work with wood only in proportion to the same attributes in the tool. It becomes a part of you, an extension of your hands. The maintenance of the tool will be automatic. It has to feel right. The cutting edges must be sharp and true. To accept anything less than the best here would be to accept screaming and shouting as a part of your daily speech.

One of the things that has drawn me to timber framing is that I can bring my hand tools to the work with no apology. It requires

The maintenance of the tool will be automatic. *Courtesy of Robert H. Brown*

them. Good, accurate mortising in the variety necessary for the many different types of joints can be done only with mallet and chisel. Power tools aren't made that can make all the cuts on a complicated scarf or a housed dovetail. The long evolution that brought such sophistication and refinement to timber framing stopped as a result of developments in the industrial era. In our work to revive the craft, we have found that it still stubbornly stands aside, demanding the hands of people working simple tools.

Like my co-workers in the shop, I have hand tools I consider personal favorites. I own a one-and-one-half-inch socket chisel with a handle, turned from maple, to fit my hand. It feels good to hold. This chisel is honed and sharpened when necessary. When I pick it up to make a mortise or shape a tenon, I know what to expect. It will respond without having to beat the daylights out of it with the mallet.

The tool I like best for timber framing is the slick. I enjoy listening to it. The slick is pushed with both hands instead of being struck with a mallet. With the noise of hammering removed, all you hear is the sound of a sharp tool against wood. The slick is refined; it is used for paring and slicing, the finishing touches. The sound it makes as it pulls a thin shaving from the wood is crisp and delicate. I like the tool for giving me those special moments during the course of a workday.

I have absolutely no reservations about the use of power tools—when they are kept in proper perspective. I feel as attached to some of them as I do to the hand tools. Their service

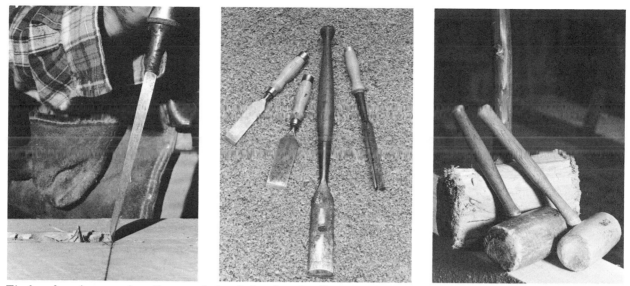

Timber framing requires the use of simple hand tools. *Courtesy of Robert H. Brown*

Power tools are helpful for many tasks, but must be kept in proper perspective.

The slick is refined; it is used for . . . the finishing touches.

is one of liberation from the tasks that are repetitive, boring, and stultifying. In this way the use of power tools is actually ennobling to the craft, because it allows more time for the part of the project that is meaningful and rewarding.

The most important thing about the work being done with timbers is the quality of the product in the end. If power tools can help the craftsman achieve his very best a little more quickly and efficiently, then they will have served their function nicely. But they would have been used wrongly if the project were forced to fit within the limitations of the tool. If we were to allow our frames to be defined by power tools, we would severely

sacrifice the beauty and excellence of the joinery, and there would be a look of naiveté from the total submission to these powerful but ignorant tools. Remember, too, that as quickly as the saw or the drill can make an accurate and precise cut, it can also inflict a mortal wound in the timber. Use the power tool carefully and with restraint.

We've discovered in our shop that the simplest tools and means tend to be the most efficient. The timbers are heavy and cumbersome—not at all easy to move around. Therefore, it is much easier to bring a portable power tool to the timber than to bring the timber to a stationary tool. This works to our advantage, because the portable tools are

79

Ed Levin, of Canaan, New Hampshire, maintains that the hand-operated mortising machine is still efficient. *Courtesy of Richard Starr*

relatively inexpensive and are extremely efficient users of energy. We've also found it easier to bring the timbers into the shop with a hand cart than to go through all the motions of starting up the old forklift. In the process less energy is consumed and we are spared the noise of the machine. In an unconscious way, the methods that seem to make timber framing click fall naturally into the category of appropriate technology. The human element is maintained because it needs to be there, and the tools that are used do not consume energy disproportionate to the work they do.

Using the body for work and learning to communicate through it is an important part of this craft. So many people today are discovering that you can't force the body to live the life of the mind. More people are out running and more people are spending time out-of-doors and in all kinds of exercise; it's good to see this new awareness of the rhythms and the messages of the body.

If you have dedicated your life to the work of your hands, these rhythms and messages are much more than an avocation. They are the experience of life. You learn to respond to the work with every sense you possess. The fingers feel things that the eyes can't see—to

This is appropriate technology? *Courtesy of Robert H. Brown*

feel if a surface is true, to discover the direction of the grain, to test the edge of a chisel; the fingers are curious. There are sounds that rasp and sounds that please. You, the craftsman, learn to hear wood, listening for cues to guide your hands and tools. And this listening, it's so much more than ears.

While you are working, the body is always in motion. Learning how to move it, what it should do in response to the needs of the task, is an acquired skill. The first efforts will be clumsy and difficult. But if you're willing to pay attention and respond to the rhythms that are present, the steps will not be hard to learn. The body wants to be braced for the use of the power saw; it wants to recoil from the blows of the mallet. You learn about slight movements—perhaps twisting or pushing the chisel just so, or perhaps a little pressure with the fingers. You learn how to make a transition from one task to another, not to waste movements. Somewhere along the line a routine develops, a smoothness; you know when to balance and when to swing. These flowing movements, this dance, are the body's reaction to your closeness to the work.

One of the great benefits of being in the business of putting houses together is that it has so much to do with people. People need places to live; we are builders. The involvement between ourselves and the people we work for is necessarily deep and personal. Caring about the work being done also means caring about the people these buildings house. When we put our best into the job, we have found that people don't hesitate to return our efforts with kindness and consideration. To be building friendships along with the houses is one of the highest rewards for the labor.

Timbers are heavy and require the hands of several people working together to transform a natural resource into a meaningful structure. In this little shop, we have become like brothers. We have learned so much from each other and had such a good time in the process that other kinds of crafts that are more individual would seem monastic in comparison. Part of the gift of each person's presence hangs lightly in the air, and though not one of us can describe it, it affects us all. Other things we give to each other are specific thoughts and ideas that are cast into the breezes that circle around the shop. They are always there for each person to watch or use, and yet sometimes nobody quite remembers their origin. And it really doesn't matter.

Courtesy of Robert H. Brown

Tom Goldschmid

Tom Page

Chris Madigan

Peter White

Photos courtesy of Robert H. Brown

What does matter is that we have the same goal.

My respect for the people who work here is complete. How good they are with their hands and how quick to respond to new challenge! To work with these people every day is to receive a daily dose of humility, and to learn daily new things: from original ideas in the use of the circular saw to the importance of maintaining a sense of humor; from learning how to "put" a timber in the frame mentally while it is still in the pile, to many valuable lessons concerning the nature of wood. Because of all that I have learned from and all that I feel toward these people, I strongly suggest to those who are beginning that they find co-workers whose goals are the same as their own. The frame will be better. The time spent will be richer.

As in the guilds of the old days, our collective work and learning improve the state of our art. Together we develop new standards, better procedures. If we flounder a bit in our attempts to bring new life to this old craft, we flounder together. We are always modifying our ideas and our methods. To keep our level of involvement high and to give more time for personal lives, we have switched to a four-day workweek.

We have come to share a strong feeling that each job be done right the first time, instead of postponing little details to be dealt with later. Later comes too quickly. We've also learned not to have too many people working on the same project. It produces confusion, and each person isn't enough a part of the job to maintain enthusiasm for it. Two seems to be a good number. In the process of learning these things together, we have improved the management of our business, the quality of our buildings, and the integrity of our lives.

If the learning and camaraderie we have seem so beneficial, it's because the element of the human being is so important to timber framing. The world has changed a lot since the days when this building technique was really alive. Some changes are good and some are bad. We should be thankful that so many needs are provided for so efficiently and be saddened by the degree that humans have been removed from their work. In the unwritten commandments that prescribe the morality of the twentieth century, there is one that tells us it is wrong to love our work, for it reduces production speed. In the strict adherence to this commandment, the fact of meaning behind technique is all but lost. Too many people who build with their hands no longer respond to the rhythm and the romance of their work. In this age, life for that person becomes an apology for the fact that machines cannot yet do that task.

But working with wood as closely as is necessary to pull forms and shapes and structures from such large timbers, maintaining traditional high standards, requires a depth of feeling as well as a knowledge of the mechanics. Had we lived in the old days, we might have learned this craft from our fathers or spent years in apprenticeship. Values and sensitivities would have been learned instinctively along with the techniques. Without these old masters, it is good that we can learn from each other the subtleties and nuances of tools and wood. And it's good we can encourage in each other the pursuit of, instead of the resistance to, those magic moments when all of the senses we possess are brought to our work.

CUTTING: A ROUTINE OF WORK

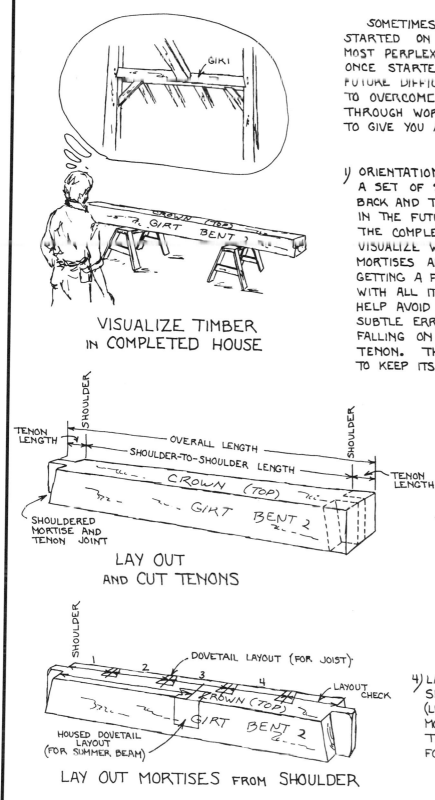

SOMETIMES, KNOWING HOW TO GET STARTED ON A MAJOR WORK IS THE MOST PERPLEXING PART OF THE PROJECT. ONCE STARTED INTO A ROUTINE, THE FUTURE DIFFICULTIES ARE OFTEN EASY TO OVERCOME. WE TAKE YOU THROUGH WORKING ONE TIMBER (A GIRT), TO GIVE YOU A SENSE OF OUR ROUTINE.

1) ORIENTATION: PLACE THE TIMBER ON A SET OF SAWHORSES. STAND BACK AND TRY TO VISUALIZE STANDING IN THE FUTURE HOUSE LOOKING AT THE COMPLETED TIMBER (LEFT). VISUALIZE WHERE THE DIFFERENT MORTISES AND TENONS WILL FALL. GETTING A FEEL FOR THE TIMBER WITH ALL ITS FUTURE JOINTS WILL HELP AVOID ILLOGICAL AND OTHER SUBTLE ERRORS SUCH AS A BAD KNOT FALLING ON THE LOWER HALF OF A TENON. THEN LABEL THE TIMBER TO KEEP ITS ORIENTATION CLEAR.

VISUALIZE TIMBER IN COMPLETED HOUSE

LAY OUT AND CUT TENONS

LAY OUT MORTISES FROM SHOULDER

2) SQUARE OFF BOTH ENDS OF THE TIMBER TO THE OVERALL LENGTH (SEE "TIMBER LAYOUT, GETTING STARTED").

3) LAY OUT AND CUT THE TENON ON ONE END (LEFT). MEASURE FROM SHOULDER OF THIS TENON (THE "SHOULDER-TO-SHOULDER" LENGTH), LAY OUT AND CUT 2ND TENON (SEE "CUTTING A TENON").

4) LAY OUT MORTISES FROM SHOULDER OF TENON (LEFT). THE DOVETAIL MORTISES ARE FOR JOISTS, THE HOUSED DOVETAIL FOR SUMMER BEAM.

CONT....

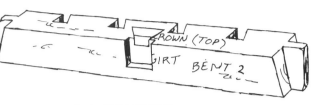

CUT MORTISES

5) CUT MORTISES BY SAWING, DRILLING, AND CHISELING (RIGHT). (SEE "CUTTING A MORTISE" AND "CUTTING A HOUSED DOVETAIL").

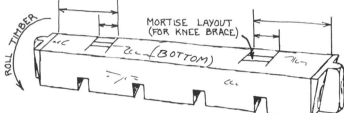

LAY OUT AND CUT MORTISES ON OTHER SIDE(S)

6) ROLL BEAM, LAY OUT AND CUT MORTISES ON OTHER SIDE(S) OF TIMBER (RIGHT). ILLUSTRATED ARE TWO KNEE BRACE MORTISES.

7) CHECK ALL TENONS AND MORTISES FOR CORRECT SIZE. A 2"-WIDE TENON CANNOT BE CUT 2$\frac{1}{16}$" WIDE AND BE EXPECTED TO FIT INTO A 2"-WIDE MORTISE.

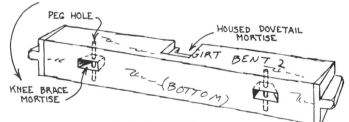

DRILL PEG HOLES

8) DRILL 1" PEG HOLES THROUGH ALL MORTISES WHICH WILL BE PEGGED (RIGHT). ALWAYS DRILL FROM THE FACE OF THE TIMBER THAT IS MOST IMPORTANT IN THE ROOM. THE DRILL BIT CAN DRIFT A LITTLE THROUGH THE TIMBER. PRECISE LOCATION OF THE HOLE IS GUARANTEED WHERE THE DRILLING IS STARTED.

9) DOUBLE CHECK THE TIMBER. IT IS EASY TO FORGET TO CUT A MORTISE.

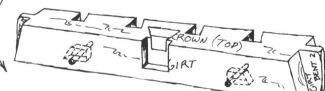

LABEL ENDS OF COMPLETED TIMBER

10) LABEL THE ENDS OF THE COMPLETED TIMBER (RIGHT). LABELS ON THE SIDES OF THE TIMBER WILL BE ERASED DURING PLANING AND SANDING.

11) IT IS EASIEST TO PLANE AND SAND ALL THE TIMBERS AT ONE TIME AFTER THE CUTTING HAS BEEN COMPLETED.

IF THOUGHT, PATIENCE, AND ATTENTION TO DETAIL ARE GIVEN TO EACH TIMBER AS IT IS CUT, THE RAISING DAY WILL BE A JOYOUS OCCASION.

TOOLS

MAN USES TOOLS AS THE MEDIUM (OR THE METHOD) TO TRANSFORM HIS THOUGHTS BY THE CONSEQUENT ACTIONS OF HIS HANDS INTO A PHYSICAL CREATION. FOR THE MOST PART, THE SIMPLER THE TOOL, THE MORE CONTROL MAN HAS OVER ITS ACTION AND, THEREFORE, THE MORE POTENTIAL FOR FINE WORKMANSHIP. IT IS INTERESTING TO DISCOVER THAT THE BASIC TOOLS WE USE FOR FRAMING TODAY ARE REMARKABLY SIMILAR TO THOSE OF 500 YEARS AGO. ON THE OTHER HAND, MODERN POWER TOOLS ARE USEFUL FOR "ROUGHING OUT", GIVING US TIME FOR THE FINE FINISHING OF THE WORK USING THE SIMPLE TOOLS.

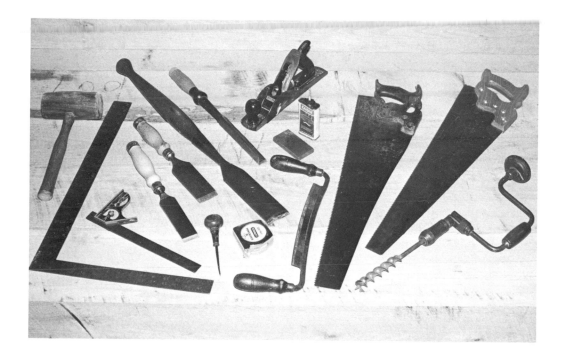

HAND TOOLS FOR TIMBER FRAMING

WE LIST ON THE NEXT THREE PAGES TOOLS WE USE FOR TIMBER FRAMING. BECAUSE SOME OF THESE TOOLS ARE REQUIRED FOR ANY TYPE OF TIMBER FRAME WHILE OTHERS MAY NOT BE NEEDED FOR A PARTICULAR PROJECT, WE HAVE GROUPED THE TOOLS INTO THE FOLLOWING CATEGORIES:

*** ESSENTIAL TOOLS FOR EVEN THE SMALLEST TIMBER FRAMING PROJECT.

** USEFUL TOOLS STRONGLY SUGGESTED FOR ANY MAJOR PROJECT.

* EXPENSIVE FINISHING TOOLS THAT IT MAY BE BEST TO RENT OR BORROW.

CONT....

CHISELS

*** <u>FRAMING CHISEL, 1½" OR 2"</u>. THESE HEAVY-
DUTY CHISELS MUST BE DESIGNED TO
WITHSTAND SEVERE STRAIN. THE
1½" IS THE MOST VERSATILE.
THE SKETCH (RIGHT)
ILLUSTRATES ITS
PRINCIPAL FEATURES.
NOTE THAT THE BACK
(THE SIDE NOT BEVELED)
MUST BE ABSOLUTELY
FLAT FOR THE CHISEL TO
CUT PROPERLY.

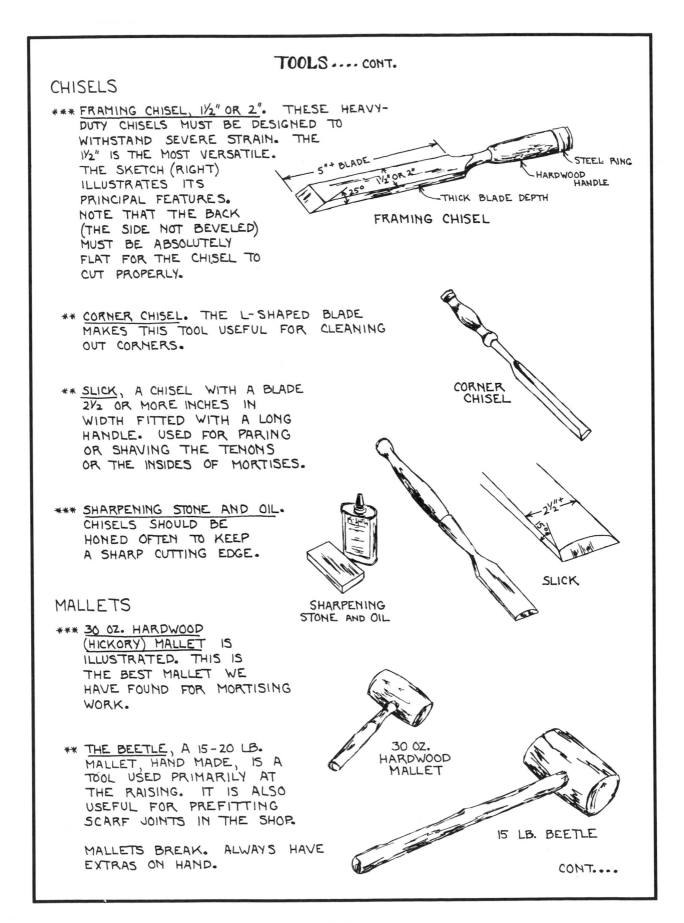

5"+ BLADE

25°

1½" OR 2"

STEEL RING
HARDWOOD HANDLE
THICK BLADE DEPTH

FRAMING CHISEL

** <u>CORNER CHISEL</u>. THE L-SHAPED BLADE
MAKES THIS TOOL USEFUL FOR CLEANING
OUT CORNERS.

CORNER CHISEL

** <u>SLICK</u>, A CHISEL WITH A BLADE
2½ OR MORE INCHES IN
WIDTH FITTED WITH A LONG
HANDLE. USED FOR PARING
OR SHAVING THE TENONS
OR THE INSIDES OF MORTISES.

*** <u>SHARPENING STONE AND OIL</u>.
CHISELS SHOULD BE
HONED OFTEN TO KEEP
A SHARP CUTTING EDGE.

2½"+

15°

SLICK

SHARPENING STONE AND OIL

MALLETS

*** <u>30 OZ. HARDWOOD
(HICKORY) MALLET</u> IS
ILLUSTRATED. THIS IS
THE BEST MALLET WE
HAVE FOUND FOR MORTISING
WORK.

30 OZ. HARDWOOD MALLET

** <u>THE BEETLE</u>, A 15-20 LB.
MALLET, HAND MADE, IS A
TOOL USED PRIMARILY AT
THE RAISING. IT IS ALSO
USEFUL FOR PREFITTING
SCARF JOINTS IN THE SHOP.

MALLETS BREAK. ALWAYS HAVE
EXTRAS ON HAND.

15 LB. BEETLE

CONT....

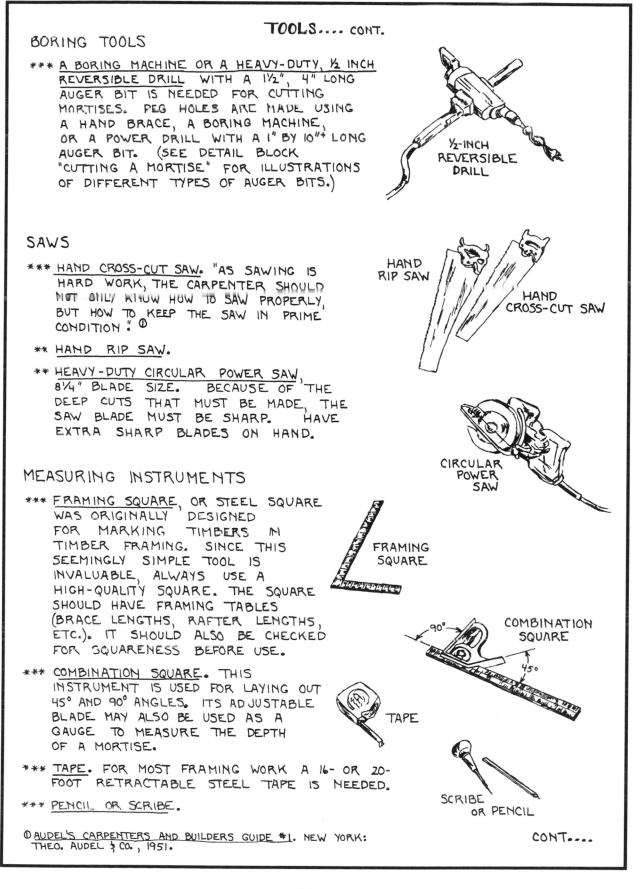

BORING TOOLS

*** <u>A BORING MACHINE OR A HEAVY-DUTY, ½ INCH REVERSIBLE DRILL WITH A 1½", 4" LONG</u> AUGER BIT IS NEEDED FOR CUTTING MORTISES. PEG HOLES ARE MADE USING A HAND BRACE, A BORING MACHINE, OR A POWER DRILL WITH A 1" BY 10"+ LONG AUGER BIT. (SEE DETAIL BLOCK "CUTTING A MORTISE" FOR ILLUSTRATIONS OF DIFFERENT TYPES OF AUGER BITS.)

½-INCH REVERSIBLE DRILL

SAWS

*** <u>HAND CROSS-CUT SAW.</u> "AS SAWING IS HARD WORK, THE CARPENTER SHOULD NOT ONLY KNOW HOW TO SAW PROPERLY, BUT HOW TO KEEP THE SAW IN PRIME CONDITION." [1]

** <u>HAND RIP SAW.</u>

** <u>HEAVY-DUTY CIRCULAR POWER SAW,</u> 8¼" BLADE SIZE. BECAUSE OF THE DEEP CUTS THAT MUST BE MADE, THE SAW BLADE MUST BE SHARP. HAVE EXTRA SHARP BLADES ON HAND.

HAND RIP SAW

HAND CROSS-CUT SAW

CIRCULAR POWER SAW

MEASURING INSTRUMENTS

*** <u>FRAMING SQUARE,</u> OR STEEL SQUARE WAS ORIGINALLY DESIGNED FOR MARKING TIMBERS IN TIMBER FRAMING. SINCE THIS SEEMINGLY SIMPLE TOOL IS INVALUABLE, ALWAYS USE A HIGH-QUALITY SQUARE. THE SQUARE SHOULD HAVE FRAMING TABLES (BRACE LENGTHS, RAFTER LENGTHS, ETC.). IT SHOULD ALSO BE CHECKED FOR SQUARENESS BEFORE USE.

FRAMING SQUARE

*** <u>COMBINATION SQUARE.</u> THIS INSTRUMENT IS USED FOR LAYING OUT 45° AND 90° ANGLES. ITS ADJUSTABLE BLADE MAY ALSO BE USED AS A GAUGE TO MEASURE THE DEPTH OF A MORTISE.

90°

COMBINATION SQUARE

45°

*** <u>TAPE.</u> FOR MOST FRAMING WORK A 16- OR 20-FOOT RETRACTABLE STEEL TAPE IS NEEDED.

TAPE

*** <u>PENCIL OR SCRIBE.</u>

SCRIBE OR PENCIL

[1] <u>AUDEL'S CARPENTERS AND BUILDERS GUIDE #1.</u> NEW YORK: THEO. AUDEL & CO., 1951.

CONT....

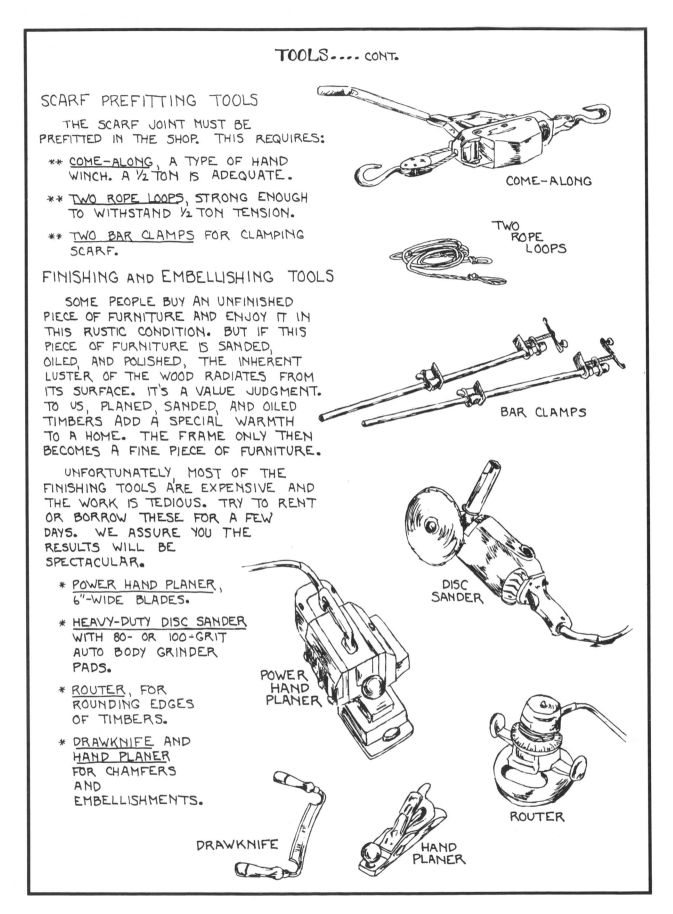

SCARF PREFITTING TOOLS

THE SCARF JOINT MUST BE PREFITTED IN THE SHOP. THIS REQUIRES:

** COME-ALONG, A TYPE OF HAND WINCH. A ½ TON IS ADEQUATE.

** TWO ROPE LOOPS, STRONG ENOUGH TO WITHSTAND ½ TON TENSION.

** TWO BAR CLAMPS FOR CLAMPING SCARF.

COME-ALONG

TWO ROPE LOOPS

FINISHING and EMBELLISHING TOOLS

SOME PEOPLE BUY AN UNFINISHED PIECE OF FURNITURE AND ENJOY IT IN THIS RUSTIC CONDITION. BUT IF THIS PIECE OF FURNITURE IS SANDED, OILED, AND POLISHED, THE INHERENT LUSTER OF THE WOOD RADIATES FROM ITS SURFACE. IT'S A VALUE JUDGMENT. TO US, PLANED, SANDED, AND OILED TIMBERS ADD A SPECIAL WARMTH TO A HOME. THE FRAME ONLY THEN BECOMES A FINE PIECE OF FURNITURE.

BAR CLAMPS

UNFORTUNATELY, MOST OF THE FINISHING TOOLS ARE EXPENSIVE AND THE WORK IS TEDIOUS. TRY TO RENT OR BORROW THESE FOR A FEW DAYS. WE ASSURE YOU THE RESULTS WILL BE SPECTACULAR.

* POWER HAND PLANER, 6"-WIDE BLADES.

* HEAVY-DUTY DISC SANDER WITH 80- OR 100-GRIT AUTO BODY GRINDER PADS.

* ROUTER, FOR ROUNDING EDGES OF TIMBERS.

* DRAWKNIFE AND HAND PLANER FOR CHAMFERS AND EMBELLISHMENTS.

DISC SANDER

POWER HAND PLANER

ROUTER

DRAWKNIFE

HAND PLANER

CUTTING A TENON

IT IS NOT DIFFICULT TO CUT A TENON, YET TO ACHIEVE THE GOAL OF AN EXACTLY LOCATED AND PERFECTLY SIZED TENON WITH SHARP RIGHT ANGLES VENTURES INTO THE REALM OF FINE WOODWORKING. ONCE AGAIN, ATTENTION TO DETAIL IS A PREREQUISITE. AS YOU WORK, KEEP IN MIND THAT THE QUALITY OF A FRAME IS DEPENDENT UPON THE QUALITY OF THE JOINERY AND THAT A TENON IS HALF OF EVERY JOINT. THOUGH THIS WORK CAN BE DONE WITH OR WITHOUT POWER TOOLS, WE ILLUSTRATE A METHOD WITH SIMPLE POWER TOOLS.

THE FIRST STEP IS SQUARING OFF THE ENDS OF THE TIMBER. THIS IS ILLUSTRATED IN CHAPTER 3, "TIMBER LAYOUT, THE FIRST STEPS." PLACE THE FRAMING SQUARE WITH THE BODY FLUSH WITH ONE EDGE OF THE TIMBER. THE TONGUE IS THEN USED TO SCRIBE A LINE ACROSS THE STICK. CONTINUE THIS LINE AROUND THE STICK. THE END OF THE LINE MUST MEET ITS BEGINNING (PHOTO 1).

IT IS OFTEN EASIEST TO SQUARE OFF BOTH ENDS OF THE TIMBER AT THE SAME TIME. REMEMBER THAT THE OVERALL LENGTH OF THE TIMBER IS THE SHOULDER-TO-SHOULDER LENGTH PLUS THE LENGTH OF THE TWO TENONS. MAKE A CUT ALONG THE LINES ON BOTH ENDS OF THE TIMBER AT THE FULL DEPTH OF YOUR SAW BLADE. WHEN THESE CUTS ARE MADE, ALWAYS LEAVE THE LINE (SEE DRAWING BELOW AND PHOTO 2). ROLL THE TIMBER AND CUT ALONG THE NEXT FACE. REPEATING THE PROCESS, MAKE FOUR CUTS ON EACH END OF THE TIMBER. DEPENDING ON THE DEPTH OF YOUR SAW BLADE, SOME WOOD MAY REMAIN IN THE CENTER. THE CUT IS EASILY FINISHED WITH A HAND CROSS-CUT SAW (PHOTO 3).

TENONS ARE LAID OUT NEXT. ILLUSTRATED IS A CENTERED 1½" THICK, 4" LONG TENON FOR THE TOP OF A POST. MARK THE TENON LENGTH (PHOTO 4) AND SQUARE THE SHOULDER AROUND THE POST (PHOTO 5). AGAIN, THE LINE MUST HAVE ITS BEGINNING AND ENDING POINTS MEET. IF NOT, THE SHOULDER OF THE JOINT IN THE ASSEMBLED FRAME WILL NOT SEAT PROPERLY AND WILL REVEAL A GAP.

SAW KERF ON SIDE OF LINE TOWARD WASTE

CONT....

CUTTING A TENON.... CONT.

1 ↗ SCRIBE LINE AROUND TIMBER, SQUARING OFF END OF TIMBER.

2 ↗ CUT ON ALL FOUR SIDES.

↙ 3 FINISH CUT WITH HAND SAW.

5 ↗ SQUARE THE SHOULDER AROUND TIMBER.

4 ↗ MARK TENON LENGTH.

CONT....

CUTTING A TENON.... CONT.

LAY OUT THE TENON USING A PLYWOOD DEPTH GAUGE AND THE BLADE OF A FRAMING SQUARE AS A TEMPLATE (PHOTOS 6 AND 7). DARKENING THE WOOD THAT IS TO BE REMOVED MAY BE HELPFUL (RIGHT).

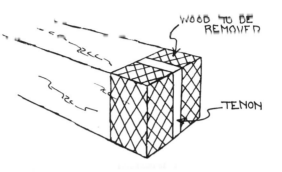

DARKENED WOOD TO BE REMOVED

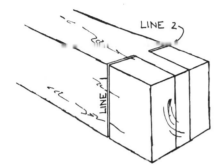

MAKE CUTS 1 AND 2 ON BOTH SIDES TO THE DEPTH OF THE TENON (SEE DRAWING LEFT AND PHOTO 8). END CUTS ALONG LINES 3 AND 4 ARE MADE INTO THE TIMBER, REMEMBERING THAT THE SAW KERF (WOOD REMOVED BY THE SAW BLADE) IS ON THE SIDE OF THE LINE OF THE WASTE (PHOTO 9). FINISH THE CUT WITH A HAND SAW.

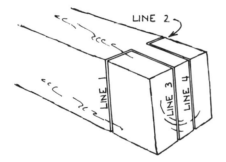

A LIGHT IMPACT WITH A MALLET WILL REMOVE THE WOOD ON EITHER SIDE OF THE TENON. CLEAN THE TENON AND SHOULDERS WITH A CHISEL (PHOTO 10). FINE ADJUSTMENTS IN THE TENON THICKNESS CAN BE MOST EASILY MADE USING A RAZOR-SHARP SLICK (PHOTO 11).

AFTER CHECKING THE TENON FOR PROPER DIMENSIONS, CHAMFER THE TENON EDGES USING A SLICK OR BLOCK PLANE (RIGHT).

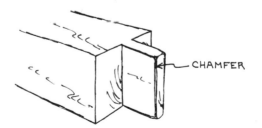

CHAMFERED TENON

CONT....

CUTTING A TENON.... CONT.

← 6 AND 7 ↗ LAY OUT TENON LOCATION.

← 8 AND 9 ↗ MAKE CUTS DOWN TO TENON.

10 ↗ REMOVE WOOD WITH MALLET AND CHISEL.   11 ↗ USE SLICK TO CLEAN TENON.

CUTTING A MORTISE

THE LAYING OUT AND CUTTING OF
A KNEE BRACE MORTISE IS ILLUSTRATED.
THE TECHNIQUE IS SIMILAR FOR STUB
AND THROUGH MORTISES.

MAKE THE MEASUREMENT FROM
THE SHOULDER OF THE TIMBER, MARK,
AND SQUARE ACROSS THE FACE (PHOTO 1).
USE THE FRAMING SQUARE AS DESCRIBED
IN CHAPTER 3 TO LAY OUT THE MORTISE
(PHOTOS 2,3 ₵ 4). MARK AND USE A
CENTER LINE AS A GUIDE FOR DRILLING
(SEE DRAWING, RIGHT).

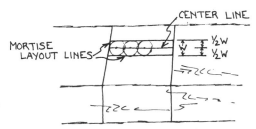

CENTER LINE AS GUIDE
FOR DRILL HOLES

TWO TYPES OF DRILL BITS
CAN BE USED. THE COMMON SELF-FEEDING
AUGER BIT IS EASIER TO USE FOR BORING, BUT
THE FORSTNER BIT PERMITS GREATER OVERLAP OF BORE HOLES
AND CONSEQUENTLY LESS CHISELING LATER (BELOW).

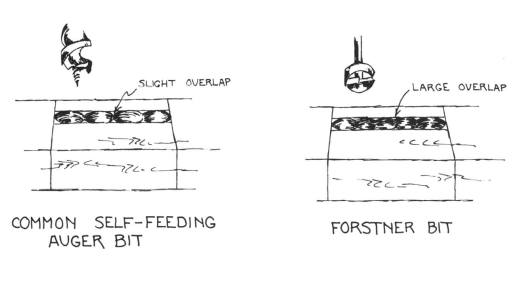

COMMON SELF-FEEDING
AUGER BIT

FORSTNER BIT

BORE A SERIES OF OVERLAPPING HOLES TO
THE REQUIRED DEPTH. THE BORE HOLE SHOULD
BE THE SAME SIZE AS THE WIDTH OF THE MORTISE
(PHOTO 5). TAKE CARE TO KEEP THE DRILL BIT
PLUMB WHILE DRILLING. WHEN CUTTING A THROUGH
MORTISE, DRILL HALFWAY THROUGH FROM EACH SIDE.

CONT....

1 MARK LOCATION OF MORTISE.

2 LAY OUT MORTISE LENGTH.

3 DRAW SIDES OF MORTISE.

4 DRAW CENTER LINE IN COMPLETED LAYOUT AS GUIDE FOR DRILLING.

5 BORE A SERIES OF HOLES.

CONT....

CUTTING A MORTISE.... CONT.

SELECT A CHISEL AS NEAR THE WIDTH OF THE MORTISE AS POSSIBLE (BUT NEVER LARGER THAN THE WIDTH). THIS CHISEL SHOULD BE A FRAMING CHISEL.

START THE CUTTING OF THE MORTISE, CHISELING LIGHTLY AROUND THE PERIMETER. ALWAYS CUT ACROSS THE GRAIN FIRST (PHOTO 6). HOLD THE CHISEL IN A VERTICAL POSITION WITH THE FLAT SIDE FACING THE OUTSIDE OF THE MORTISE (RIGHT).

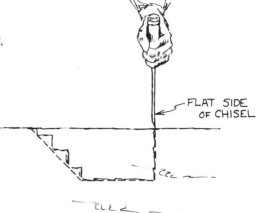

FLAT SIDE OF CHISEL

FLAT SIDE OF CHISEL
TO OUTSIDE OF MORTISE

DRIVE THE CORNER CHISEL AT THE CORNERS TO THE FULL DEPTH OF THE MORTISE (PHOTO 7). USE THE STRAIGHT CHISEL TO CLEAN THE SIDES AND REMOVE THE WOOD (PHOTO 8). ALWAYS LOOSEN THE CHISEL BY A MOVEMENT TOWARD THE MORTISE. A MOVEMENT IN THE OPPOSITE DIRECTION WILL INJURE THE ENDS OF THE MORTISE AND MAY BREAK THE CHISEL HANDLE.

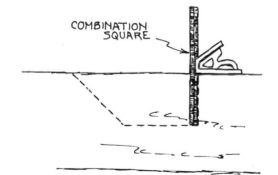

COMBINATION SQUARE

CHECKING DEPTH
OF MORTISE

NOTE THAT IN A KNEE BRACE MORTISE ONE END IS DRILLED SHALLOW AND CHISELED OUT AT AN ANGLE.

USE THE BROAD FLAT BLADE OF THE SLICK TO CLEAN AND STRAIGHTEN THE SIDES OF THE MORTISE (PHOTO 9). YOU CAN USE A COMBINATION SQUARE TO CHECK THE DEPTH AND SIDES (LEFT).

INSERT A MOCK KNEE BRACE TO CHECK FOR PROPER FIT (PHOTO 10).

CONT....

6 ↗ CHISEL LIGHTLY AROUND PERIMETER. CUT ACROSS GRAIN FIRST.

7 ↗ DRIVE CORNER CHISEL INTO CORNERS.

8 → CHISEL SIDES WITH STRAIGHT CHISEL.

9 ↗ CLEAN AND STRAIGHTEN SIDES WITH A SLICK.

10 ↗ TEST MORTISE WITH MOCK TENON.

CUTTING THE HOUSED DOVETAIL MORTISE

THIS ILLUSTRATION OF CUTTING THE HOUSED DOVETAIL JOINT DEMONSTRATES WOOD REMOVAL TECHNIQUES APPLICABLE TO OTHER COMPLEX JOINTS.

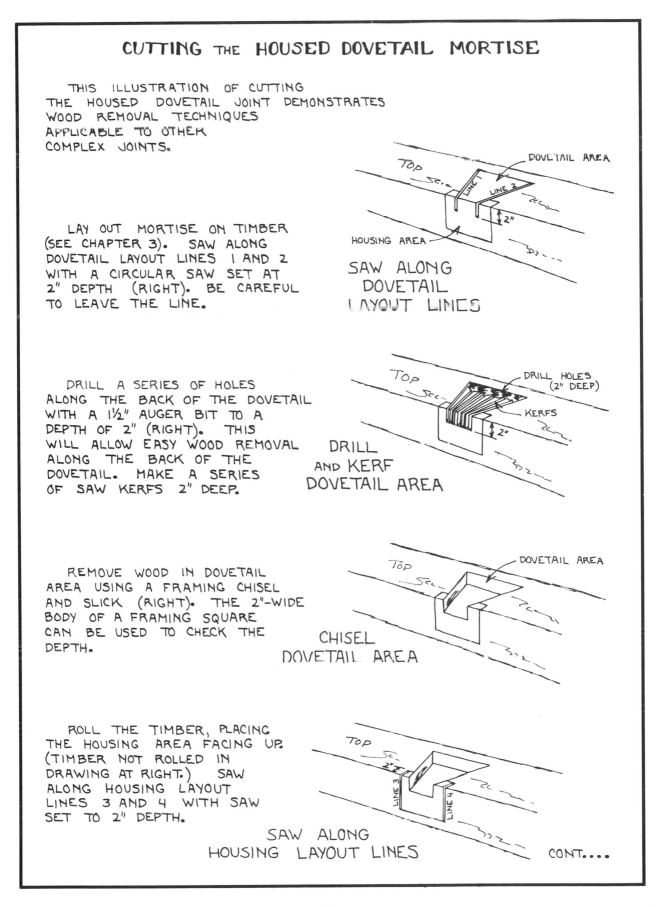

LAY OUT MORTISE ON TIMBER (SEE CHAPTER 3). SAW ALONG DOVETAIL LAYOUT LINES 1 AND 2 WITH A CIRCULAR SAW SET AT 2" DEPTH (RIGHT). BE CAREFUL TO LEAVE THE LINE.

SAW ALONG DOVETAIL LAYOUT LINES

DRILL A SERIES OF HOLES ALONG THE BACK OF THE DOVETAIL WITH A 1½" AUGER BIT TO A DEPTH OF 2" (RIGHT). THIS WILL ALLOW EASY WOOD REMOVAL ALONG THE BACK OF THE DOVETAIL. MAKE A SERIES OF SAW KERFS 2" DEEP.

DRILL AND KERF DOVETAIL AREA

REMOVE WOOD IN DOVETAIL AREA USING A FRAMING CHISEL AND SLICK (RIGHT). THE 2"-WIDE BODY OF A FRAMING SQUARE CAN BE USED TO CHECK THE DEPTH.

CHISEL DOVETAIL AREA

ROLL THE TIMBER, PLACING THE HOUSING AREA FACING UP. (TIMBER NOT ROLLED IN DRAWING AT RIGHT.) SAW ALONG HOUSING LAYOUT LINES 3 AND 4 WITH SAW SET TO 2" DEPTH.

SAW ALONG HOUSING LAYOUT LINES

CONT....

CUTTING THE HOUSED DOVETAIL MORTISE....CONT.

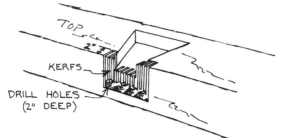

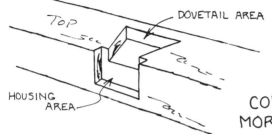

DRILL AND KERF·
HOUSING AREA

DRILL A SERIES OF 2"-DEEP HOLES ALONG THE BOTTOM OF THE HOUSING AS SHOWN (LEFT). MAKE A SERIES OF SAW KERFS WITHIN THE HOUSING AREA, 2" DEEP. THIS ALLOWS THE WOOD TO BE MORE EASILY REMOVED.

REMOVE WOOD WITH CHISELS. CLEAN CORNERS WITH CORNER CHISEL. FINAL CLEANING OF THE MORTISE MAY BE DONE USING A SLICK. CHECK THE MORTISE WITH THE LAYOUT TEMPLATE.

COMPLETED
MORTISE

CUTTING THE HOUSED DOVETAIL TENON

LAY OUT THE TENON AS SHOWN
IN CHAPTER 3. TRY TO VISUALIZE
THE TENON WITHIN THE TIMBER
(RIGHT). THERE ARE TWO PARTS TO
THIS TENON, THE DOVETAIL AND
THE HOUSING.

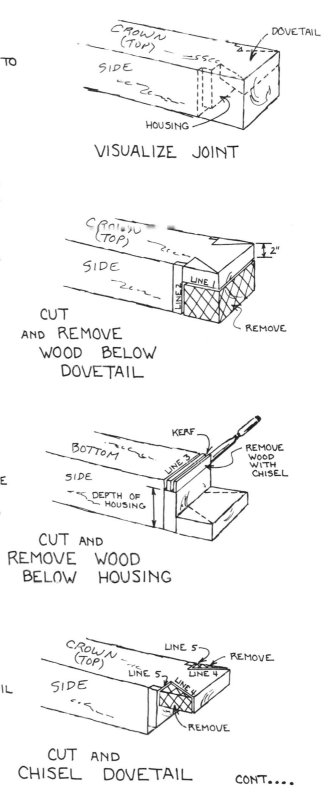

VISUALIZE JOINT

ROLL TIMBER ONTO SIDE AND
SAW ALONG LINE 1 AT FULL DEPTH
OF CIRCULAR SAW (RIGHT, TIMBER
NOT ROLLED IN DRAWING). ROLL
TIMBER TWICE TO OPPOSITE
SIDE UP AND REPEAT. USE
A HAND SAW TO FINISH THIS CUT.
ROLL TIMBER UPSIDE DOWN
AND SAW ACROSS BOTTOM OF
TIMBER ON LINE 2. DEPTH OF
SAW IS 2" LESS THAN DEPTH OF
TIMBER. FINISH CUT WITH HAND
SAW. THE SHADED BLOCK OF
WOOD SHOWN SHOULD FALL
OUT. A TAP WITH A MALLET
MAY BE NEEDED.

CUT
AND REMOVE
WOOD BELOW
DOVETAIL

WITH TIMBER UPSIDE DOWN,
SAW LINE 3 AND KERF WITH THE
SAW SET AT THE SAME DEPTH
TO REMOVE WOOD BELOW HOUSING
AREA (RIGHT). FINISH
REMOVING WOOD WITH CHISEL
AS SHOWN. REMOVING THIS
WOOD WITH SAW KERFS AND A
CHISEL SHOULD GIVE A VERY
PRECISE DIMENSION TO THE
DEPTH OF THE HOUSING.

CUT AND
REMOVE WOOD
BELOW HOUSING

ROLL TIMBER TO HAVE DOVETAIL
ON TOP. SAW DOVETAIL LINES 4
AND 5 (RIGHT). FINISH CUTS
WITH HAND SAW.
REMOVE WOOD (SHADED AREA)
AND CLEAN DOVETAIL
WITH CHISEL.

CUT AND
CHISEL DOVETAIL

CONT....

CUTTING THE HOUSED DOVETAIL TENON.... CONT.

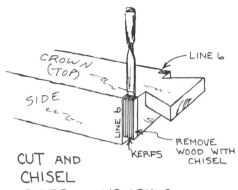

CROWN (TOP)

SIDE

LINE 6

LINE 6

KERFS

REMOVE WOOD WITH CHISEL

CUT AND CHISEL SIDES OF HOUSING

ROLL TIMBER ON ONE SIDE AND THEN ON THE OTHER, CUTTING LINE 6 AND KERFING AREA TO BE REMOVED AS SHOWN AT LEFT (TIMBER NOT ROLLED IN DRAWING). CHISEL AND CLEAN AROUND HOUSING.

CHAMFER DOVETAIL AND HOUSING AREA (LOWER LEFT). THIS WILL MAKE ASSEMBLING EASIER. DO NOT CHAMFER SHOULDER.

LARGE TIMBERS ARE NOT EASY TO MOVE. WE THEREFORE MINIMIZE ROLLING BY:
1) CUTTING TENONS ON BOTH ENDS SIMULTANEOUSLY.
2) MAKING ALL REQUIRED CUTS ON ONE SIDE BEFORE ROLLING TIMBER TO THE NEXT SIDE. FOR CLARITY'S SAKE, OUR ILLUSTRATION WAS NOT DONE THIS WAY.

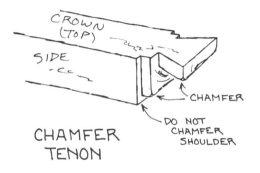

CROWN (TOP)

SIDE

CHAMFER

DO NOT CHAMFER SHOULDER

CHAMFER TENON

CUTTING A SCARF JOINT

   A SCARF JOINT IS USED TO SPLICE TOGETHER
TWO TIMBERS. WE ILLUSTRATED THREE TYPES IN THE
LAST CHAPTER. THE EFFECTIVENESS OF A SCARF JOINT IS IN
RELATION TO HOW WELL IT FITS.   THE TIGHTER WE CAN
MAKE THIS SPLICE, THE STRONGER THE JOINT WILL BE.

   IT IS VITAL TO HAVE A SHARP SAW BLADE,
FOR THERE IS A GREAT AMOUNT OF RIPPING
REQUIRED. THE LAYING OUT OF THE JOINT
USING A TEMPLATE WAS EXPLAINED
IN CHAPTER 3. IT IS IMPORTANT TO
REMEMBER THAT THE TEMPLATE
MUST BE HELD FLUSH TO THE
BOTTOM OF THE TIMBER
AND THAT TRANSFER LINES
ARE USED FOR ACCURATELY
PLACING THE TEMPLATE ON
THE OPPOSITE SIDE OF THE
TIMBER.
AS YOU ARE CUTTING, TRY
TO VISUALIZE THE JOINT. YOU
ARE WORKING TO REVEAL A JOINT
THAT IS ALREADY WITHIN THE
TIMBER (RIGHT). DARKENING THE AREA
WHICH IS TO BE REMOVED HELPS IN
THIS VISUALIZATION.

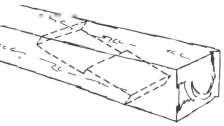

VISUALIZE
SCARF JOINT
WITHIN TIMBER

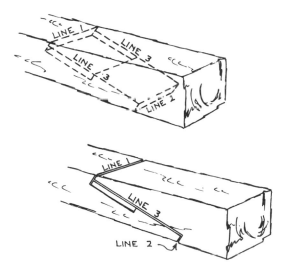

CUT LINES 1 AND 2,
THEN LINE 3 (BOTH SIDES OF TIMBER).

   WE ILLUSTRATE THE
CUTTING OF A STOPPED
SPLAYED SCARF. CUT
ALONG LINES 1 AND 2
(LEFT) AT THE ANGLE
DETERMINED BY THE
TEMPLATE. RIP CUT
LINE 3 (LEFT) FROM
BOTH SIDES OF THE
TIMBER WITH THE SAW
BLADE SET AT FULL
DEPTH. WHEN CUTTING,
ALWAYS LEAVE THE
LINE. FINISH THE CUT
WITH A HAND SAW
AND REMOVE THIS
WOOD.

CONT....

CUTTING A SCARF JOINT.... CONT.

MAKE A SERIES OF SAW KERFS
ACROSS THE STEP WITH THE
CIRCULAR SAW SET TO THE
DEPTH OF LINE 4 (RIGHT). REMOVE
THIS WOOD WITH A CHISEL AND
SLICK. TAKE SPECIAL CARE
TO KEEP LINE 4 STRAIGHT
AND SHARP.

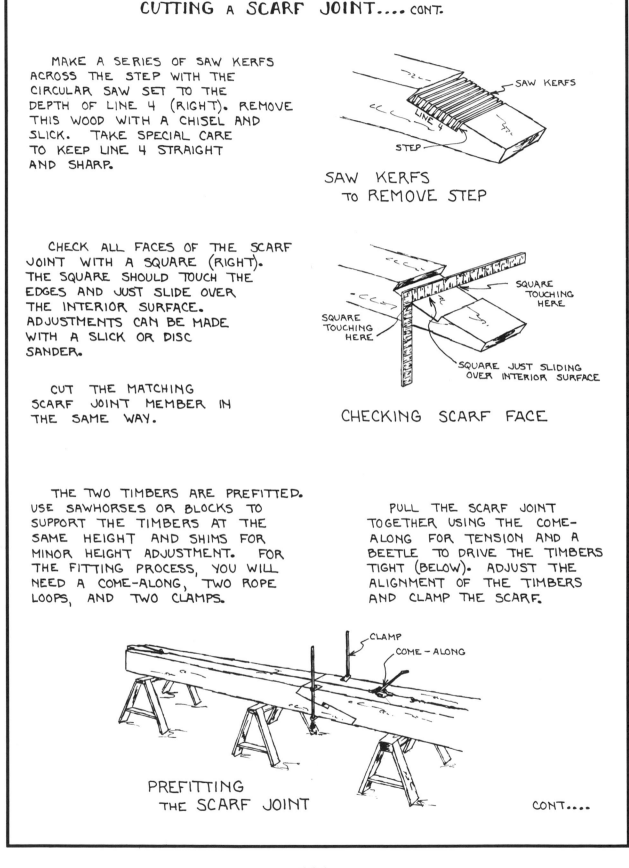

SAW KERFS
TO REMOVE STEP

CHECK ALL FACES OF THE SCARF
JOINT WITH A SQUARE (RIGHT).
THE SQUARE SHOULD TOUCH THE
EDGES AND JUST SLIDE OVER
THE INTERIOR SURFACE.
ADJUSTMENTS CAN BE MADE
WITH A SLICK OR DISC
SANDER.

CUT THE MATCHING
SCARF JOINT MEMBER IN
THE SAME WAY.

CHECKING SCARF FACE

THE TWO TIMBERS ARE PREFITTED.
USE SAWHORSES OR BLOCKS TO
SUPPORT THE TIMBERS AT THE
SAME HEIGHT AND SHIMS FOR
MINOR HEIGHT ADJUSTMENT. FOR
THE FITTING PROCESS, YOU WILL
NEED A COME-ALONG, TWO ROPE
LOOPS, AND TWO CLAMPS.

PULL THE SCARF JOINT
TOGETHER USING THE COME-
ALONG FOR TENSION AND A
BEETLE TO DRIVE THE TIMBERS
TIGHT (BELOW). ADJUST THE
ALIGNMENT OF THE TIMBERS
AND CLAMP THE SCARF.

PREFITTING
THE SCARF JOINT

CONT....

CUTTING A SCARF JOINT.... CONT.

UNDOUBTEDLY, AT LEAST ONE SURFACE OF THE SCARF WILL NOT FIT TIGHTLY, WHILE OTHERS WILL BE TIGHT. MAKE IMPROVEMENTS IN THE FIT BY SAWING ALONG LINES 1 AND 2 WITH A HAND CROSS-CUT SAW (REFERRED TO AS "KERFING THE JOINT") (SEE DRAWING AT RIGHT). THIS WILL MAKE THE GAP UNIFORM. TAKE CARE NOT TO SAW TOO FAR, A VERY COMMON ERROR. CLOSE THE GAP BY LOOSENING THE CLAMPS AND TIGHTENING THE COME-ALONG. SEVERAL KERFS MAY BE NECESSARY TO CLOSE LARGE GAPS.

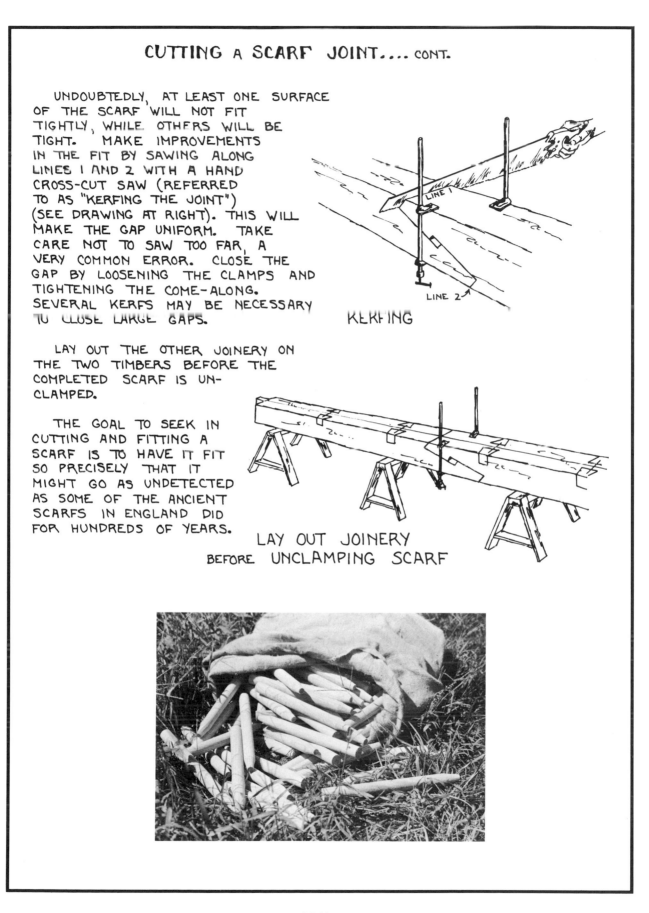

KERFING

LAY OUT THE OTHER JOINERY ON THE TWO TIMBERS BEFORE THE COMPLETED SCARF IS UN-CLAMPED.

THE GOAL TO SEEK IN CUTTING AND FITTING A SCARF IS TO HAVE IT FIT SO PRECISELY THAT IT MIGHT GO AS UNDETECTED AS SOME OF THE ANCIENT SCARFS IN ENGLAND DID FOR HUNDREDS OF YEARS.

LAY OUT JOINERY
BEFORE UNCLAMPING SCARF

105

PEGS
(ALSO KNOWN AS PINS, TRUNNELS, AND TREENAILS)

PEGS ARE THE NAILS OF TIMBER FRAMING. THEY SHOULD BE 1" IN DIAMETER, STRAIGHT-GRAINED, AND MADE OF HARDWOOD, IDEALLY WHITE OAK OR LOCUST. PEGS OFTEN FUNCTION SOMEWHAT LIKE COTTER PINS HOLDING JOINTS TOGETHER, THE GEOMETRY OF THE JOINT ALLOWING THE TIMBERS TO BEAR THE MAJOR FORCES. IN A FEW RARE CASES WHERE A MAJOR SHEARING FORCE WILL ACT UPON THE PEG (SUCH AS IN THE FRAMING OF GAMBREL ROOF RAFTERS), USE AN EXTRA-LARGE 1½" DIAMETER PEG.

PEGS DRIVEN BY BLOWS FROM A 15-20 LB. BEETLE STAY PUT AS A RESULT OF THE FRICTION DEVELOPED BETWEEN THE PEG AND THE TIMBER (RIGHT). TIMBER FRAMERS IN NEW ENGLAND HAVE DEVELOPED DIFFERENT TYPES OF PEGS IN ORDER TO MAXIMIZE THIS FRICTIONAL FORCE.

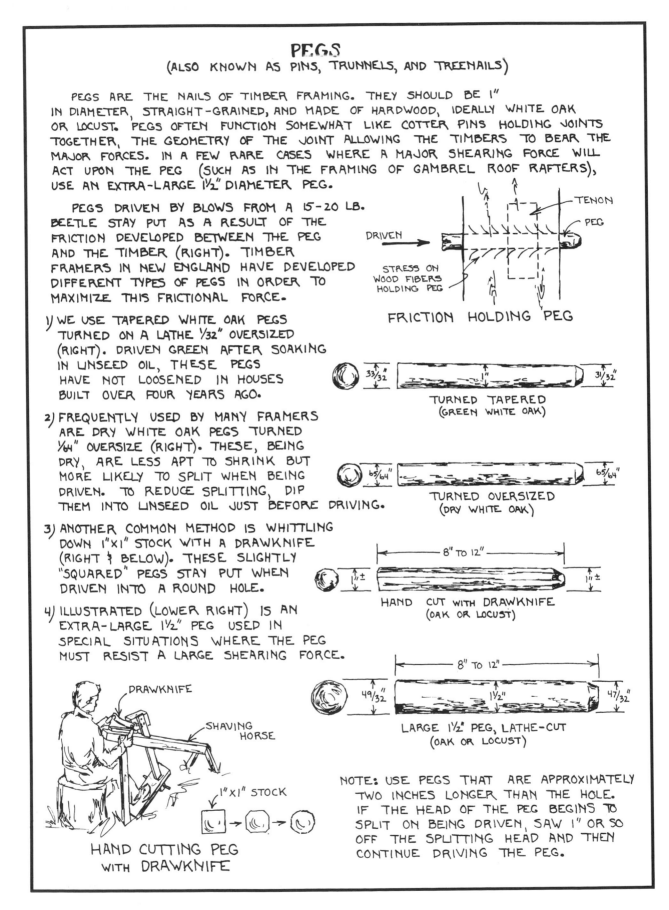

FRICTION HOLDING PEG

TENON
PEG
DRIVEN
STRESS ON WOOD FIBERS HOLDING PEG

1) WE USE TAPERED WHITE OAK PEGS TURNED ON A LATHE 1/32" OVERSIZED (RIGHT). DRIVEN GREEN AFTER SOAKING IN LINSEED OIL, THESE PEGS HAVE NOT LOOSENED IN HOUSES BUILT OVER FOUR YEARS AGO.

TURNED TAPERED
(GREEN WHITE OAK)
33/32" ... 1" ... 31/32"

2) FREQUENTLY USED BY MANY FRAMERS ARE DRY WHITE OAK PEGS TURNED 1/64" OVERSIZE (RIGHT). THESE, BEING DRY, ARE LESS APT TO SHRINK BUT MORE LIKELY TO SPLIT WHEN BEING DRIVEN. TO REDUCE SPLITTING, DIP THEM INTO LINSEED OIL JUST BEFORE DRIVING.

TURNED OVERSIZED
(DRY WHITE OAK)
65/64" ... 65/64"

3) ANOTHER COMMON METHOD IS WHITTLING DOWN 1"x1" STOCK WITH A DRAWKNIFE (RIGHT & BELOW). THESE SLIGHTLY "SQUARED" PEGS STAY PUT WHEN DRIVEN INTO A ROUND HOLE.

8" TO 12"
1"± ... 1"±
HAND CUT WITH DRAWKNIFE
(OAK OR LOCUST)

4) ILLUSTRATED (LOWER RIGHT) IS AN EXTRA-LARGE 1½" PEG USED IN SPECIAL SITUATIONS WHERE THE PEG MUST RESIST A LARGE SHEARING FORCE.

8" TO 12"
49/32" ... 1½" ... 47/32"
LARGE 1½" PEG, LATHE-CUT
(OAK OR LOCUST)

DRAWKNIFE
SHAVING HORSE

1"x1" STOCK

HAND CUTTING PEG
WITH DRAWKNIFE

NOTE: USE PEGS THAT ARE APPROXIMATELY TWO INCHES LONGER THAN THE HOLE. IF THE HEAD OF THE PEG BEGINS TO SPLIT ON BEING DRIVEN, SAW 1" OR SO OFF THE SPLITTING HEAD AND THEN CONTINUE DRIVING THE PEG.

FINISHING AND EMBELLISHMENTS

FINISHING

THE TIMBER FRAMERS IN OUR AREA USE SEVERAL DIFFERENT METHODS OF FINISHING TIMBERS:

1) ONE METHOD, GOUGING THE TIMBERS, IS DONE TO GIVE A HAND-HEWN EFFECT. TO OUR EYES, IT MERELY LOOKS GOUGED.

2) ANOTHER METHOD IS SIMPLY OILING THE ROUGH-SAWED TIMBERS WITH BOILED LINSEED OIL AFTER THEY HAVE BEEN RAISED. A SIMPLE, HONEST LOOK.

3) THE METHOD WE USE INCLUDES PLANING AND SANDING THE TIMBERS, REMOVING SCARS AND WANE WITH A DRAWKNIFE, AND ROUTING THE EDGES WITH A QUARTER ROUND BIT. THE FRAME IS TOUCHED UP WITH A SANDER AFTER IT IS RAISED AND THEN OILED WITH BOILED LINSEED OIL. ALTHOUGH THIS SEEMS A MONUMENTAL TASK, A SMALL FRAME WILL TAKE ONLY A FEW DAYS TO FINISH USING A POWER HAND PLANER AND DISC SANDER (SEE "FINISHING TOOLS").

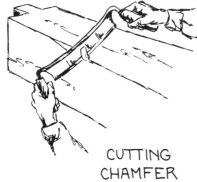

CUTTING
CHAMFER
WITH
DRAWKNIFE

EMBELLISHMENTS

EMBELLISHMENTS ADD LITTLE TO A FRAME POORLY CUT AND ASSEMBLED, BUT ACCENTUATE A FINE QUALITY FRAME. BECAUSE THE FULL ARRAY OF METHODS OF CUTTING AND CARVING EMBELLISHMENTS GOES FAR BEYOND THE SCOPE OF THIS BOOK, WE SUGGEST READING A BOOK ON CABINET FINISHING OR WOOD-CARVING TECHNIQUES.

SHOWN AT LEFT IS A DRAWKNIFE BEING USED TO CUT A CHAMFER.

EXAMPLES OF TRADITIONAL COLONIAL AND ENGLISH EMBELLISHMENTS ARE SHOWN ON THE NEXT THREE PAGES TO GIVE AN IDEA OF THE RANGE OF POSSIBILITIES. THOUGH THE EARLY AMERICAN BUILDERS USED FEW EMBELLISHMENTS, THOSE THEY DID USE OFTEN HAD STRUCTURAL AS WELL AS AESTHETIC REASONS.

POSTS WERE FREQUENTLY WIDER AT THE TOP, OR "GUNSTOCKED" (SEE TWO DRAWINGS, TOP NEXT PAGE). AESTHETICALLY INTERESTING, IT ALSO ADDED THE EXTRA WOOD NEEDED AT THIS JOINT. ILLUSTRATED ARE A SIMPLE CHAMFERED GUNSTOCK (TOP LEFT, NEXT PAGE) AND A MORE ELABORATELY CARVED ONE (TOP RIGHT, NEXT PAGE).

CONT....

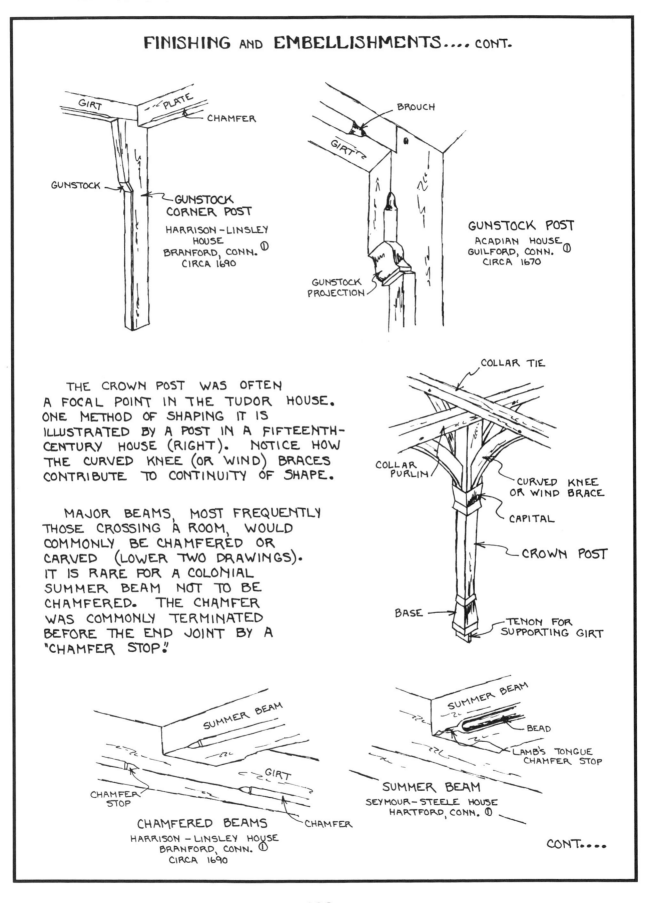

GIRT
PLATE
CHAMFER
GUNSTOCK
GUNSTOCK
CORNER POST
HARRISON — LINSLEY
HOUSE
BRANFORD, CONN. ①
CIRCA 1690

BROUCH
GIRT
GUNSTOCK POST
ACADIAN HOUSE
GUILFORD, CONN. ①
CIRCA 1670
GUNSTOCK
PROJECTION

THE CROWN POST WAS OFTEN
A FOCAL POINT IN THE TUDOR HOUSE.
ONE METHOD OF SHAPING IT IS
ILLUSTRATED BY A POST IN A FIFTEENTH-
CENTURY HOUSE (RIGHT). NOTICE HOW
THE CURVED KNEE (OR WIND) BRACES
CONTRIBUTE TO CONTINUITY OF SHAPE.

MAJOR BEAMS, MOST FREQUENTLY
THOSE CROSSING A ROOM, WOULD
COMMONLY BE CHAMFERED OR
CARVED (LOWER TWO DRAWINGS).
IT IS RARE FOR A COLONIAL
SUMMER BEAM NOT TO BE
CHAMFERED. THE CHAMFER
WAS COMMONLY TERMINATED
BEFORE THE END JOINT BY A
"CHAMFER STOP."

COLLAR TIE
COLLAR
PURLIN
CURVED KNEE
OR WIND BRACE
CAPITAL
CROWN POST
BASE
TENON FOR
SUPPORTING GIRT

SUMMER BEAM
GIRT
CHAMFER
STOP
CHAMFERED BEAMS
HARRISON — LINSLEY HOUSE
BRANFORD, CONN. ①
CIRCA 1690

SUMMER BEAM
BEAD
LAMB'S TONGUE
CHAMFER STOP
SUMMER BEAM
SEYMOUR — STEELE HOUSE
HARTFORD, CONN. ①

CONT....

FINISHING AND EMBELLISHMENTS.... CONT.

TUDOR ENGLAND DEVELOPED A TRADITION OF
RICHLY MOLDED AND CARVED BEAMS. THIS TRADITION
ORIGINATED FROM EARLY COMPETITION BETWEEN MASONS
AND CARPENTERS. THE CARPENTERS STROVE TO HAVE
TIMBERS CONSIDERED PART OF THE FINISHED INTERIOR
OF THE HOUSE AS WELL AS ITS
STRUCTURAL FRAMEWORK.

TWO EXAMPLES OF
THIS WORK ARE SHOWN
(RIGHT AND BELOW).
NOTICE IN THE
FRAMEWORK BELOW
THE SUBTLE,
INTERESTING EFFECT
OF THE KNEE BRACE
CURVED ONLY
ON THE LOWER
SIDE.

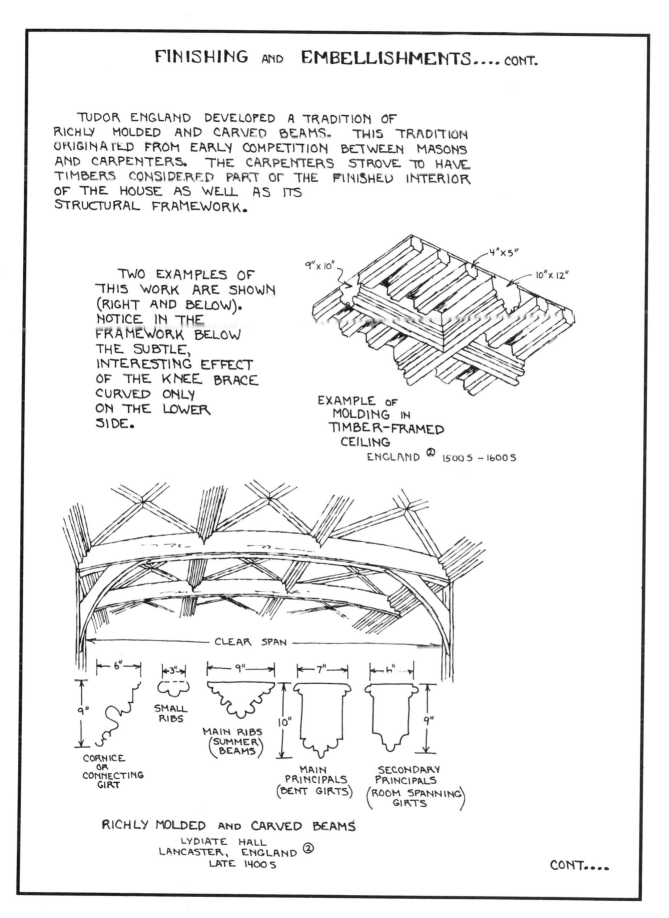

EXAMPLE OF
MOLDING IN
TIMBER-FRAMED
CEILING
ENGLAND ② 1500S - 1600S

RICHLY MOLDED AND CARVED BEAMS
LYDIATE HALL
LANCASTER, ENGLAND ②
LATE 1400S

CONT....

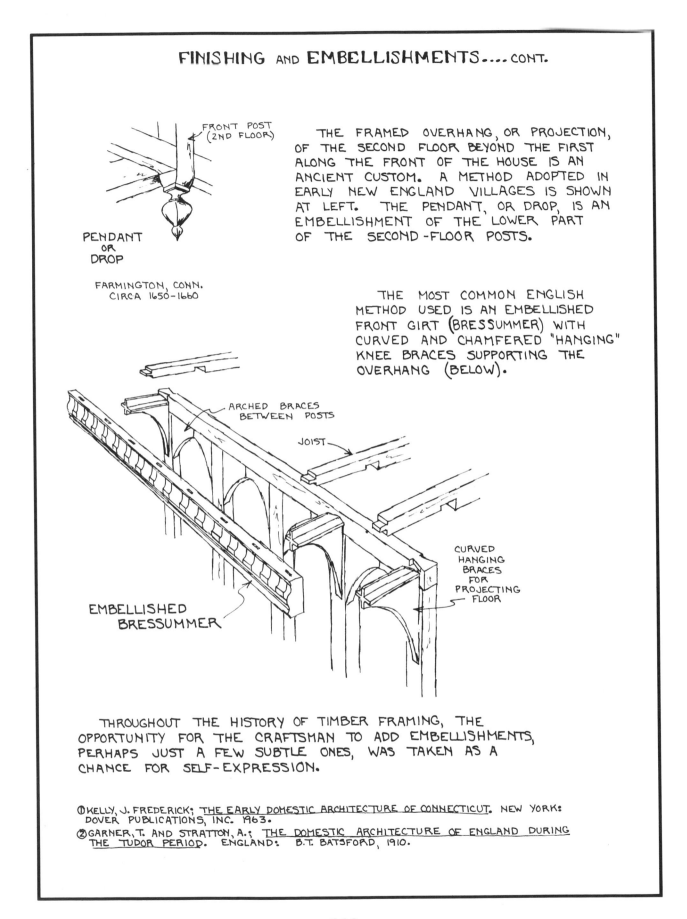

FRONT POST
(2ND FLOOR)

PENDANT
OR
DROP

FARMINGTON, CONN.
CIRCA 1650-1660

THE FRAMED OVERHANG, OR PROJECTION, OF THE SECOND FLOOR BEYOND THE FIRST ALONG THE FRONT OF THE HOUSE IS AN ANCIENT CUSTOM. A METHOD ADOPTED IN EARLY NEW ENGLAND VILLAGES IS SHOWN AT LEFT. THE PENDANT, OR DROP, IS AN EMBELLISHMENT OF THE LOWER PART OF THE SECOND-FLOOR POSTS.

THE MOST COMMON ENGLISH METHOD USED IS AN EMBELLISHED FRONT GIRT (BRESSUMMER) WITH CURVED AND CHAMFERED "HANGING" KNEE BRACES SUPPORTING THE OVERHANG (BELOW).

ARCHED BRACES
BETWEEN POSTS

JOIST

CURVED
HANGING
BRACES
FOR
PROJECTING
FLOOR

EMBELLISHED
BRESSUMMER

THROUGHOUT THE HISTORY OF TIMBER FRAMING, THE OPPORTUNITY FOR THE CRAFTSMAN TO ADD EMBELLISHMENTS, PERHAPS JUST A FEW SUBTLE ONES, WAS TAKEN AS A CHANCE FOR SELF-EXPRESSION.

① KELLY, J. FREDERICK; THE EARLY DOMESTIC ARCHITECTURE OF CONNECTICUT. NEW YORK: DOVER PUBLICATIONS, INC. 1963.
② GARNER, T. AND STRATTON, A.; THE DOMESTIC ARCHITECTURE OF ENGLAND DURING THE TUDOR PERIOD. ENGLAND: B.T. BATSFORD, 1910.

CHAPTER FIVE
PUTTING IT ALL TOGETHER
ASSEMBLY AND RAISING

Courtesy of Martha Carlson

The truth is that when a free spirit exists, it has to materialize itself in some form of work, and for this the hands are needed. Everywhere we find traces of man's handiwork and through these we can catch a glimpse of his spirit and the thoughts of his time.

—Maria Montessori: *The Absorbent Mind*

A properly fitted timber frame, with high quality joinery, stands apart from twentieth-century construction methods. It's something natural and real In the age of synthetics and plastic. Instead of relying on many 2 by 4's and hundreds of pounds of nails, this building technique is based only on large timbers cut from native trees, and wooden pegs. Instead of being a system based on speed in production and simplified labor, timber framing is used because of its beauty and strength and because it requires skill and personal involvement with the work.

People who build with timbers are building a home strong enough and durable enough to have its age measured not in decades but in centuries, an extremely optimistic statement in an age rife with doomsayers.

It should be obvious that one does not choose timber framing because it is quicker. It isn't. With this fact in mind, we would hope that the owners and builders who are thoughtful enough to want to put a building together in this manner will also be patient enough to do the job right.

In today's home-building industry, along with all the good building materials in short supply, there exists an extreme lack of patience. Technological advances of this century have done fantastic things for the building trades and for the home buyer, but the repeated use of these quick and easy tools and materials seems to have sapped the industry of the ability to slow down when fastidiousness and persistence are required. In this environment, quality is plywood nailed on six-inch centers instead of twelve, or a

A properly fitted timber frame draws strength from good joinery and bracing.

sheetrocked wall that is true within one-eighth of an inch. These are good values, yes, but if one is armed with nail guns and steel studs, these goals are not difficult to achieve. Because of this, it seems that more often we hear people brag about how quickly a building was put together than how well. But there is a price to pay for this speed, for surely if the endless movement of the assembly line is symbolic of the frenetic pace of our era, then the sterile environment created by today's industry to house our families is a symbol of the deteriorating quality of our lives.

The process of fitting the timbers on the site in preparation for the raising demands time and patience. Good joints in these massive timbers don't just pop together. The misunderstanding of this fact is one significant reason why the traditional quality of timber frames is having a difficult time reemerging today. Our inspection of old buildings in Europe and in America reveals that most of the ancient joints are so well fitted that they have remained tight even through centuries. Some of the frames put together today seem to have been assembled very quickly, with little or no regard for the quality of the joinery. Did the builder expect them to drop together like Lincoln logs? Perhaps the problem is that he

is trying to get the assembly of a timber frame to fit into the time frame of the modern kit house that goes up overnight, or maybe the stud-built home down the street that went up in a week. I'm convinced that if we're going to learn to master the old methods, we'll also have to embrace many of the old values. A good place to start is to remove some of the constraints of time and to learn to be patient.

I hope it is clear that the reasons for demanding good fits are not just aesthetic. Building a timber-framed home is great fun, but it is also serious business. Unlike other modes of construction, timber framing does not have a great number of pieces to compensate for individual defects, nor does it depend on sheathing for rigidity. Instead, it is independently strong, drawing strength from good joinery and bracing in large timbers. The point is this: properly assembled joints are very important, as they will not only affect the beauty and value of the home being constructed but will also lock together ten to fifteen tons of timbers that will be over the heads of many generations of inhabitants.

Obviously, joining large timbers is a difficult process. I'll confess that even the best efforts produce many frustrations. We have not put together a perfect frame. We doubt if one has ever been built. But the best of efforts

112

MOVING TIMBERS

TIMBERS USED IN A FRAME, ESPECIALLY OF HARD WOOD, CAN BE EXTREMELY HEAVY. BECAUSE AN 8" X 8" OAK TIMBER, 16 FT. LONG, WEIGHS APPROXIMATELY 350-400 POUNDS, YOU MUST USE CARE AND FORESIGHT. LIFT WITH YOUR LEGS, NOT WITH YOUR BACK. TRY ALWAYS TO USE WALKING BEAMS, ROLLERS, LEVERS, CARRYING STICKS AND/OR A LARGE NUMBER OF PEOPLE WHEN MOVING TIMBERS.

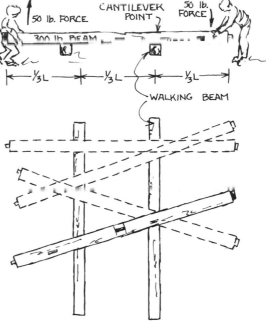

CARRYING STICKS
CARRYING STICKS AND FOUR PEOPLE WILL DISTRIBUTE A LOAD EVENLY (ABOVE).

ROLLERS UNDER BEAM
A ROLLER PLACED AT MID-SPAN AND ANOTHER PLACED AT THE STARTING END OF A TIMBER WILL ALLOW EASY MOVING OF THE TIMBER ON RELATIVELY FLAT SURFACES (BELOW). 4" P.V.C. PIPE WORKS WELL. NOTE: TIMBER MOVES IN DIRECTION OF ROLLERS.

WALKING BEAMS
TWO PEOPLE AND 50 lb. OF LIFTING AND PUSHING CAN MOVE A 300 lb. TIMBER (ABOVE).

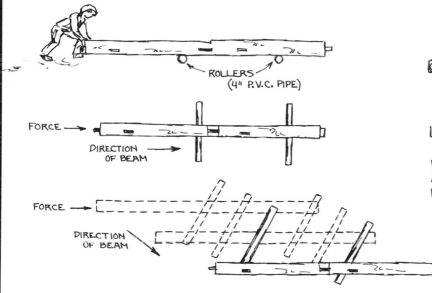

LEVER ACTION
LEVER ACTION CAN BE USEFUL TO RAISE A TIMBER TO A DESIRED HEIGHT (ABOVE).

Framing for first-floor deck.

have helped us to improve the state of our art. As we have improved, we have come to feel that, like other aspects of woodworking, assembly of the piece is the most important part of the process. And certainly, like a very large and functional piece of furniture, it deserves the patience and attention to detail that would be given to a table or a chair.

We have learned (mostly the hard way) to try to break the building down to its lowest common denominator and to proceed one step at a time. I once asked an elderly mason who does a great deal of stone and brickwork in our area what the secret is to his beautiful work. He gave a typically brief response: "Why, I lay one brick at a time, each one perfectly." This philosophy is a good one to remember on any building project, and especially when the enormity of the project starts to feel overwhelming. It feels encouraging to complete little tasks even if the larger one still seems out of reach.

We like to start by sorting the timbers. Separating the sticks into different groups such as sill members, bents, trusses, joists, and so on will help to reduce confusion. This is a good time to take inventory to be certain that all the needed timbers are on the building site. Even after doing many timber frames, we have found that important pieces will sometimes be overlooked.

Before the deck is started, the foundation must be checked to be certain it is level, square, and that the dimensions are correct. If the owner worked on the foundation himself, we have found that it is usually quite accurate. If an outside contractor was hired to do the work, you never know what to expect. The contractor for one of our customers poured the foundation a foot too long. On another job it was poured six inches too long, six inches out of square, four inches out of level, and all the window openings had caved in! Of course, this was the extreme and could not be built upon; smaller discrepancies should be expected and adjustments can be made as the sills are put into place.

The heavy and awkward work required to lay a framed deck is much like the hard and dusty work of moving and sawing planks for a piece of furniture before the sensitive work can begin. It's part of a bargain that is made—the grunt work and sweat that tempers the sheer pleasure of working with wood in this manner. Lifting the girders onto the foundation and setting the girders between the sill is difficult, yes, but it is also the first major step in the building process and, consequently, rewarding. There is no clear-cut procedure for solving these problems, as each house and each site has its own idiosyncrasies, and new solutions must be found for

114

each situation. There are various solutions to the problem of getting these timbers into position, but none are magic. We have found that this part of the project seems to boil down to a physical struggle between ourselves and certain gravitational laws.

Since gravity is the law, and since attempts to defy it are variable, it is best to move very slowly and carefully, always having "thought" the timber into position before actually putting it there. For instance, if a timber needed to be shimmed to bring it up to level on an irregular foundation, that fact would have been noted and shims would have been placed in position ready to adjust the timber to the proper elevation. It would not have to be lifted again later. Since all the scarf joints and corner joints would have been prefit during the cutting stage, joints will fit with relatively little effort; but it is important to remember that many of these interlocking joints, like the pieces of a jigsaw puzzle, depend on a certain order of assembly. This order should be planned very carefully so that each piece slides into position only once.

We've learned that one can't be too critical about being certain the deck frame is level, square, and straight. Whatever inconsistencies that might exist in the sills and girders will be repeated again in the posts and girts placed on top of them. This point was made very clear to us once when we had raised a frame on a deck built by another contractor. We were having a terrible time aligning the bents and getting proper fits on the girts before it was discovered the deck was out of level by over an inch from corner to corner. Immediately, we jacked and shimmed the deck frame until it was level. In the space of those few minutes, the bents were properly aligned, the girts tilted into a proper fit, and the frame went from disaster to one of the best we have done.

When all the framing members are securely joined on the foundation (see "Framing a Deck," pages 116–17), the planking is nailed down and the deck is complete. It feels satisfying to have this part of the job done and to be operating on a level and clean surface conducive to the really fine work necessary for fitting the bents.

Before the bents are assembled, just a little planning is in order. It may seem elementary that bents should be built and stacked in a sequence logical for the way they will be raised, but, believe me, it's easy to make a mistake here and it is worth a moment of pause: a stack of two-ton bents cannot be shuffled like a stack of cards, and the assembled bent is very difficult to move if it obstructs another part of the raising (see "Assembling a Bent," pages 122–23). Remember, too, that if the post layout is consistent, it is possible to put the bents up in the wrong order or to raise the whole building backward. I heard a story about a fellow who came to see his house after the raising day, only to find the ridge line running north-south instead of east–west. The frame had to be taken apart and raised again a few days later.

If the raising is to be done by hand, it probably won't make any difference whether you start at one end of the deck or the other, unless there happens to be a large tree close to one end of the deck, onto which a pulley can be attached, to aid in pulling up the first bent. If a crane is assisting the raising, you may be limited by where the operator can reasonably set up his machine. Should the crane be unable to set up perpendicular to the broadside of the building, then the bent farthest from the machine would go up first.

A statement attributed to Ben Franklin expresses his secret of longevity by proclaiming that "I never run when I can walk. I never walk when I can stand still. I never stand still when I can sit. I never sit when I can lie down." We might paraphrase him and suggest that you "never carry a timber that can slide. Never slide a timber that can be rolled. Never lift a timber at all that doesn't have to be moved." When the deck is on and the foundation is backfilled, moving the timbers into position is much easier because rollers and walking beams can be used to their best advantage (see "Moving Timbers," page 113).

I have found the fitting and assembly of the bents on the building site to be the most enjoyable part of timber framing. Each bent is a significant woodworking project, worthy of the best possible effort. Not only is it important because it is within the bent that the full weight of the building is borne, but also the joinery here is the most sophisticated and is almost always fully revealed to the inside of the home. The quality of the joinery in the bents will set the tone for the quality of the home, just as the difference between a butt joint and dovetails at the corner of a box

FRAMING A DECK

STARTING AT ONE CORNER, PLACE SILL TIMBERS ONE BY ONE. PULL EACH SCARF JOINT TIGHTLY TOGETHER USING A COME-ALONG (BELOW). CHECK THE TWO TIMBERS FOR LINEAR ALIGNMENT BY USING A TAUT STRING TIED TO TWO 1" BLOCKS (SEE DRAWING). DRILL AND PEG THE SCARF JOINT. ASSEMBLE CORNER JOINTS BUT DO NOT PEG UNTIL THE ENTIRE SILL HAS BEEN ASSEMBLED AND SQUARED.

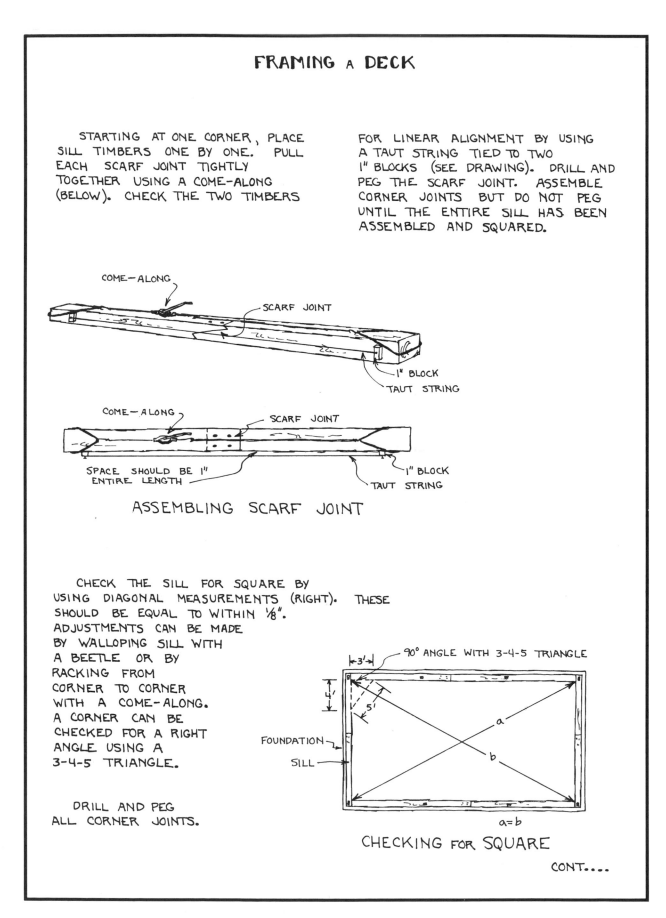

ASSEMBLING SCARF JOINT

CHECK THE SILL FOR SQUARE BY USING DIAGONAL MEASUREMENTS (RIGHT). THESE SHOULD BE EQUAL TO WITHIN $\frac{1}{8}$". ADJUSTMENTS CAN BE MADE BY WALLOPING SILL WITH A BEETLE OR BY RACKING FROM CORNER TO CORNER WITH A COME-ALONG. A CORNER CAN BE CHECKED FOR A RIGHT ANGLE USING A 3-4-5 TRIANGLE.

DRILL AND PEG ALL CORNER JOINTS.

CHECKING FOR SQUARE

CONT....

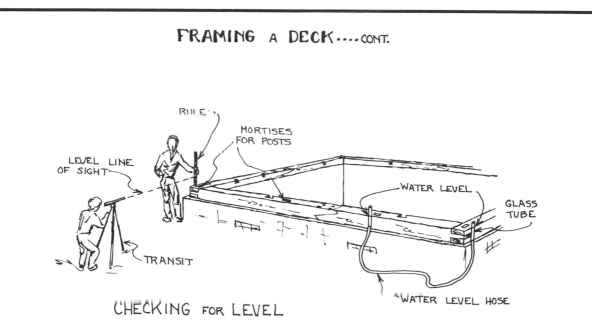

CHECKING FOR LEVEL

IF THE FOUNDATION WAS NOT CONSTRUCTED PERFECTLY LEVEL, SOME SHIMMING OR PLANING OF THE SILLS WILL BE NECESSARY. THE ELEVATION AT THE LOCATIONS OF THE POST MORTISES MUST ALL BE EXACTLY THE SAME. OTHERWISE, RACKING OF THE HOUSE FRAME WILL OCCUR. USE A WATER LEVEL OR A TRANSIT (ABOVE).

GIRDERS AND JOISTS ARE THEN DROPPED INTO PLACE (BELOW). IF INTERMEDIATE CELLAR POSTS ARE NEEDED, THEY ARE PLACED AND TEMPORARILY BRACED BEFORE ASSEMBLING THE GIRDER BEAMS. A SUBFLOOR SHOULD BE LAID OVER THE DECK FRAME PRIOR TO ASSEMBLING BENTS AND RAISING THE FRAME.

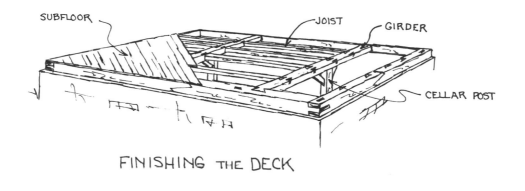

FINISHING THE DECK

Kerfing the shoulder is often helpful in obtaining a tight fit.

A come-along is used to pull joints tightly together.

defines whether it will be an apple crate or a jewelry box.

As the work starts to progress on the bents, step by step, a rhythm begins to develop—a measurement, a trial fit, more measurements, reclamping, a shave or a kerf, and then drilling and driving a peg through the joint. This work seems to be done best by just a couple of people. Two are enough to move timbers into position and both can remain busy even while adjustments are being made. And as their energy is being fed by the quality of the work, joint by joint and bent by bent, these people can be very efficient.

Trial-fitting the joints has always been a part of good timber framing. Just as in furniture or cabinetmaking, it is simply the only way to get a joint to fit well. I have a hobby of studying old barns and houses in my travels around New England, and have noticed that almost all of the frames show the signs of having been trial-fitted before being pegged into the frame. One sure sign occurs when a timber has been scribed to fit the irregular surface of the piece it joins. Another indication is slight variations in lengths of very tightly fitted braces. These variations would probably be the result of an exact measurement having been taken after a trial fit. The colonists even developed a specially tapered metal drift pin so that pieces could be tempo-

rarily joined to check the fit and to get an accurate brace length. There is evidence, too, that the master joiners who put together the great Dutch barns in upper New York State actually completely assembled the broadsides of the frame to test-fit the whole unit. After that, they took them apart so that bents could then be assembled.

The most advanced timber framers were the early English craftsmen whose fabulous halls and cathedrals demonstrate rich detail and extremely sophisticated joinery. The scribed fits in the hewn timbers show a great deal of hand work at each joint. I find it humbling that the intricate work created by these early joiners was accomplished with just a few rough tools, and inspiring to know that some of their buildings have lasted eight centuries and longer. It's another reminder that a few extra minutes or an hour to ensure a good fit is time well spent.

Despite some effort to the contrary, we have found it necessary to use trial-fitting as a part of our procedure too. Large timbers in the rough-sawn condition are never perfect. Dimensional variations are practically a rule, but it is not uncommon to discover the more serious problem of finding a timber to be out of square. We have also learned to expect the organic inconsistencies of a twist or a bow or both. These things considered,

118

CONTEMPLATING THE RAISING
(FOR A CRANE RAISING)

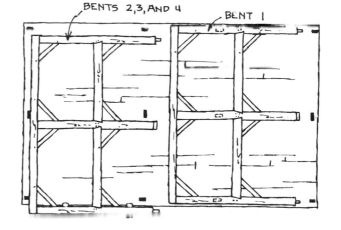

BENTS 2, 3, AND 4   BENT 1

PLANNING
BENT ASSEMBLAGE

BEFORE THE BENTS ARE ASSEMBLED ON THE DECK, CAREFUL THOUGHT SHOULD BE GIVEN TO HOW AND IN WHICH ORDER THEY WILL BE RAISED. THEY SHOULD BE POSITIONED SO THAT THE MINIMUM AMOUNT OF MOVEMENT WILL BE NEEDED TO RAISE THEM INTO PLACE.

BENTS ARE NORMALLY ASSEMBLED IN THE REVERSE ORDER OF THAT IN WHICH THEY WILL BE ERECTED. A METHOD WE FIND EFFICIENT IS ILLUSTRATED.

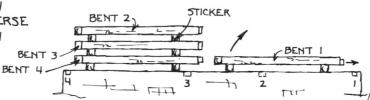

BENT 2   STICKER
BENT 3
BENT 4

BENT 1

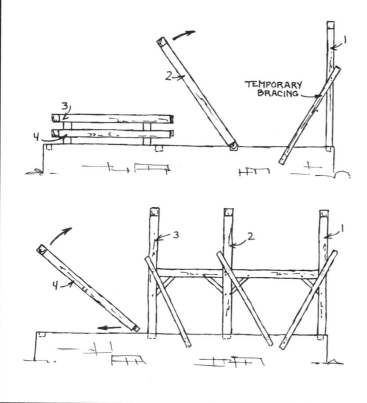

TEMPORARY BRACING

NOTE THAT STICKERS, OR BLOCKS, ARE PLACED UNDER EACH BENT (ABOVE). THIS IS NECESSARY SO THAT ROPES CAN BE PLACED AROUND THE TIMBERS FOR NECESSARY CLAMPING. BENT 4 IS ASSEMBLED FIRST OVERHANGING THE EDGE OF THE DECK SO THAT THE MORTISES IN THE DECK ARE NOT BLOCKED (UPPER DRAWING). THEN BENTS 3 AND 2 ARE ASSEMBLED ON TOP (ABOVE). BENT 1 IS ASSEMBLED LAST WITH TENONS ON BOTTOM OF POSTS ADJACENT TO THE RECEIVING MORTISES IN DECK.

When the joint fits well, tension can be easily applied with clamps and come-alongs. It is then ready to be drilled and pegged.

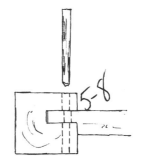

IN DRAW-BORING,
HOLES ARE OFFSET
TO FORCE A TIGHT FIT
WHEN THE PIN IS DRIVEN.

and taken together with the problems of getting absolutely perfect cuts in such large timbers, there is certainly no reason to expect that the joints always fit without some fussing.

We use clamps and come-alongs for trial assembly.

With these mechanical advantages, it is easy to put pieces together and apply tension for testing joints and checking measurements. When everything is ready for pegging, tension can be quickly reapplied and the joint can be drilled and pegged with absolutely no guesswork (see "Assembling a Bent," pages 122–23). We believe this simple mechanical system—ropes, come-alongs, and clamps—is far superior to the old-fashioned method of draw-boring, which inevitably involved some guesswork.

Coming home from another day of assembling one of our frames, we were feeling rather frustrated because some of the joints had not come together as we had hoped. On our way we stopped for a cup of coffee in a small café and had the coincidental opportunity to talk with an elderly gentleman who had vivid memories of several raisings he had attended as a child in the early 1900s. One particular remark he overheard at a raising was interesting to us because it concurred with the difficulty we had just experienced. The master carpenter on the job made the statement that "anybody can put a tenon into a mortise and make a frame, but

120

"Anybody can put a tenon into a mortise and make a frame, but very few can make the braces fit."

very few can make the braces fit." This was welcome information. It was encouraging to find that we weren't the first joiners who have suffered over this matter.

We are convinced that the knee brace is the most difficult piece in the frame to fit accurately. It works primarily in compression, resisting racking in the building, which is caused most often by the pressure of wind loads. Without the effect of the brace, the integral rigidity of the frame would be severely limited. For this reason we like to use the fully housed brace because it is the strongest. However, it is also somewhat more difficult to master. With the fully housed connection, the cut shoulder, as well as the tenon against the back wall of the mortise, can both 'come into play, weathering the forces on the building. A quick look at some of the timber frames put up today would support the remark we heard from the gentleman in the café. Some people put up frames, but eliminate braces. Some put in braces, but eliminate tenons. Others use tenons, but eliminate the housed mortise. And they all add up to shortcuts on a very important element in the frame.

Of these alternatives, the let-in brace is somewhat of a compromise because it depends on sheathing to hold it into the frame. The brace that is only nailed to the frame—that is, not attached with any internal joinery—is the worst possible method; it isn't strong and, therefore, it is not appropriate to good timber framing. Although the technique of fitting the fully housed brace is more difficult to learn, it is worth the trouble. Assembling the bents on the deck provides the environment to start learning that technique.

Obviously, if the wood were absolutely perfect and if all cuts were made to pinpoint precision, the Pythagorean theorem would rule and the braces would always fit the first time. But this is not to be expected. The wood will neither grow nor be milled without some inconsistencies, and the cuts in the timbers will be made by human beings. If the back wall of either brace mortise is not cut exactly to the right measurement or not quite square, the brace will not fit. Therefore, it is best to trial-fit the timbers without the brace; then make sure the beam is square with the post, and check for other variables that might exist. Adjust the brace accordingly. It is also a good idea at this point to check the relation-

121

ASSEMBLING a BENT

THIS STAGE OF THE JOB IS A CULMINATION OF ALL THE WORK PUT INTO LAYOUT AND CUTTING. PATIENCE AND CARE ARE REQUIRED. A GOOD FIT MEANS THAT WOOD IS TIGHT TO WOOD.

LAY OUT TIMBERS ON DECK WITH STICKERS (RIGHT). CHECK SIZES OF MORTISES AND TENONS PRIOR TO ASSEMBLING A JOINT.

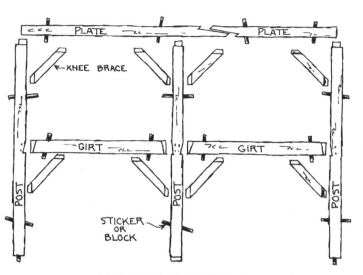

LAYING OUT TIMBERS (TOP VIEW)

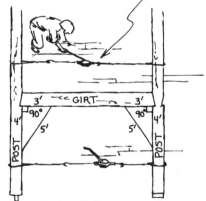

COME—ALONG AND ROPES TO PULL TOGETHER BENT TIMBERS

TRIAL FIT (TOP VIEW)

TRIAL FIT THE FIRST GIRT WITHOUT BRACES (LEFT). USE 3-4-5 TRIANGLES FOR PLACING GIRT AT RIGHT ANGLES WITH POST. KERFING MAY BE REQUIRED.

CHECK BRACE LENGTHS K (LOWER LEFT). NOTE: $L_1^2 + L_2^2 = K^2$. ADJUST LENGTH OF BRACE IF MEASUREMENT DIFFERS FROM BRACE LENGTH BY MORE THAN 1/16TH INCH.

REASSEMBLE WITH KNEE BRACES (BELOW). CHECK CORNERS FOR 90° BY THE 3-4-5 TRIANGLE METHOD. WHEN ALL JOINTS ARE TIGHT AND POSTS ARE AT 90° TO GIRT, DRILL AND PEG.

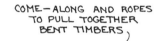

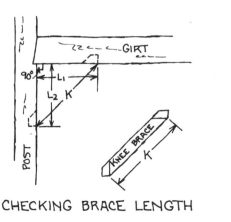

CHECKING BRACE LENGTH

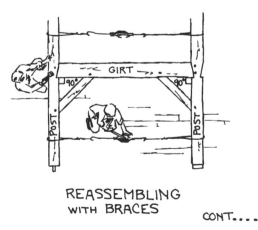

REASSEMBLING WITH BRACES

CONT....

ASSEMBLING A BENT....CONT.

TOP PLATES ARE ASSEMBLED AFTER ALL GIRTS ARE PEGGED IN PLACE.

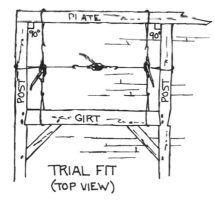

TRIAL FIT
(TOP VIEW)

TRIAL FIT PLATE WITHOUT BRACES (ABOVE). USE 3-4-5 TRIANGLE OR MEASURE DIAGONALS TO CHECK ANGLES TO BE 90°.

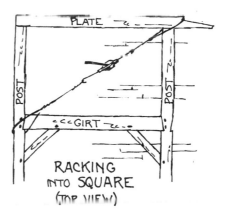

RACKING
INTO SQUARE
(TOP VIEW)

IF TOP SECTION OF BENT IS OUT OF SQUARE, USE A COME-ALONG DIAGONALLY TO RACK INTO SQUARE (ABOVE).

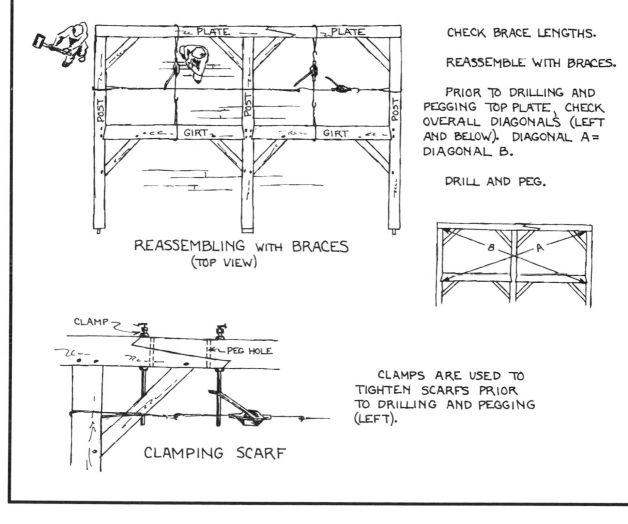

REASSEMBLING WITH BRACES
(TOP VIEW)

CHECK BRACE LENGTHS.

REASSEMBLE WITH BRACES.

PRIOR TO DRILLING AND PEGGING TOP PLATE, CHECK OVERALL DIAGONALS (LEFT AND BELOW). DIAGONAL A = DIAGONAL B.

DRILL AND PEG.

CLAMPING SCARF

CLAMPS ARE USED TO TIGHTEN SCARFS PRIOR TO DRILLING AND PEGGING (LEFT).

ASSEMBLING ROOF TRUSSES

ROOF TRUSSES ARE NORMALLY ASSEMBLED ON
THE GROUND PRIOR TO BEING RAISED. A ROOF TRUSS
MAY BE ASSEMBLED AS PART OF A BENT AND RAISED
WITH THE BENT OR, IF USING A CRANE, THE TRUSS MAY
BE LIFTED AFTER THE MAIN BENTS HAVE
BEEN ERECTED.

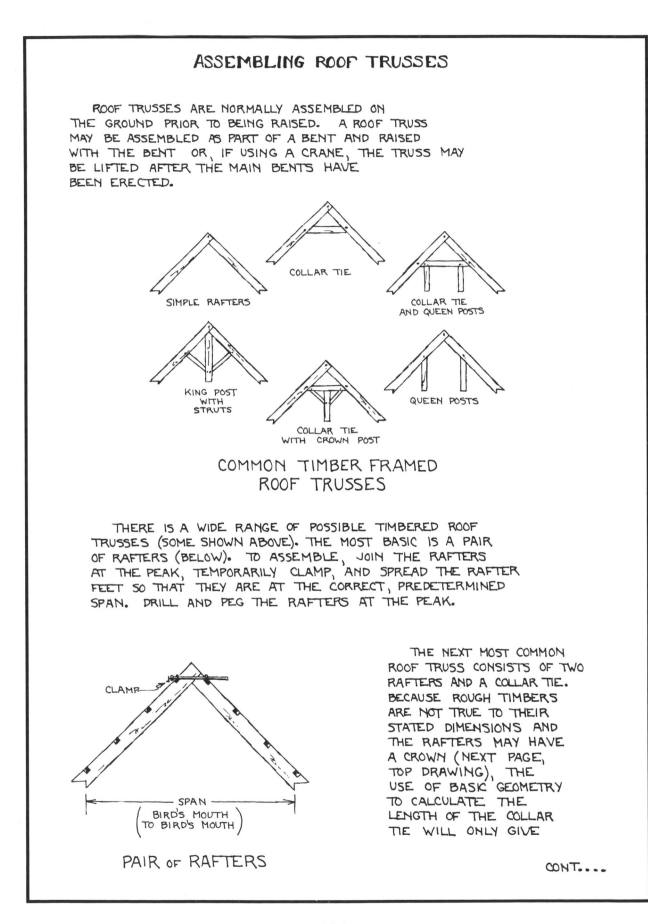

SIMPLE RAFTERS

COLLAR TIE

COLLAR TIE
AND QUEEN POSTS

KING POST
WITH
STRUTS

COLLAR TIE
WITH CROWN POST

QUEEN POSTS

COMMON TIMBER FRAMED
ROOF TRUSSES

THERE IS A WIDE RANGE OF POSSIBLE TIMBERED ROOF
TRUSSES (SOME SHOWN ABOVE). THE MOST BASIC IS A PAIR
OF RAFTERS (BELOW). TO ASSEMBLE, JOIN THE RAFTERS
AT THE PEAK, TEMPORARILY CLAMP, AND SPREAD THE RAFTER
FEET SO THAT THEY ARE AT THE CORRECT, PREDETERMINED
SPAN. DRILL AND PEG THE RAFTERS AT THE PEAK.

CLAMP

SPAN
(BIRD'S MOUTH
TO BIRD'S MOUTH)

PAIR OF RAFTERS

THE NEXT MOST COMMON
ROOF TRUSS CONSISTS OF TWO
RAFTERS AND A COLLAR TIE.
BECAUSE ROUGH TIMBERS
ARE NOT TRUE TO THEIR
STATED DIMENSIONS AND
THE RAFTERS MAY HAVE
A CROWN (NEXT PAGE,
TOP DRAWING), THE
USE OF BASIC GEOMETRY
TO CALCULATE THE
LENGTH OF THE COLLAR
TIE WILL ONLY GIVE

CONT....

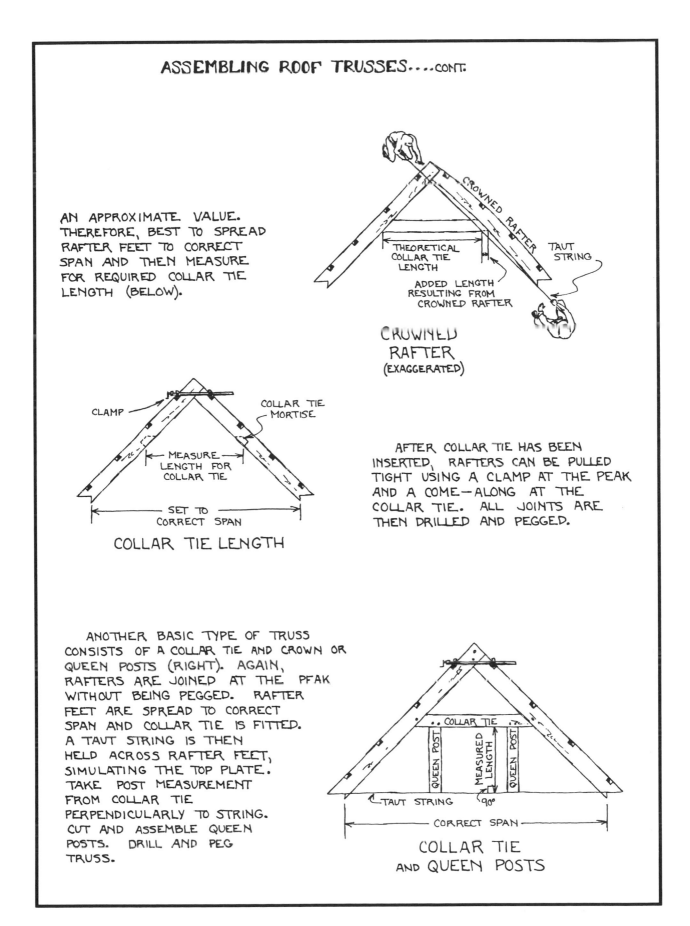

AN APPROXIMATE VALUE. THEREFORE, BEST TO SPREAD RAFTER FEET TO CORRECT SPAN AND THEN MEASURE FOR REQUIRED COLLAR TIE LENGTH (BELOW).

CROWNED RAFTER
(EXAGGERATED)

CLAMP

COLLAR TIE MORTISE

MEASURE LENGTH FOR COLLAR TIE

SET TO CORRECT SPAN

COLLAR TIE LENGTH

AFTER COLLAR TIE HAS BEEN INSERTED, RAFTERS CAN BE PULLED TIGHT USING A CLAMP AT THE PEAK AND A COME—ALONG AT THE COLLAR TIE. ALL JOINTS ARE THEN DRILLED AND PEGGED.

ANOTHER BASIC TYPE OF TRUSS CONSISTS OF A COLLAR TIE AND CROWN OR QUEEN POSTS (RIGHT). AGAIN, RAFTERS ARE JOINED AT THE PEAK WITHOUT BEING PEGGED. RAFTER FEET ARE SPREAD TO CORRECT SPAN AND COLLAR TIE IS FITTED. A TAUT STRING IS THEN HELD ACROSS RAFTER FEET, SIMULATING THE TOP PLATE. TAKE POST MEASUREMENT FROM COLLAR TIE PERPENDICULARLY TO STRING. CUT AND ASSEMBLE QUEEN POSTS. DRILL AND PEG TRUSS.

COLLAR TIE
AND QUEEN POSTS

ship of the knee-brace tenon and its corresponding mortise. Finally, reassemble the unit, check that the post and the beam are square, drill, and peg (see "Assembling a Bent," pages 122–23).

Putting the rafters together is similar to working with the braces in that they are both parts of a triangle. The difference is that the rafter represents the sides, while the brace is the hypotenuse. In either case the angles and lengths must be correct or major problems will have been created. If a collar tie is being joined between the rafters, it is best to take an accurate measurement of its length with the rafters temporarily fitted. An incorrect length at the height of the collar tie could drastically change the length between the feet of the rafters.

With all the bents stacked in position, trusses assembled and stacked, and all connecting pieces and braces checked and put in a position where they can be located quickly and without confusion, the raising is ready to begin.

Historically, the day of the raising was a time of great anticipation and excitement. For the owner, the building about to go up, whether it was a house or a barn, was necessary for survival. The preparation of the timbers alone—from felling the trees to trial-fitting the joints—often required more than a year of labor. If the owner hired people to do the work for him, this labor represented a substantial investment, perhaps two hundred and fifty dollars or more. For the many neighbors and friends on their way to the "raisin'," this was to be a chance for socializing and fun as well as a tremendous community work effort. The isolated rural families looked on this day as an opportunity to bring the community together for a day of neighborliness, country dancing, good food, and bad jokes. Everyone involved looked back upon this day as symbolic of something special in his life; its completion was another historical landmark. Family histories referred to "the year after the barn was raised" or "the summer of old Mr. Clarke's raising." And old-timers, even today, will have their memories jogged a bit and details will become a little more specific if the discussion turns to a raising they had attended.

Most of the old buildings went up because of a well-coordinated human effort—brute strength with little or no mechanical assistance. The intensity of the effort needed to

Driving tongue into fork for the joint at rafter peak.

Putting the rafters together is similar to working with braces.

Bents stacked in position ready for the raising.

raise a barn that might be as large as fifty by a hundred feet provided drama, especially at the moment when the huge fabric of timbers rose from the floor. A good description of the raising of the bents comes from Anne Gertrude Sneller, in *A Vanished World*.

When the moment came for lifting the first bent from the ground, a line of men took

126

The raisin' is a chance for socializing and fun as well as a tremendous work effort of the community. *Courtesy of Fred Benton*

The Reverend Elijah Kellogg wrote a number of books for boys that were popular in the mid-1800s. He was especially noted for his accurate and colorful descriptions of the tasks of life performed by the average man. The characters in this story are about to raise another "broadside," or bent.

"You've got to lift now, I tell you, for it's a master heavy frame," said Uncle Isaac. "We'll make two lifts of it; take it breast high, then take a breath, and up with it. Are you ready men?"

"Ready," was the reply.

"Well, say when you're mad."

"Mad," shouted Joe Griffin.

"Up with him, breast high."

Up went the great mass of timber, with a shout, breast high, while the boys propped it with shores, that they might take a breath.

"Be ready with your pike-poles, boy; up with him."

Placing their shoulders beneath the corner and middle-posts, and applying the pike-poles, as the frame was elevated beyond the reach of their hands, it rose slowly, but with extreme difficulty for the timber was of enormous size, and it was difficult for men enough to get hold to lift to advantage.

"Lift," shouted Uncle Isaac, "till the sparks fly out of your eyes; it must go up. if it comes back it will kill the whole of us."

By dint of severe effort, it at last stood erect, in which position it was secured by braces and stay laths. The remaining broadside was now raised to a position nearly erect, where it was held by spurshores to permit of being inclined, in order to enter the girths and beams of the ends.

The young men now sprang like squirrels upon the broadsides, that trembled in the air, in order to enter and fasten the ends of the braces and timbers, that were lifted up to them by those below. Men were clinging to all parts of the broadsides, already raised, with broadaxe in one hand and pins in the other, and walking along timbers that quivered on the pike-poles of those beneath, or hanging with their breast over a timber, to enter the end of a beam or girth. On every side resounded the cries "Three with a witness," "Four with a witness," "Brace number four," "Brace number five," "Give beam," "Rack off," "Rack to."

their places before the heavy beams. Pike poles could not be used till after the bent was high enough up in the air so that poles could be slipped under it. Pike poles were long or short according to the height needed, with a sharp steel tip. The head carpenter was usually chosen leader to give the signals, for he knew best how all must be put together, and his keen eye could see in an instant any slackening in the line before the right height was reached. A last survey—then he waved his arms and shouted "He-oh-heave." With the cry of Heave every man strained to lift his part of the bent the required distance and hold it there till other men could thrust poles into it. There was a breathing space and then again all eyes on the leader: "He-oh-heave!" and another yard was gained. Every bent was raised the same way and interlocked with those already up. By the time the last bent was in place, the skeleton of the barn was standing up for all to see. No other part of barn building was so hard or so full of risk as the raising.

These were strong men. These men, whose united efforts could raise mammoth frames, also cleared their land of stone and stump, spent entire days and weeks behind horse

". . . then he waved his arms and shouted 'He-oh-heave!'" . . . "Lift, . . . till the sparks fly out of your eyes; it must go up: if it comes back it will kill the whole of us." *Courtesy of* The Barn

and plow, built miles of stone walls, and cut ten or twenty cords of wood for winter's warmth with only an axe and saw. In the days before industrialization on the farm, men were measured by their ability to work. The raising of the frame, then, also became a stage for each man to demonstrate his strength to the other. Even considering their physical preparedness, they sometimes failed in the effort. Because there were so many people under the heavy bents as they were raised, once the lift was started it had to go all the way. If it didn't, someone would surely be seriously hurt or killed; sometimes people were injured in the effort of lifting. As Kellogg put it, "To be smart on a frame was considered a great accomplishment, and many were injured for life by hard lifts at raisings."

Here in Alstead, New Hampshire, we are lucky to be living in a rich garden of a community, in a place where the needs of one man still brings fifty together. Here, many small buildings still go up "by dint of severe effort." But we realize we are living in another age—in some ways a better one—where life is not so physically demanding. When our community gathers together for a raising, it is unlikely that more than half the participants spend their days in physical labor. Some are businessmen or teachers or technicians, and the rest of us don't work nearly as hard as they did a hundred years ago. Together, we are not prepared for the job of lifting a large building by hand. Because of this, we think it is most sensible today to hire a crane, if only to erect the heaviest units. The crane is only on the site for four to eight hours. The average cost is about three hundred and fifty dollars. It seems like a small price to pay for a safe raising.

128

Frames being raised "by dint of severe effort." *Courtesy of Charles R. Goldschmid*

RAISING A FRAME BY HAND

WITH A COMMUNITY EFFORT, IT IS POSSIBLE TO RAISE A SMALL SOFTWOOD FRAME BY HAND. BUT BEAR IN MIND THE DANGERS INVOLVED. THE BENTS SHOWN IN THIS SERIES ILLUSTRATE A SIZE THAT SHOULD BE SAFE FOR A HAND RAISING. WE RECOMMEND USING A CRANE FOR RAISING MOST FRAMES.

PEOPLE NEEDED
- 1 PERSON: PRESUMABLY THE MOST EXPERIENCED, TO DIRECT AND GIVE ORDERS.
- 1 PERSON: TO HOLD THE SAFETY ROPE TO PREVENT THE BENT GOING OVER.
- 8 OR MORE PEOPLE: TO SLIDE AND RAISE THE BENTS, TWO SHOULD HELP DIRECT THE ENDS OF THE POSTS INTO THEIR MORTISES.

PRIOR TO RAISING A BENT
- CHECK MORTISES IN DECK TO BE CERTAIN POSTS WILL FIT PROPERLY.
- HAVE BRACING STOCK, HAMMER AND NAILS NEARBY FOR TEMPORARY BRACING.
- HAVE A BEETLE ON HAND; IT MAY BE USEFUL FOR ALIGNING POSTS INTO MORTISES.
- CLEAR THE DECK OF ANY DEBRIS.

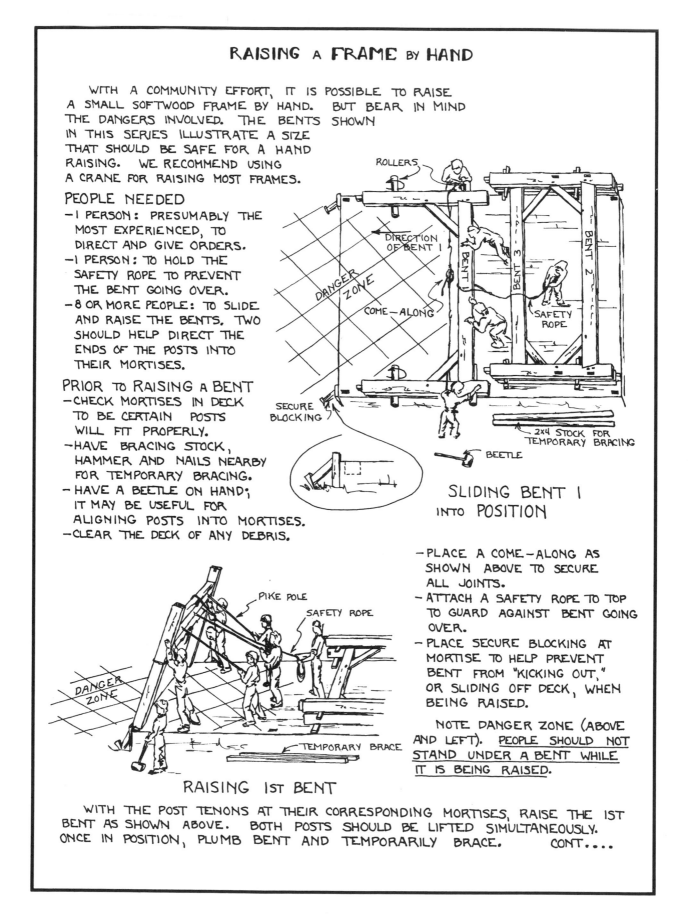

SLIDING BENT 1 INTO POSITION

- PLACE A COME-ALONG AS SHOWN ABOVE TO SECURE ALL JOINTS.
- ATTACH A SAFETY ROPE TO TOP TO GUARD AGAINST BENT GOING OVER.
- PLACE SECURE BLOCKING AT MORTISE TO HELP PREVENT BENT FROM "KICKING OUT," OR SLIDING OFF DECK, WHEN BEING RAISED.

NOTE DANGER ZONE (ABOVE AND LEFT). PEOPLE SHOULD NOT STAND UNDER A BENT WHILE IT IS BEING RAISED.

RAISING 1ST BENT

WITH THE POST TENONS AT THEIR CORRESPONDING MORTISES, RAISE THE 1ST BENT AS SHOWN ABOVE. BOTH POSTS SHOULD BE LIFTED SIMULTANEOUSLY. ONCE IN POSITION, PLUMB BENT AND TEMPORARILY BRACE. CONT.....

RAISE THE 2ND BENT IN
THE SAME MANNER, AND TEMPORARILY
BRACE. WITH A COME-ALONG
LOOSELY CONNECTING THE TWO
BENTS AND A PERSON HOLDING
THE SAFETY ROPE, REMOVE
TEMPORARY BRACING
FROM SECOND BENT.
LEAN THE BENT SLIGHTLY
OUTWARD TO ALLOW
CONNECTING GIRTS AND
KNEE BRACES TO BE
SIMULTANEOUSLY INSERTED
INTO PLACE (RIGHT). PULL
BENTS TIGHTLY TOGETHER
WITH COME-ALONGS AND
ADD TEMPORARY BRACING.
SUMMER BEAM(S) CAN NOW
BE LOWERED INTO PLACE.
SUMMER BEAM DOVETAIL JOINTS
WILL HELP LOCK BENTS TOGETHER.

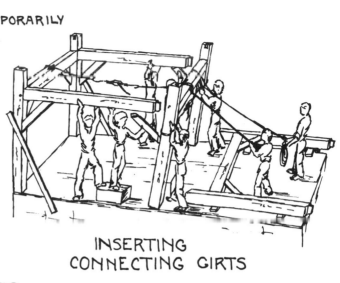

INSERTING
CONNECTING GIRTS

RAISE THE 3RD BENT AND ADD CONNECTING GIRTS AND KNEE
BRACES AS BEFORE. IF BENT 1 WAS PROPERLY PLUMBED, KNEE BRACES
CUT TO CORRECT LENGTHS AND ALL JOINTS ARE TIGHT, BENTS
2 AND 3 WILL ALSO BE PLUMB. SOME MINOR CORRECTIONS CAN
BE MADE BY PLACING COME-ALONGS DIAGONALLY TO ADJUST THE FRAME
INTO SQUARE. BECAUSE TIMBERS MAY BE CROWNED OR SLIGHTLY
TWISTED, THE SHOULDERS OF SOME JOINTS MAY NOT BE TIGHT. THIS
CAN BE CORRECTED BY HAND SAWING, OR "KERFING", THE SHOULDER
ON EITHER SIDE OF THE TENON (SEE CRANE RAISING). BE CAREFUL
NOT TO CUT INTO TENON.

ONCE THE FRAME HAS BEEN PROPERLY SQUARED AND JOINTS ARE
TIGHT, DRILL AND PEG JOINTS.

DROP SUMMER
BEAM(S) AND JOISTS
INTO POSITION.
USING COME-ALONGS
AND KERFING WHERE
NECESSARY, PULL
JOINTS TIGHT. LAY
TEMPORARY DECKING
(IF NOT THE PERMANENT
DECKING) TO PROVIDE
A SAFE FLOOR ON
WHICH TO ASSEMBLE
AND RAISE RAFTERS.

CONT....

LIFT IST PAIR OF RAFTERS TO 2ND-FLOOR DECK USING ROPE AND SEVERAL PEOPLE (RIGHT). BE SURE TO FASTEN ROPE AROUND A MORTISE IN THE RAFTER TO PREVENT IT FROM SLIPPING.

ASSEMBLE RAFTERS IN POSITION TO BE RAISED AS SHOWN BELOW. BRACE THE RAFTERS TOGETHER WITH A TEMPORARY "COLLAR TIE" TO PREVENT STRAIN ON THE TONGUE AND FORK JOINT WHILE BEING RAISED.

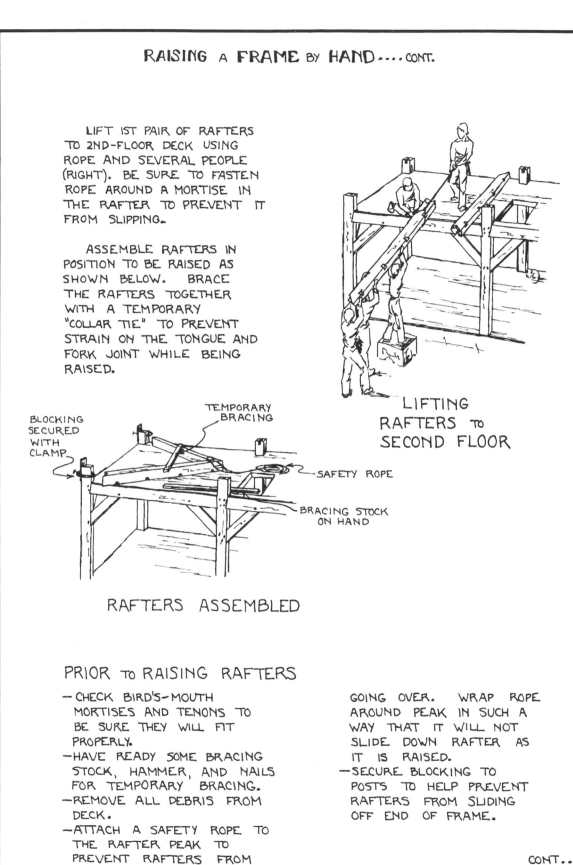

LIFTING RAFTERS TO SECOND FLOOR

RAFTERS ASSEMBLED

PRIOR TO RAISING RAFTERS

—CHECK BIRD'S-MOUTH MORTISES AND TENONS TO BE SURE THEY WILL FIT PROPERLY.

—HAVE READY SOME BRACING STOCK, HAMMER, AND NAILS FOR TEMPORARY BRACING.

—REMOVE ALL DEBRIS FROM DECK.

—ATTACH A SAFETY ROPE TO THE RAFTER PEAK TO PREVENT RAFTERS FROM GOING OVER. WRAP ROPE AROUND PEAK IN SUCH A WAY THAT IT WILL NOT SLIDE DOWN RAFTER AS IT IS RAISED.

—SECURE BLOCKING TO POSTS TO HELP PREVENT RAFTERS FROM SLIDING OFF END OF FRAME.

CONT....

RAISING A FRAME BY HAND....CONT.

RAISE AND LIFT RAFTERS INTO POSITION AS SHOWN (RIGHT). ONCE IN PLACE, PLUMB RAFTERS AND TEMPORARILY BRACE. NOTE DANGER ZONE. <u>NO ONE SHOULD BE STANDING UNDER AREA WHERE RAFTERS ARE BEING RAISED.</u>

ASSEMBLE AND RAISE 2ND PAIR OF RAFTERS IN THE SAME MANNER, AND TEMPORARILY BRACE. PLACE PURLINS BETWEEN RAFTERS STARTING ON

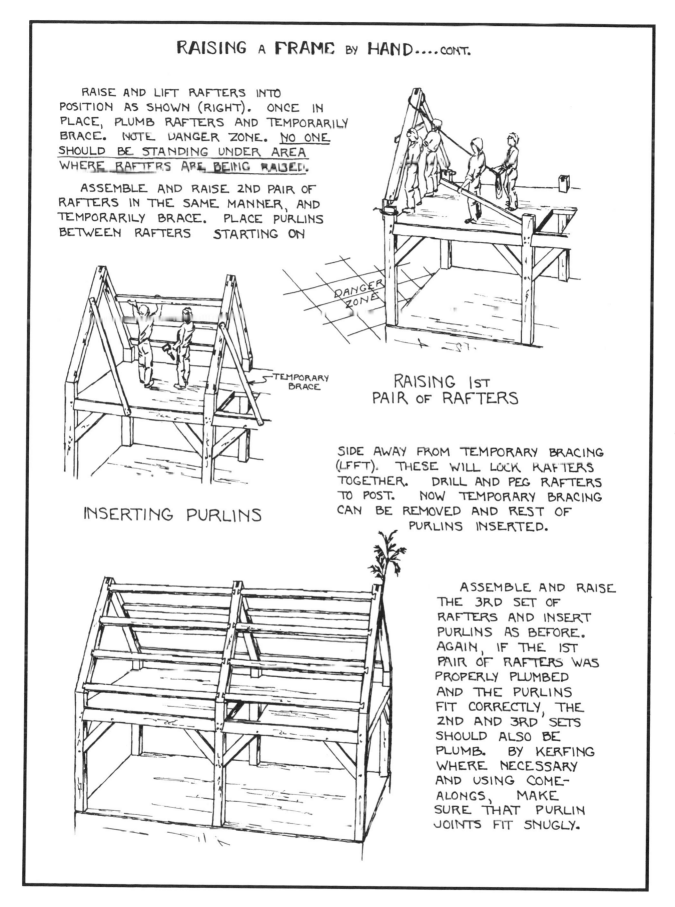

RAISING 1st PAIR of RAFTERS

TEMPORARY BRACE

INSERTING PURLINS

SIDE AWAY FROM TEMPORARY BRACING (LEFT). THESE WILL LOCK RAFTERS TOGETHER. DRILL AND PEG RAFTERS TO POST. NOW TEMPORARY BRACING CAN BE REMOVED AND REST OF PURLINS INSERTED.

ASSEMBLE AND RAISE THE 3RD SET OF RAFTERS AND INSERT PURLINS AS BEFORE. AGAIN, IF THE 1ST PAIR OF RAFTERS WAS PROPERLY PLUMBED AND THE PURLINS FIT CORRECTLY, THE 2ND AND 3RD SETS SHOULD ALSO BE PLUMB. BY KERFING WHERE NECESSARY AND USING COME-ALONGS, MAKE SURE THAT PURLIN JOINTS FIT SNUGLY.

133

Pike poles used to help raise rafters. *Courtesy of Pamela Hitchcock*

One hundred fifty people came to help Frances and Richard raise their frame. They're rightfully proud. *Courtesy of Fred Benton*

The aid of the crane makes the raising safer.

Bents are raised to hanging vertical position, then lowered into place. *Courtesy of Tafi Brown*

The last bent is swung out and then lowered into position. We have used a large come-along to hold the shed tightly to the main bent. In most cases, it is better to raise the shed separately. *Courtesy of Tafi Brown*

When bents are up and temporarily braced, girts and braces are put into position. *Courtesy of Tafi Brown*

There are many ways to spread the bents when fitting the connecting girts. *Courtesy of Tafi Brown*

And there are many ways to hold a brace. *Courtesy of Tafi Brown*

RAISING A FRAME BY CRANE

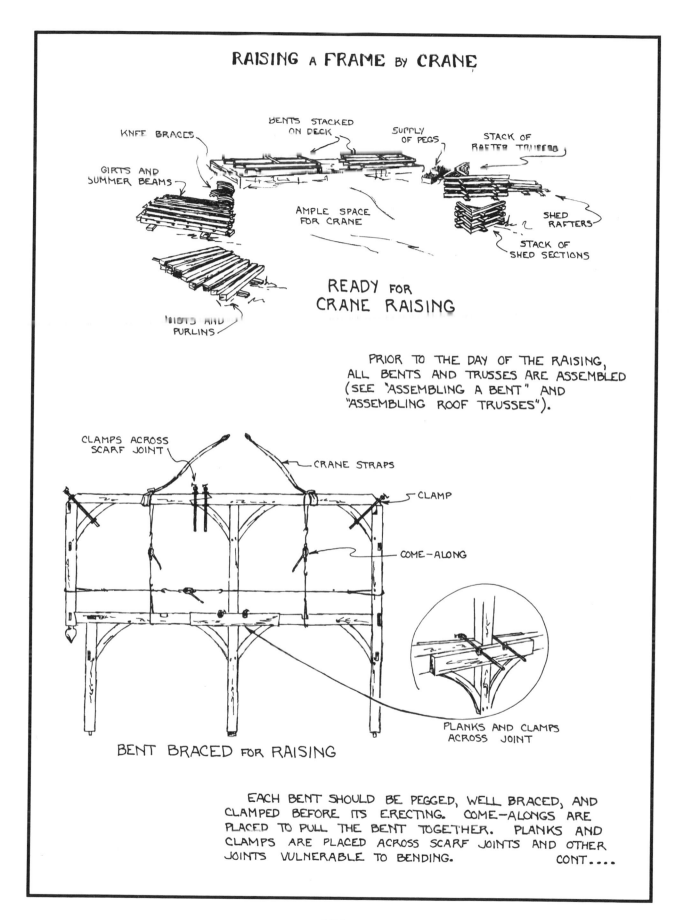

KNEE BRACES

BENTS STACKED ON DECK

SUPPLY OF PEGS

STACK OF RAFTER TRUSSES

GIRTS AND SUMMER BEAMS

AMPLE SPACE FOR CRANE

SHED RAFTERS

STACK OF SHED SECTIONS

JOISTS AND PURLINS

READY FOR CRANE RAISING

PRIOR TO THE DAY OF THE RAISING, ALL BENTS AND TRUSSES ARE ASSEMBLED (SEE "ASSEMBLING A BENT" AND "ASSEMBLING ROOF TRUSSES").

CLAMPS ACROSS SCARF JOINT

CRANE STRAPS

CLAMP

COME-ALONG

PLANKS AND CLAMPS ACROSS JOINT

BENT BRACED FOR RAISING

EACH BENT SHOULD BE PEGGED, WELL BRACED, AND CLAMPED BEFORE ITS ERECTING. COME-ALONGS ARE PLACED TO PULL THE BENT TOGETHER. PLANKS AND CLAMPS ARE PLACED ACROSS SCARF JOINTS AND OTHER JOINTS VULNERABLE TO BENDING.   CONT....

The benefits of a crane are clear when the trusses are raised. *Courtesy of Tafi Brown*

With the setting of the purlins, the rafters are connected. *Courtesy of Tafi Brown*

RAISING A FRAME BY CRANE....CONT.

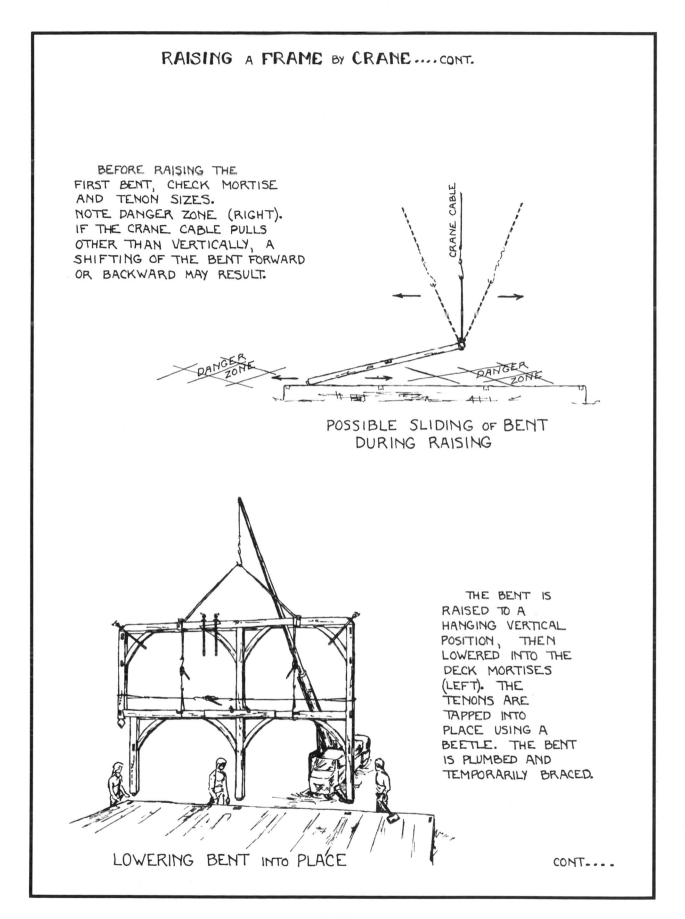

BEFORE RAISING THE
FIRST BENT, CHECK MORTISE
AND TENON SIZES.
NOTE DANGER ZONE (RIGHT).
IF THE CRANE CABLE PULLS
OTHER THAN VERTICALLY, A
SHIFTING OF THE BENT FORWARD
OR BACKWARD MAY RESULT.

CRANE CABLE

DANGER ZONE

DANGER ZONE

POSSIBLE SLIDING OF BENT
DURING RAISING

THE BENT IS
RAISED TO A
HANGING VERTICAL
POSITION, THEN
LOWERED INTO THE
DECK MORTISES
(LEFT). THE
TENONS ARE
TAPPED INTO
PLACE USING A
BEETLE. THE BENT
IS PLUMBED AND
TEMPORARILY BRACED.

LOWERING BENT INTO PLACE

CONT....

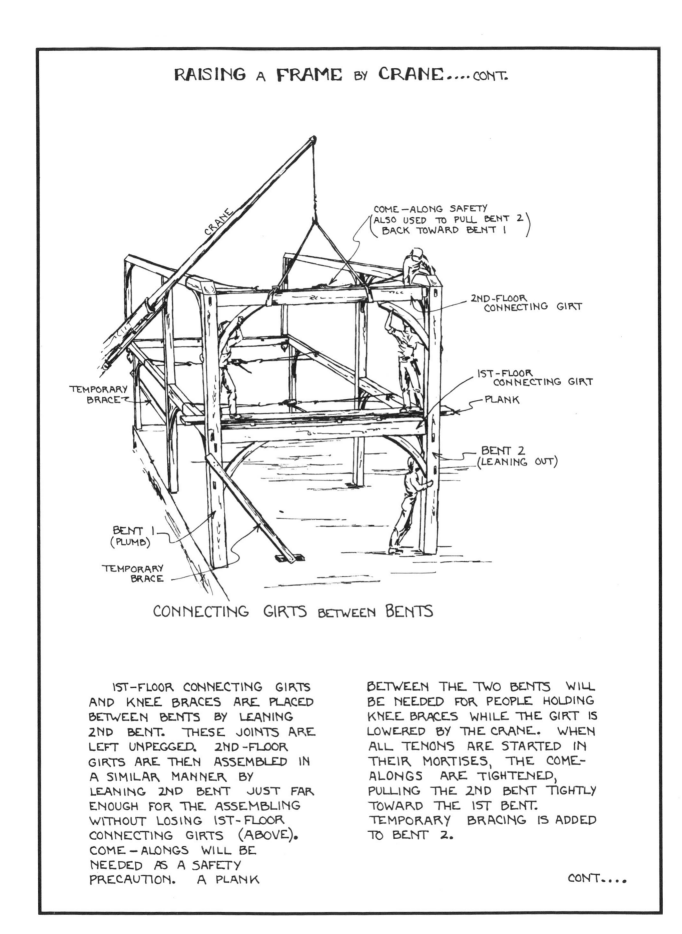

CRANE

COME—ALONG SAFETY
(ALSO USED TO PULL BENT 2
BACK TOWARD BENT 1)

2ND-FLOOR
CONNECTING GIRT

1ST-FLOOR
CONNECTING GIRT

PLANK

BENT 2
(LEANING OUT)

TEMPORARY
BRACE

BENT 1
(PLUMB)

TEMPORARY
BRACE

CONNECTING GIRTS BETWEEN BENTS

1ST-FLOOR CONNECTING GIRTS AND KNEE BRACES ARE PLACED BETWEEN BENTS BY LEANING 2ND BENT. THESE JOINTS ARE LEFT UNPEGGED. 2ND-FLOOR GIRTS ARE THEN ASSEMBLED IN A SIMILAR MANNER BY LEANING 2ND BENT JUST FAR ENOUGH FOR THE ASSEMBLING WITHOUT LOSING 1ST-FLOOR CONNECTING GIRTS (ABOVE). COME—ALONGS WILL BE NEEDED AS A SAFETY PRECAUTION. A PLANK BETWEEN THE TWO BENTS WILL BE NEEDED FOR PEOPLE HOLDING KNEE BRACES WHILE THE GIRT IS LOWERED BY THE CRANE. WHEN ALL TENONS ARE STARTED IN THEIR MORTISES, THE COME—ALONGS ARE TIGHTENED, PULLING THE 2ND BENT TIGHTLY TOWARD THE 1ST BENT. TEMPORARY BRACING IS ADDED TO BENT 2.

CONT....

RAISING A FRAME BY CRANE....CONT.

ONCE ALL BENTS HAVE BEEN RAISED AND CONNECTING GIRTS PLACED AND TEMPORARILY BRACED, SUMMER BEAMS CAN BE LOWERED INTO PLACE (RIGHT). THESE TIMBERS WITH THEIR DOVETAIL JOINTS WILL HELP LOCK THE BENTS TOGETHER.

IF POSTS ARE PLUMB AND JOINTS ARE TIGHT, PEGGING JOINTS IN THE MAIN FRAME CAN BEGIN. SINCE PLUMBING POSTS, FITTING AND PEGGING JOINTS WILL TAKE SEVERAL HOURS OF FUSSING, IT IS ADVISABLE TO TEMPORARILY BRACE THE FRAME AND CONTINUE WITH THE CRANE WORK.

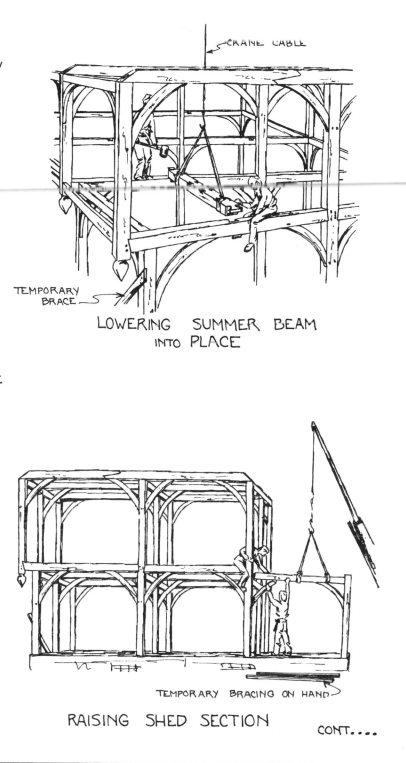

CRANE CABLE

TEMPORARY BRACE

LOWERING SUMMER BEAM INTO PLACE

LEAN-TO, OR SHED, SECTIONS ARE RAISED (RIGHT) AND HELD TO THE FRAME WITH COME-ALONGS OR TEMPORARY BRACING. THEY ARE NOT YET PEGGED, FOR THEY WILL NEED TO BE SLIGHTLY SPREAD WHEN JOINING SHED RAFTERS.

TEMPORARY BRACING ON HAND

RAISING SHED SECTION

CONT....

143

ALL THROUGH THIS RAISING PROCESS, MORTISE
AND TENON KNEE BRACES ARE BEING SET. (IF
LAPPED DOVETAIL KNEE BRACES WERE USED, THEY
WOULD BE FITTED LATER.) IT IS VITAL THAT LOCATIONS
FOR KNEE BRACE MORTISES BE CHECKED AND LENGTHS
OF KNEE BRACES ADJUSTED USING THE PYTHAGOREAN
THEOREM, $L_1^2 + L_2^2 = K^2$ (RIGHT). AN ERROR OF $\frac{1}{16}''$
OR GREATER WILL CAUSE THE FRAME TO BE THROWN
OUT OF SQUARE.

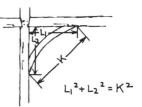

$$L_1^2 + L_2^2 = K^2$$

NO MATTER HOW HARD ONE MAY TRY,
THERE WILL BE SOME ASSEMBLED JOINTS
IN WHICH SHOULDERS ARE NOT TIGHT. BEFORE
PEGGING, THIS FAULT CAN BE CORRECTED BY
HAND SAWING, OR "KERFING", AROUND THE
SHOULDER OF THE JOINT, BEING CAREFUL NOT
TO CUT INTO THE TENON (LEFT).

KERFING

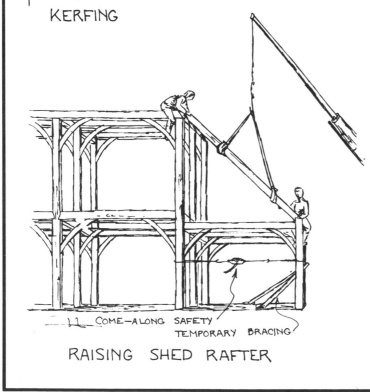

SHED RAFTERS ARE
LIFTED WITH STRAPS OFF-
SET ALLOWING THE LOWER
TENON TO START FIRST
(LEFT). THE SHED
SECTION IS SPREAD FROM
THE BUILDING WITH
A COME—ALONG
PREVENTING PULL-OUT
OF SHED GIRT. THE
UPPER RAFTER TENON
CAN THEN BE INSERTED
AND SHED SECTION
PULLED TIGHTLY INTO
THE MAIN FRAME. IF
ALL JOINTS ARE TIGHT
IN THIS SHED SECTION,
JOINTS CAN BE DRILLED
AND PEGGED. OTHERWISE,
TEMPORARILY BRACE
UNTIL LATER WHEN
JOINTS CAN BE KERFED
AND FUSSED WITH.

COME—ALONG SAFETY
TEMPORARY BRACING

RAISING SHED RAFTER

CONT....

ROOF TRUSSES ARE THE
LAST MAJOR TIMBERS TO BE
RAISED. IF TRUSSES WERE
PROPERLY CUT AND
ASSEMBLED, THEY CAN
BE SIMPLY RAISED,
LOWERED INTO
POSITION, PLUMBED,
AND TEMPORARILY
BRACED (RIGHT).
THE TEMPORARY
BRACING AND
COME—ALONGS ARE
NEEDED TO HOLD
RAFTERS UNTIL
PURLINS ARE PLACED.
ROOF TRUSSES ARE
NORMALLY PEGGED
AT THE PLATE
AFTER THE PURLINS
HAVE BEEN SET.

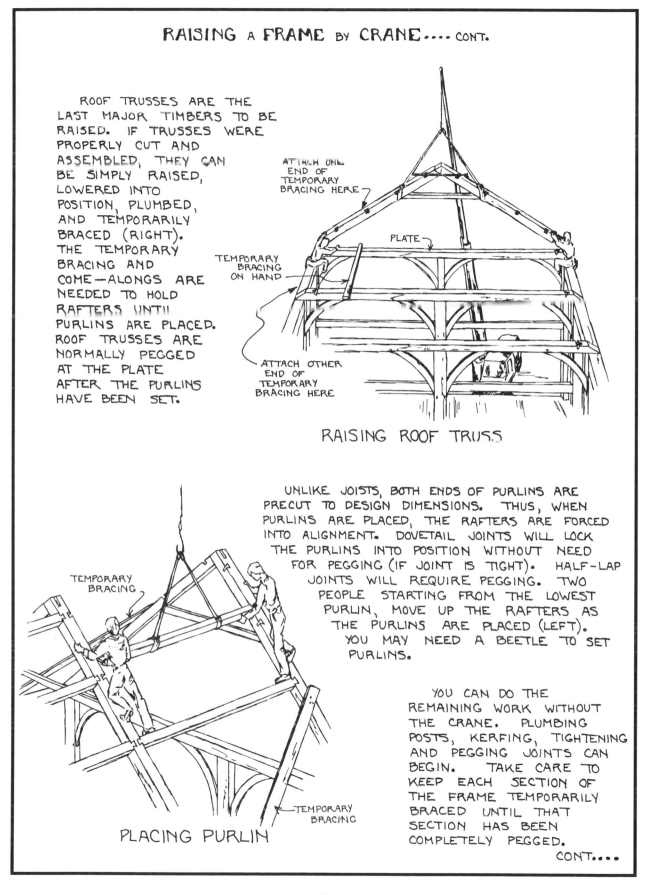

ATTACH ONE
END OF
TEMPORARY
BRACING HERE

PLATE

TEMPORARY
BRACING
ON HAND

ATTACH OTHER
END OF
TEMPORARY
BRACING HERE

RAISING ROOF TRUSS

UNLIKE JOISTS, BOTH ENDS OF PURLINS ARE
PRECUT TO DESIGN DIMENSIONS. THUS, WHEN
PURLINS ARE PLACED, THE RAFTERS ARE FORCED
INTO ALIGNMENT. DOVETAIL JOINTS WILL LOCK
THE PURLINS INTO POSITION WITHOUT NEED
FOR PEGGING (IF JOINT IS TIGHT). HALF-LAP
JOINTS WILL REQUIRE PEGGING. TWO
PEOPLE STARTING FROM THE LOWEST
PURLIN, MOVE UP THE RAFTERS AS
THE PURLINS ARE PLACED (LEFT).
YOU MAY NEED A BEETLE TO SET
PURLINS.

TEMPORARY
BRACING

YOU CAN DO THE
REMAINING WORK WITHOUT
THE CRANE. PLUMBING
POSTS, KERFING, TIGHTENING
AND PEGGING JOINTS CAN
BEGIN. TAKE CARE TO
KEEP EACH SECTION OF
THE FRAME TEMPORARILY
BRACED UNTIL THAT
SECTION HAS BEEN
COMPLETELY PEGGED.

TEMPORARY
BRACING

PLACING PURLIN

CONT....

BY THE TIME THE JOISTS
ARE TO BE SET INTO THE
FRAME (RIGHT), ALL THE
OTHER FRAME MEMBERS HAVE
BEEN JOINED AND PEGGED.
THE FRAME IS NOW RIGID.
CROWNED OR TWISTED TIMBERS
OR UNDER- OR OVERSIZED
GIRTS AND SUMMER BEAMS
WILL CAUSE SLIGHT
VARIATIONS IN THE
LENGTHS OF JOISTS. IT IS
NOT UNCOMMON FOR A
VARIATION OF ¼" TO RESULT.
TO AVOID GAPS AT THE
ENDS OF THE JOISTS
IT IS ADVISABLE TO
MEASURE EACH SPAN
BEFORE CUTTING THE
SECOND END OF THE JOIST.

SETTING JOISTS

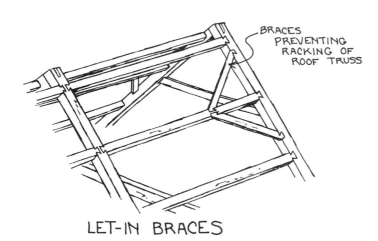

BRACES
PREVENTING
RACKING OF
ROOF TRUSS

LET-IN BRACES

RAFTERS SHOULD BE
CHECKED FOR PLUMB
BY HANGING A PLUMB
BOB FROM RAFTER PEAK.
MINOR ADJUSTMENT
CAN BE MADE USING
COME-ALONGS TO RACK
THE ROOF FRAME.
PLACE LAPPED BRACES
BETWEEN RAFTERS
AND PURLINS TO
ADD RIGIDITY TO THE
ROOF FRAME.

CONT....

RAISING a FRAME by CRANE.... CONT.

AFTER THE LAST JOIST HAS BEEN SET AND ALL JOINTS HAVE BEEN PEGGED, THE FINISHING OF THE FRAME STARTS. EVEN THOUGH THE TIMBERS HAVE ALREADY BEEN PLANED AND SANDED, ROPE, BEETLE, AND SCUFF MARKS WILL HAVE SCARRED THE TIMBERS DURING THE RAISING. IF THE FRAME IS TO BE A BARN, NO OTHER WORK IS NEEDED. BUT, IF IT IS TO BE A HOME, THE TIMBERS SHOULD NOW BE SANDED AND OILED. A DISC AND ORBITAL SANDER WITH 80- OR 100-GRIT PAPER AND A FEW DAYS OF PERSEVERANCE WILL TRANSFORM THE TIMBERS OF A ROUGH FRAME INTO AN IMPRESSIVE PIECE OF FURNITURE. THE SAFEST WAY TO DO THIS WORK ON THE 2ND FLOOR IS AFTER THE SUBFLOOR HAS BEEN LAID. IF POSSIBLE, BUILD THE ROOF OVER THE FRAME BEFORE SANDING TO PROTECT THE BEAMS FROM WATER STAINS. RIGHT AFTER THE SANDING, APPLY A GENEROUS COAT OF BOILED LINSEED OIL TO BRING OUT THE LUSTER OF THE WOOD.

PINE BOUGH

THE CELEBRATION

A POEM TO DEDICATE THE FRAME.
A PINE BOUGH PLACED TO PAY HOMAGE TO THE WOOD.
AND A SHARING OF JOY AND CELEBRATION AMONG
    THE COMMUNITY OF PEOPLE WHO JOINED TOGETHER
    TO RAISE THIS MIGHTY FRAME.

The raising moves along until the last purlin has been set.

Whether the frame is to be raised entirely by hand or with a crane, careful planning is necessary. As the work gets started, one person can take charge of preparing the bents. He should make sure that all clamps and come-alongs are in position and that the bent is well reinforced and ready to be lifted. Another person can make sure that all the connecting pieces are located and ready to go. Traditionally, the master or "boss" carpenter is the caller. With the hand raising, he is extremely important to the safety of the job, as he must be certain that the lifting of the bent is well coordinated. With the crane raising, he is the one to direct the crane operator. Other people, with good balance, are needed "upstairs" as the timbers are placed. John Burroughs, the naturalist and essayist, describes what this man was like.

He was bold and strong and quick. He helped guide and superintend the work. He was the first one up on the bent, catching a pin or a brace and putting it in place. He walked the lofty and perilous plate with the great beetle in hand, put the pins in the holes, and swinging the heavy instrument through the air, drove the pins home. He was as much at home up there as a squirrel.

During the raising process, everyone on the job should be careful not to leave tools or loose pieces of wood on the timbers overhead. Every tool not in use should be handed down to the floor and every knee brace or joist not being put into position should be left on the ground. Accidents are avoided most easily if every person present is aware of the dangers and learns to watch out not only for himself but also for others. An otherwise successful

Courtesy of Tafi Brown

raising could be saddened if anybody were to get hurt.

There's another caution hidden in this amusing quote from an old man who grew up near Cooperstown, New York: "As the labor was gratuitous, the whiskey went round freely and many a serious injury was the result. But no matter. The whiskey must go round or the frame would not go up."

In order to keep the raising going along smoothly and without hesitation, it is best to leave most pieces unpegged by placing temporary braces on the bents and moving on. This procedure will allow a couple of people to come back on a less hectic day to spend undistracted time snugging up each joint.

And so the raising moves quickly along until the last purlin has been set and the frame stands complete. Now the lines in the drawings are much more than dreams and that first moment of hesitation before the saw bit into the wood is only a distant memory. Now you are happy that there was no compromise on either the choice of the wood or the quality of the joints. Now that one extra effort as the timbers were joined makes a pleasing difference. With so many hours of work and planning left behind and this extremely exhausting but satisfying day of labor just completed, you will well understand why, historically, raising day doesn't just end with the placing of the last timber. More often, it turns into a party.

To signify a safe and successful raising, to pay respect to the wood that has given life to the frame, a traditional pine bough is attached to the peak of the building. Some of the old-timers marked the occasion further

149

by breaking a bottle of rum at the ridge and delivering a few lines of verse composed for the occasion. A frame was raised in 1818 for a doctor and given this dedication:

Here is a fine frame raised on Taunton Hill.
The owner is rich and getting richer still.
May health come upon us like showers of grace,
And the owner get rich by the sweat of his face.

And of course it would be silly to pass up this opportunity to dance. Anne Gertrude Sneller records that

as soon as the last nail had been driven, there was a dance on the big barn floor. On that ninety foot long floor the dancers had room aplenty to bow, circle, gallop and swing. The musicians, never more than three for such occasions, sat in the empty hayloft and played until two o'clock in the morning.

The festivities of the evening signify more than the completion of the frame. They also celebrate the beginning of a new age of hope. Historically, poor quality housing has been the mark of wandering tribes, invading armies, and treasure seekers. The barbaric Huns and the western gold miners are examples. They lived in their environment only for what they could take from it and were contemptuous of indigenous culture. Our civilization is not just passing through, and we have learned that our environment has very little left to take from it.

This building, with its roots in the past, was built with an eye toward the future. This structure will serve a most noble function; it will be a comfortable and dignified dwelling for many generations of people. All of those who dance to the tune of the fiddle and the flute this night can feel they have contributed to the enrichment and to the cultivation of our civilization.

PART III: DESIGN THOUGHTS

CHAPTER SIX
BUILDING
FOR STRENGTH
A STRUCTURAL LOOK

Courtesy of Tafi Brown

*All good observation is more or less a refining
and transmuting process, and the secret is to
know the crude material when you see it.*

—John Burroughs: *The Birds of John Burroughs*

THE environment in which a tree grows—
the soil, light, moisture, and wind—affects its structure and shape and the strength of the wood it yields. We rarely have control over the tree's environment. The tree has experienced droughts and storms that occurred before many of us were born. But for our shelter, we can evaluate the timber that this tree gives. We look at a variety of factors and how they affect the strength of the wood.

Determining the quality of a timber is not a clear-cut process. You need to look at the grain. Is it straight and clear with few knots, or is the grain diagonal, with numerous knots disturbing it? You look for shakes, checks, and splits. Minor checks will have minimal effect, but a timber with deep shakes and splits will be drastically weaker. The structural capacity of each timber in the pile is different, but they all should find a use.

Large knots and twisted grain in a timber would suggest that it not be used as a major load-bearing beam. But the same timber might be adequate for a post or sill. Judging the available timbers this way, you should be able to find an appropriate place in the framework for all the pieces.

We take a brief look in this chapter at characteristics and strengths of different species of wood. I can recount an experience that undeniably shows the variation in wood strengths.

A few winters ago, I was cabin-sitting for Tom and Jamie (the artist for this book), who were away for a few weeks. As I was working one evening under the light of their kerosene lamps, reviewing the chapter on structural design, a major ice and snow storm was hitting this part of New Hampshire. The following morning the sun was out; I headed down the hill to fetch water from a nearby stream. The forest had been transformed

151

TABLE 1
INHERENT CHARACTERISTICS OF WOOD SPECIES*

	Compressive Strength C(psi)[1]	Modulus of Elasticity E(psi)[2]	Maximum Allowable Horizontal Shear h(psi)[3]	Maximum Allowable Fiber Stress in Bending f(psi)[4]
Red or White Oak**	1200	1,600,000	150	1600
Douglas Fir	1200	1,600,000	120	1500
Eastern and Sitka Spruce	800	1,200,000	100	1200
Pine	700	1,000,000	80	900

* *Allowable properties for structural design.*
** *Exclusion: Burr Oak, Overcup Oak, Post Oak.*

Safety factors based on maximum strengths in clear specimens, *U.S.D.A. Wood Handbook,* 1974.
1. Safety factor 2.5 (green)
2. Seasoned wood
3. Safety factor 6.0 (green)
4. Safety factor 4.5 (green)

that night. There was a groaning and creaking from the trees that were heavily laden with ice and snow. A snapping sound, somewhat like gunshots, could be heard every once in a while. All around, there were trees bowed to the ground or snapped off midway up the trunk. After a closer look, I realized that nearly all of the trees that had snapped (or as an engineer might say, "reached their failure point on the stress-strain curve") were pines, hemlocks, and other softwoods. The hardwoods, such as oak and maple, were still erect, and some, such as birch and beech, were bowed to the ground without breaking.

On the way back from the stream, as I was taking this in and realizing how well this illustrated the variation in strengths of different species of wood, a pine branch snapped off and fell across the path behind me. It was time to view nature's example of structural characteristics of wood from the safety of the cabin.

Perhaps it was from ice storms and similar natural situations such as this one that the early colonial settlers acquired their intuitive understanding of the differences in strengths among various species of wood. These differences, for example, would require that a pine beam be of a larger dimension than an oak beam bearing the same load. Table 1 gives design values for oak, Douglas fir, spruce, and pine. Values for other woods

not listed can be found in the References.

To be able to design the timbers for a frame, you need to have a general understanding of the physics of forces and their effect upon the frame. For those unfamiliar with physics and math, the information on pages 155 to 166 will serve as an elementary introduction. If you have technical knowledge, this will be an opportunity to review the basic principles of the physics of forces and structural design. You may also wish to look at the design equations in Appendices 1 and 2. (We give beam design tables for sizing timbers later in this chapter and in Appendix 3.) These tables are applicable to the framing methods shown in this book. If you have a unique framing system, you may wish to have an engineer check your design.

In most parts of the country, your work on frame design—including joinery specifications and the sizing of timbers—will not be complete until it has met with the approval of the local building inspector. Before you meet with him, make sure you fully understand all the elements of the frame. He may have specific questions about how your structure will carry the loads and resist the forces as described in his building code. Because there is some discrepancy in the matter, he may also want to know what wood values were used to evaluate the timbers and what your source was for these values. We have

TABLE 2
LOADS

DEAD LOAD: Weight of building without occupants and furnishings

    FLOORS—7½ pounds per square foot (psf)
    ROOF—7½ psf

LIVE LOAD: Occupants and furnishings (National Building Code)
    1st Floor (living space)—40psf
    2nd Floor (bedrooms)—30psf
    Attic (unoccupied)—20psf

SNOW LOAD: Check local conditions. 10 to 40 psf
National Building Code allows reduction of snow load for steeply pitched roof if the snow load in your area is greater than 20 psf. Check with local building inspector.

$$\text{Reduction in Load (psf)} = (S/40 - 1/2) \times (P-20)$$

S = Snow load in your area in psf.
P = Roof pitch in degrees (example: a 12-pitch roof is 45).

WIND LOAD: Highly variable. Check with building inspector.

NOTE: *If BOCA or another building code is applicable in your area, it should be used for allowable design loads.*

The shouldering of major load-bearing beams prevents shear failure at the joint (see "Tenons: Checking for Shear," page 167). *Courtesy of Tafi Brown*

By locating a scarf joint above a knee brace, additional strength is gained.

Braces divide nonrigid rectangular areas into rigid triangular trusses. *Courtesy of Tafi Brown*

found that the *Wood Handbook,* by the United States Department of Agriculture, is authoritative.

Unfortunately, most building codes have no provision for timber frames. They are written for standard framing stock on sixteen- or twenty-four-inch centers. When the building inspector is informed that you in-

tend to frame with posts that are twelve to sixteen feet apart, you might find yourself faced with a blank stare of disbelief. And a fight. He may want the plans to be reviewed and stamped by a registered engineer. Try to develop a positive relationship with the inspector. At least you share the common interest that your house be structurally sound.

WOOD: EVALUATING ITS STRENGTH

BRIEFLY REVIEWED HERE ARE SOME BASIC CHARACTERISTICS OF WOOD AND HOW THEY AFFECT THE STRENGTH OF THE TIMBER. GUIDELINES ARE GIVEN FOR ACCEPTABLE AND USABLE TIMBERS.

MOISTURE CONTENT

MOST STRUCTURAL PROPERTIES OF WOOD ARE IMPROVED 25% OR MORE BY SEASONING. THIS IMPROVEMENT WILL BE PARTIALLY OFFSET BY A WEAKENING OF THE TIMBERS FROM THE FORMATION OF CHECKS. THEREFORE, DESIGNING THE TIMBERS USING STRENGTH VALUES FOR GREEN LUMBER GIVES US A MARGIN OF SAFETY.

SLOPE OF GRAIN

A DIAGONAL, OR CROSS GRAIN, OF 1:10 GIVES A 20% REDUCTION IN STRENGTH. THEREFORE, AVOID USE OF WOOD WITH DIAGONAL GRAIN GREATER THAN 1:20 (10% REDUCTION IN STRENGTH), OR REDUCE DESIGN STRENGTH ACCORDINGLY.

DIAGONAL
GRAIN OF 1:10

KNOTS

KNOTS ARE CAUSED BY THE FORMATION OF BRANCHES IN THE TREE TRUNK AND CONSEQUENT DISTURBANCE OF THE GRAIN. KNOTS SHOULD GENERALLY BE LESS THAN 1½" IN WIDTH. BOTH THE KNOT AND THE GRAIN DISTURBANCE CAUSED BY THE KNOT WEAKEN THE TIMBER. IT IS BEST TO USE TIMBERS WITH MAJOR KNOTS AS POSTS OR SILLS. OTHERWISE, ORIENT THE BEAM SO THAT THE KNOT FALLS ON THE UPPER SURFACE (COMPRESSION SIDE) OF THE BEAM.

MAJOR
KNOT

SHAKES, CHECKS, AND SPLITS

THESE ARE CAUSED BY SEPARATION OF FIBERS. SHAKES FOLLOW CURVATURE OF GROWTH RINGS. WOOD EXHIBITING MAJOR SHAKES IS NOT SUITABLE FOR TIMBER FRAMING. CHECKS AND SPLITS FOLLOW DIRECTION OF RAYS. THESE DEFECTS REDUCE, PRINCIPALLY, THE SHEAR STRENGTH OF A TIMBER (SEE "STRUCTURAL CHARACTERISTICS OF TIMBERS"). ALTHOUGH DIFFICULT TO COMPUTE MATHEMATICALLY, A REDUCTION IN STRENGTH FROM SHAKES AND SPLITS FORMED DURING DRYING IS COMPENSATED FOR BY AN INCREASE IN STRENGTH FROM MOISTURE REDUCTION.

CHECKS
AND SPLITS

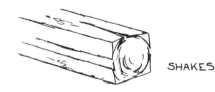

SHAKES

INSECT ATTACK AND DECAY

THE EFFECT ON STRENGTH IS AGAIN DIFFICULT TO DETERMINE. USE AN INSECTICIDE TO TREAT WOOD THAT SHOWS INSECT ATTACK. PROBING WITH A PENKNIFE IS USEFUL IN EVALUATING THE EXTENT OF DECAY. IT IS BETTER TO REJECT A TIMBER THAN TO RISK STRUCTURAL FAILURE.

FORCES AND HOW THEY INTERACT

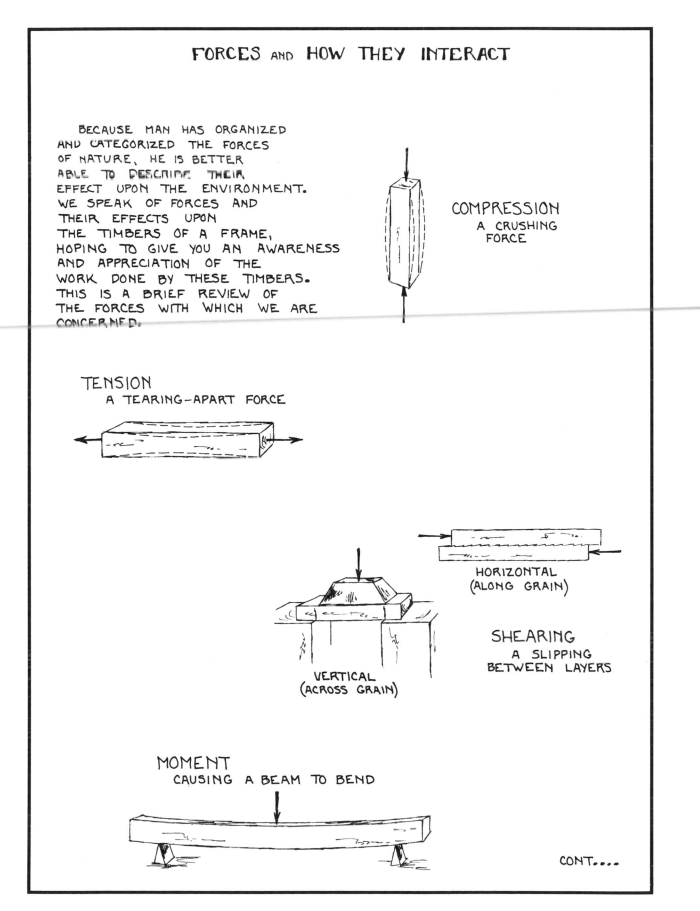

BECAUSE MAN HAS ORGANIZED AND CATEGORIZED THE FORCES OF NATURE, HE IS BETTER ABLE TO DESCRIBE THEIR EFFECT UPON THE ENVIRONMENT. WE SPEAK OF FORCES AND THEIR EFFECTS UPON THE TIMBERS OF A FRAME, HOPING TO GIVE YOU AN AWARENESS AND APPRECIATION OF THE WORK DONE BY THESE TIMBERS. THIS IS A BRIEF REVIEW OF THE FORCES WITH WHICH WE ARE CONCERNED.

COMPRESSION
A CRUSHING FORCE

TENSION
A TEARING-APART FORCE

HORIZONTAL
(ALONG GRAIN)

SHEARING
A SLIPPING BETWEEN LAYERS

VERTICAL
(ACROSS GRAIN)

MOMENT
CAUSING A BEAM TO BEND

CONT....

FORCES AND HOW THEY INTERACT.... CONT.

FORCES ACTING ON A POST

THESE VERTICAL TIMBERS ARE PRINCIPALLY EXPOSED TO COMPRESSION FORCES. THE DOWNWARD FORCE IS REFERRED TO AS THE <u>LOAD</u> AND THE FORCE PUSHING BACK AS THE <u>REACTION</u>. FOR EQUILIBRIUM, THESE MUST BE EQUAL BUT OPPOSITE.

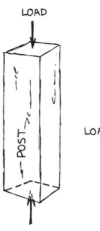

LOAD = REACTION

FORCES ACTING ON A BEAM

THESE HORIZONTAL TIMBERS ARE AFFECTED BY FORCES AND MOMENTS. A <u>MOMENT</u> IS A RESULT OF FORCE TIMES DISTANCE FROM A POINT. THE RELATIONSHIP OF THE FORCES GIVES A DIRECTION CLOCKWISE OR COUNTERCLOCKWISE.

THE 100-POUND FORCE ILLUSTRATED (LEFT) GIVES A 1,000 ft. lb. MOMENT TRYING TO TURN THE TIMBER CLOCKWISE. THE 200-POUND FORCE GIVES A 1,000 ft. lb. MOMENT COUNTER-CLOCKWISE. FOR EQUILIBRIUM BOTH MOMENTS MUST BE EQUAL IN VALUE BUT OPPOSITE IN DIRECTION.

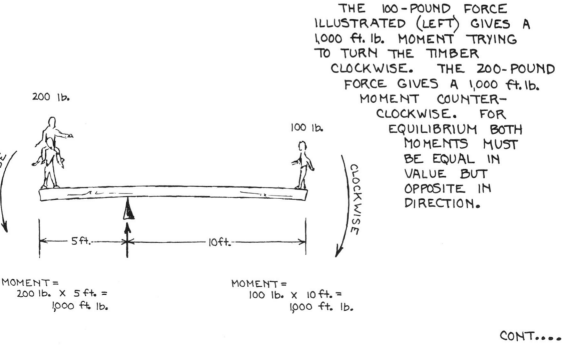

MOMENT =
200 lb. X 5 ft. =
1,000 ft. lb.

MOMENT =
100 lb. X 10 ft. =
1,000 ft. lb.

CONT....

FORCES AND HOW THEY INTERACT.... CONT.

WE, THEREFORE, HAVE TWO RULES THAT APPLY TO ALL TIMBERS AND TO THE FRAME AS A WHOLE:

> 1. ALL LOADS MUST BE BALANCED BY EQUAL REACTIONS.
>
> 2. ALL CLOCKWISE MOMENTS MUST BE BALANCED BY EQUAL COUNTERCLOCKWISE MOMENTS.

BELOW IS AN EXAGGERATED VIEW OF A TYPICAL BEAM WITH A LOAD LOCATED IN THE CENTER. THIS IS SIMILAR TO THE PREVIOUS DRAWING, FLIPPED UPSIDE-DOWN.

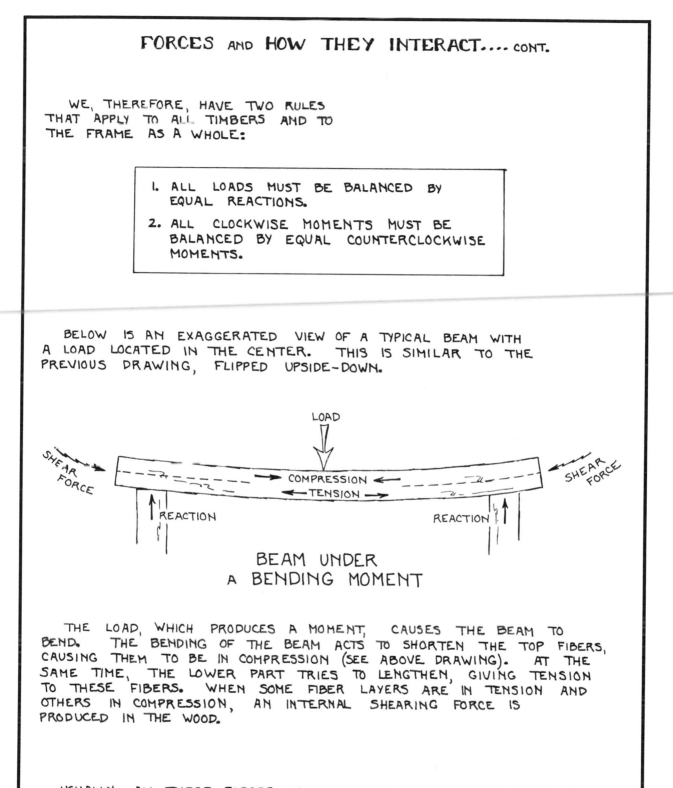

BEAM UNDER
A BENDING MOMENT

THE LOAD, WHICH PRODUCES A MOMENT, CAUSES THE BEAM TO BEND. THE BENDING OF THE BEAM ACTS TO SHORTEN THE TOP FIBERS, CAUSING THEM TO BE IN COMPRESSION (SEE ABOVE DRAWING). AT THE SAME TIME, THE LOWER PART TRIES TO LENGTHEN, GIVING TENSION TO THESE FIBERS. WHEN SOME FIBER LAYERS ARE IN TENSION AND OTHERS IN COMPRESSION, AN INTERNAL SHEARING FORCE IS PRODUCED IN THE WOOD.

USUALLY, ALL THREE FORCES — COMPRESSION, TENSION, AND SHEARING — ARE PRESENT IN A BEAM BEARING A LOAD. WE WILL LATER SEE THAT THE INTERACTION BETWEEN THESE FORCES ILLUSTRATED, THE DIMENSIONS OF THE TIMBER, AND THE INHERENT CHARACTERISTICS OF THE WOOD DETERMINE THE STRENGTH OF A TIMBER IN A FRAME.

THOUGHTS on STRUCTURAL DESIGN

CHAPTER 2 ILLUSTRATED A SERIES OF STRUCTURALLY SOUND BENTS. HERE ARE SOME OF THE DESIGN CONSIDERATIONS.

FRAME RACKING

BRACING TIMBERS THAT MEET AT RIGHT ANGLES IS NECESSARY FOR FRAME RIGIDITY WITHIN A BENT AND BETWEEN BENTS (RIGHT).

THE ADDITION OF BRACES DIVIDES NONRIGID RECTANGULAR AREAS INTO RIGID TRIANGULAR TRUSSES.

RAFTER SPREADING

1½- OR 2-STORY FRAMES MAY HAVE RAFTER SPREADING WITHOUT PROPER TYING (BELOW).

ADDING COLLAR TIE AND STRUTS PREVENTS SPREADING.

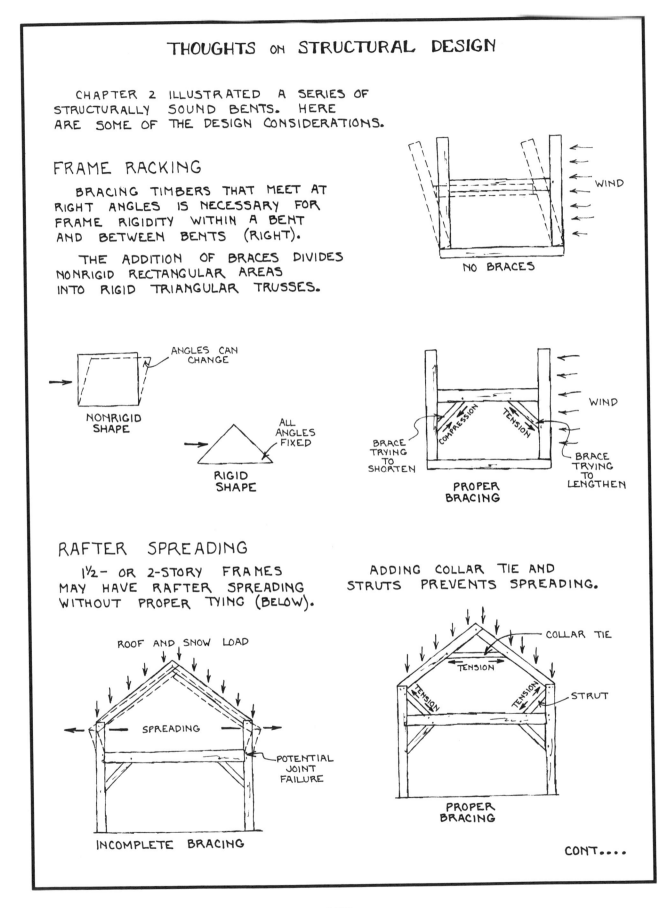

WIND

NO BRACES

ANGLES CAN CHANGE

NONRIGID SHAPE

ALL ANGLES FIXED

RIGID SHAPE

WIND

COMPRESSION   TENSION

BRACE TRYING TO SHORTEN

BRACE TRYING TO LENGTHEN

PROPER BRACING

ROOF AND SNOW LOAD

SPREADING

POTENTIAL JOINT FAILURE

INCOMPLETE BRACING

COLLAR TIE

TENSION

TENSION   TENSION

STRUT

PROPER BRACING

CONT....

RAFTER SAGGING

UNSUPPORTED AND/OR UNDERSIZED RAFTERS MAY SAG FROM ROOF AND SNOW LOAD (RIGHT).

PREVENT RAFTER SAGGING BY SHORTENING THE CLEAR SPAN WITH QUEEN POSTS OR BY INCREASING THE SIZE OF THE TIMBER.

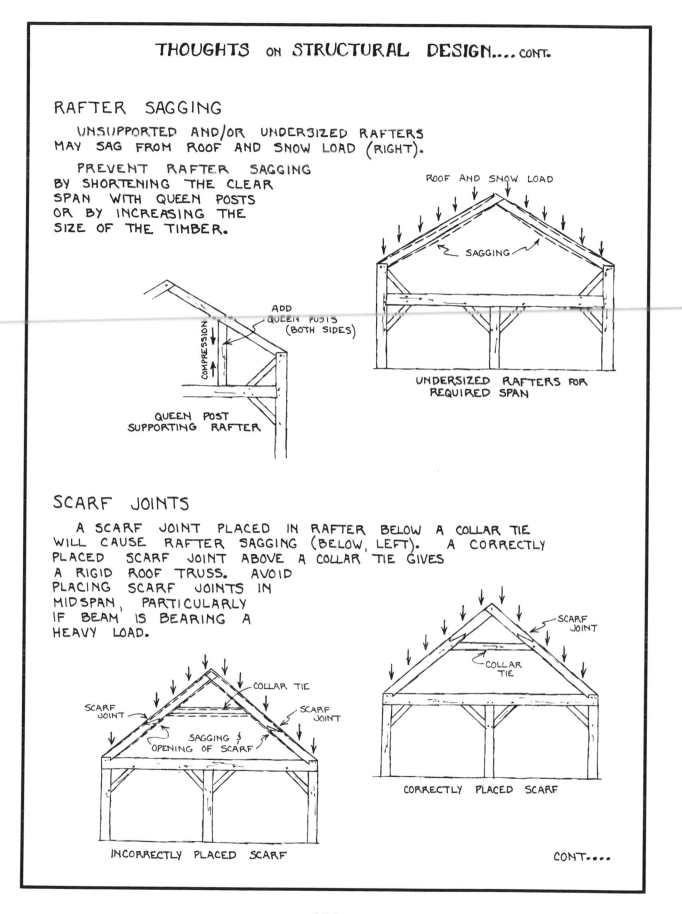

ROOF AND SNOW LOAD

SAGGING

UNDERSIZED RAFTERS FOR REQUIRED SPAN

ADD QUEEN POSTS (BOTH SIDES)

COMPRESSION

QUEEN POST SUPPORTING RAFTER

SCARF JOINTS

A SCARF JOINT PLACED IN RAFTER BELOW A COLLAR TIE WILL CAUSE RAFTER SAGGING (BELOW, LEFT). A CORRECTLY PLACED SCARF JOINT ABOVE A COLLAR TIE GIVES A RIGID ROOF TRUSS. AVOID PLACING SCARF JOINTS IN MIDSPAN, PARTICULARLY IF BEAM IS BEARING A HEAVY LOAD.

SCARF JOINT

COLLAR TIE

SCARF JOINT

SCARF JOINT

COLLAR TIE

SAGGING & OPENING OF SCARF

INCORRECTLY PLACED SCARF

CORRECTLY PLACED SCARF

CONT....

THOUGHTS ON STRUCTURAL DESIGN.... CONT.

UNFORTUNATELY, WHEN A NEW SCIENCE OR CRAFT EMERGES OR REEMERGES, ERRORS AND MISTAKES WILL UNDOUBTEDLY OCCUR. AS I WAS REVIEWING THE RECENT PUBLICATIONS ON TIMBER FRAMING AND SAW DESIGNS WITH MAJOR STRUCTURAL ERRORS, THE POTENTIAL FOR A CATASTROPHE FROM AN IMPROPERLY FRAMED HOUSE ALARMED ME. I POINT OUT HERE SOME OF THESE ERRORS TO AVERT THEIR USE AND TO ENCOURAGE AN AWARENESS OF THE DANGERS OF IMPROPERLY FRAMING A HOUSE.

CASE I: JOINERY AT GIRT AND POST

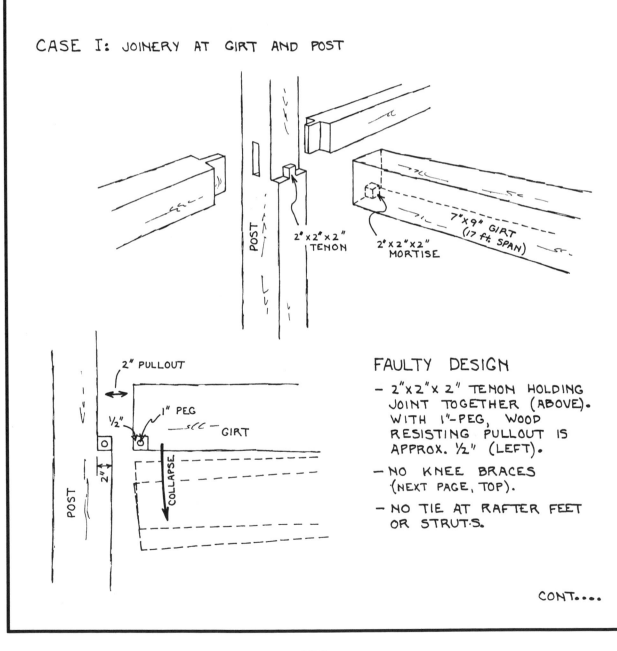

POST

2" x 2" x 2" TENON

2" x 2" x 2" MORTISE

7" x 9" GIRT (17 ft SPAN)

2" PULLOUT

1" PEG

½"

GIRT

POST

2"

COLLAPSE

FAULTY DESIGN

- 2" x 2" x 2" TENON HOLDING JOINT TOGETHER (ABOVE). WITH 1"-PEG, WOOD RESISTING PULLOUT IS APPROX. ½" (LEFT).

- NO KNEE BRACES (NEXT PAGE, TOP).

- NO TIE AT RAFTER FEET OR STRUTS.

CONT....

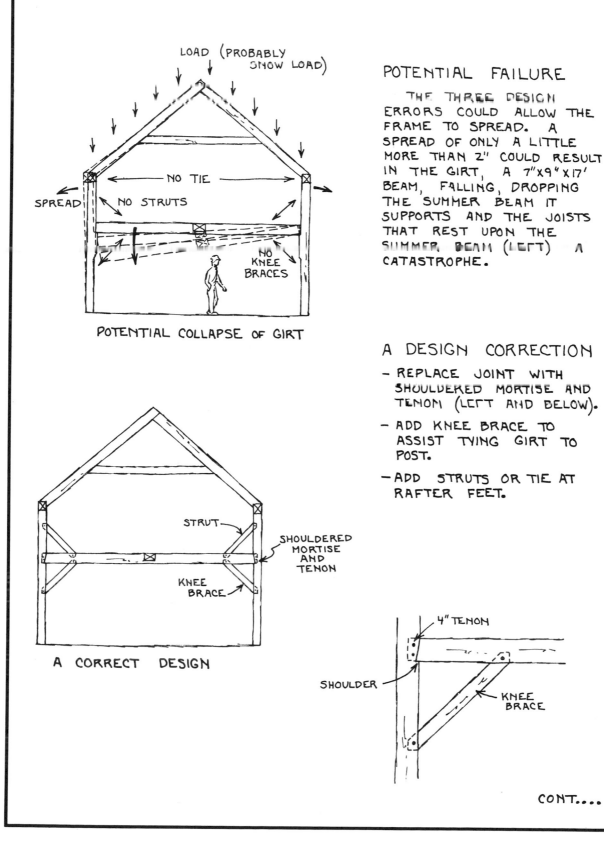

LOAD (PROBABLY SNOW LOAD)

NO TIE

SPREAD

NO STRUTS

NO KNEE BRACES

POTENTIAL COLLAPSE OF GIRT

POTENTIAL FAILURE

THE THREE DESIGN ERRORS COULD ALLOW THE FRAME TO SPREAD. A SPREAD OF ONLY A LITTLE MORE THAN 2" COULD RESULT IN THE GIRT, A 7"X9"X17' BEAM, FALLING, DROPPING THE SUMMER BEAM IT SUPPORTS AND THE JOISTS THAT REST UPON THE SUMMER BEAM (LEFT) A CATASTROPHE.

A DESIGN CORRECTION

- REPLACE JOINT WITH SHOULDERED MORTISE AND TENON (LEFT AND BELOW).

- ADD KNEE BRACE TO ASSIST TYING GIRT TO POST.

- ADD STRUTS OR TIE AT RAFTER FEET.

STRUT

SHOULDERED MORTISE AND TENON

KNEE BRACE

A CORRECT DESIGN

4" TENON

SHOULDER

KNEE BRACE

CONT....

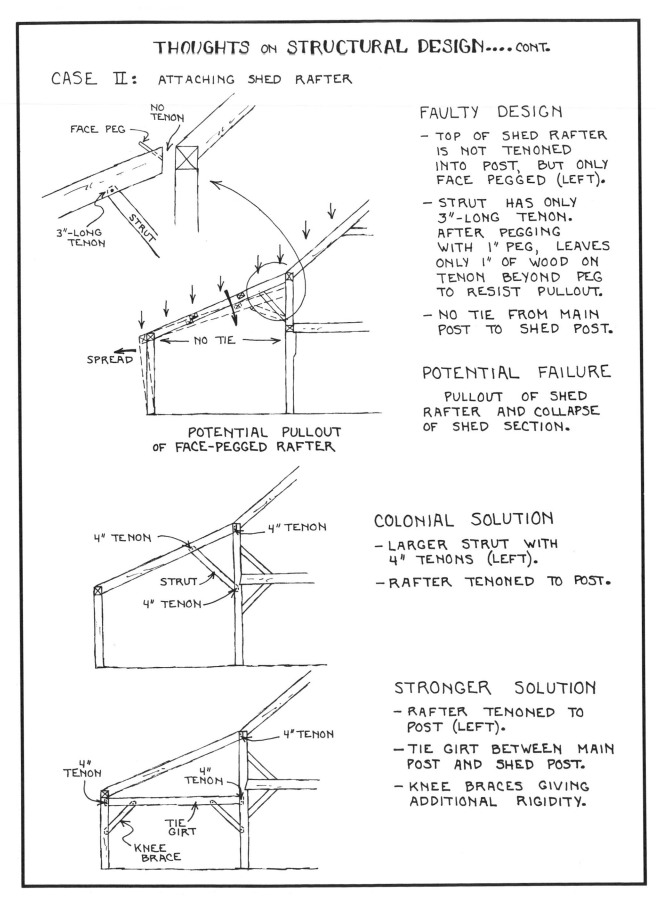

THOUGHTS on STRUCTURAL DESIGN.... cont.

CASE II: ATTACHING SHED RAFTER

NO TENON

FACE PEG

3"-LONG TENON

STRUT

POTENTIAL PULLOUT
OF FACE-PEGGED RAFTER

NO TIE

SPREAD

FAULTY DESIGN

- TOP OF SHED RAFTER IS NOT TENONED INTO POST, BUT ONLY FACE PEGGED (LEFT).

- STRUT HAS ONLY 3"-LONG TENON. AFTER PEGGING WITH 1" PEG, LEAVES ONLY 1" OF WOOD ON TENON BEYOND PEG TO RESIST PULLOUT.

- NO TIE FROM MAIN POST TO SHED POST.

POTENTIAL FAILURE

PULLOUT OF SHED RAFTER AND COLLAPSE OF SHED SECTION.

4" TENON   4" TENON

STRUT

4" TENON

COLONIAL SOLUTION

- LARGER STRUT WITH 4" TENONS (LEFT).
- RAFTER TENONED TO POST.

4" TENON

4" TENON   4" TENON

TIE GIRT

KNEE BRACE

STRONGER SOLUTION

- RAFTER TENONED TO POST (LEFT).
- TIE GIRT BETWEEN MAIN POST AND SHED POST.
- KNEE BRACES GIVING ADDITIONAL RIGIDITY.

STRUCTURAL CHARACTERISTICS OF TIMBERS
HOW TIMBERS REACT TO LOADS

THE EARLY AMERICANS WORRIED LITTLE ABOUT DESIGNING THE TIMBERS OF THEIR HOUSES AND BARNS. THEY KNEW FROM YEARS OF TRADITION AND EXPERIENCE WHICH SIZE TIMBERS WOULD BE NEEDED FOR EACH POSITION WITHIN THE FRAME. STRUCTURAL CHARACTERISTICS OF TIMBERS WERE SIMPLY COMMON SENSE TO THESE BUILDERS. ALTHOUGH THIS KNOWLEDGE CAN ONLY BE DEVELOPED THROUGH EXPERIENCE, WE ATTEMPT HERE TO GIVE SOME INSIGHT INTO HOW TIMBERS REACT TO LOAD.

POSTS

POSTS ARE DESIGNED TO RESIST CRUSHING AND BUCKLING.

CRUSHING

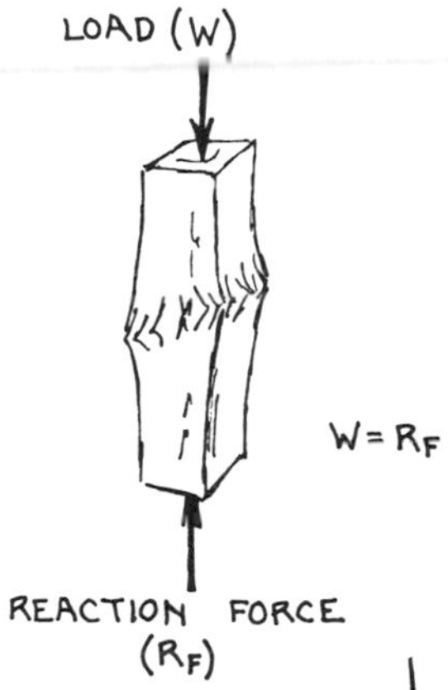

LOAD (W)

$W = R_F$

REACTION FORCE
(R_F)

MOST WOODS ARE EXTREMELY STRONG IN RESISTING A COMPRESSIVE OR CRUSHING FORCE. TABLE 6-1 GIVES VALUES OF DIFFERENT WOODS IN RESISTING COMPRESSION. CALCULATION OF MAXIMUM LOAD IN COMPRESSION IS GIVEN BY:

$$W = C \times A$$

W = MAXIMUM SAFE LOAD
C = MAXIMUM COMPRESSIVE STRENGTH (TABLE 6-1)
A = CROSS-SECTIONAL AREA OF POST REMAINING AT WEAKEST SPOT (WHERE MOST MORTISES ARE LOCATED)

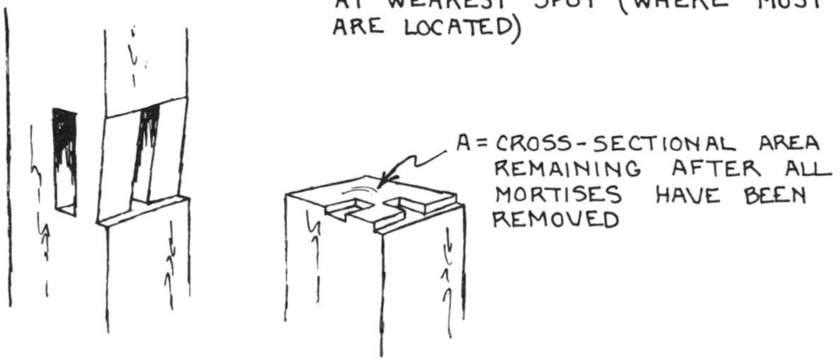

A = CROSS-SECTIONAL AREA REMAINING AFTER ALL MORTISES HAVE BEEN REMOVED

BUCKLING

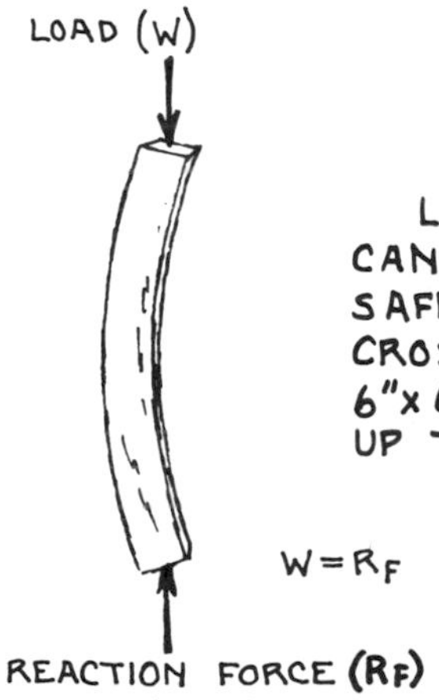

LOAD (W)

LONG, SLENDER POSTS CAN FAIL BY BUCKLING. A SAFE DESIGN IS TO HAVE THE CROSS-SECTION OF A POST AT LEAST 6"x 6" UP TO 8-FOOT LENGTHS AND 8"x8" UP TO 16-FOOT LENGTHS.

$W = R_F$

CONT....

REACTION FORCE (R_F)

BEAMS

THE DESIGN OF BEAMS IS MORE COMPLICATED THAN POST DESIGN BECAUSE THREE DIFFERENT CRITERIA MUST BE SATISFIED: RESISTANCE TO FIBER FAILURE, TO EXCESSIVE BENDING, AND TO SHEAR FAILURE.

FIBER FAILURE

LARGE BEAMS DON'T EASILY BREAK. BECAUSE WOOD IS EXTREMELY STRONG IN TENSION PARALLEL TO THE GRAIN, IT IS RARE FOR A BEAM TO FAIL BY THE LOWER FIBERS TEARING APART (BELOW). BUT FIBER FAILURE CAN OCCUR. I'VE SEEN IT IN AN 8"X 8" ROOF TIMBER SUPPORTING A BELL TOWER. WE THEREFORE MUST DESIGN A TIMBER TO MEET THIS REQUIREMENT. THE VALUE f (MAXIMUM ALLOWABLE FIBER STRESS IN BENDING), SHOWN IN TABLE 6-1, GIVES THE STRENGTH OF THE WOODS' FIBERS TO RESIST THIS TYPE OF FAILURE.

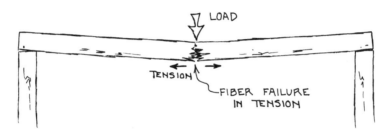

EXCESSIVE BENDING AND DEFLECTION

BOUNCY FLOORS ARE NOT UNSAFE BUT ARE VERY ANNOYING. TYPICAL BUILDING CODES REQUIRE:

> FLOORS: MAXIMUM DEFLECTION TO BE LESS THAN 1/360 OF SPAN.
> ROOFS: MAXIMUM DEFLECTION TO BE LESS THAN 1/240 OF SPAN.

AS AN EXAMPLE, A FLOOR WITH A 15-FT. SPAN (180") IS DESIGNED WITH A MAXIMUM DEFLECTION OF 1/360 X 180", WHICH EQUALS 1/2". YOUR TIMBERS SHOULD BE LARGE ENOUGH TO HAVE SUFFICIENT STIFFNESS TO AVOID SAGGING AND BOUNCY ROOF AND FLOORS. THE VALUE "E" (MODULUS OF ELASTICITY), GIVEN IN TABLE 6-1, EXPRESSES THE STIFFNESS OF A WOOD TO RESIST BENDING.

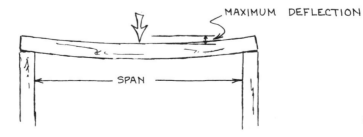

CONT....

STRUCTURAL CHARACTERISTICS OF TIMBERS.... CONT.
HOW TIMBERS REACT TO LOADS

SHEAR FAILURE

SHEAR FAILURE IS RARE, BUT COULD HAPPEN IN A TIMBER BEARING A GREAT LOAD. THIS COULD ALSO OCCUR IN A CANTILEVER BEAM. HERE THE TIMBER FAILS FROM ITS FIBERS SLIPPING OVER EACH OTHER. THE FIBERS ARE NOT TORN, BUT THE COHESION BETWEEN THE FIBERS IS EXCEEDED, CAUSING SLIPPAGE AND THUS FAILURE. THIS MIGHT BE SIMILAR TO BENDING A TELEPHONE BOOK AND SEEING THE PAGES SLIDE OVER EACH OTHER. THE VALUE "h" (MAXIMUM ALLOWABLE HORIZONTAL SHEAR STRESS) IN TABLE 6-1 CHARACTERIZES A WOOD'S RESISTANCE TO SHEARING.

WHAT DETERMINES THE BEAM'S SIZE?

A BEAM MUST SATISFY ALL THREE OF THE ABOVE CRITERIA. THEREFORE, THE ONE THAT MINIMIZES THE LOAD THAT A TIMBER CAN CARRY WILL BE THE ONE THAT DETERMINES THE TIMBER'S SIZE.

FOR EXAMPLE, IF A TIMBER CAN BEAR 5,000 lb. IN SHEARING, 5,000 lb. IN FIBER STRENGTH, BUT ONLY 3,000 lb. WITHOUT EXCESSIVE BENDING, THE MAXIMUM LOAD THIS TIMBER CAN BEAR IS 3,000 lb.

TO ILLUSTRATE, WE TAKE A HYPOTHETICAL TIMBER WITH FIXED WIDTH AND DEPTH (RIGHT AND BELOW). AT SHORT SPANS, THE FACTOR LIMITING THE SIZE OF THE LOAD THAT CAN BE BORNE BY THE TIMBER IS SHEAR FAILURE. AT A LONGER SPAN, THE LIMITING FACTOR IS FIBER FAILURE. AT EVEN LONGER SPANS, EXCESSIVE BENDING AND DEFLECTION LIMIT THE LOAD SIZE. THESE LIMITING FACTORS REDUCE THE TOTAL LOAD THAT THE BEAM CAN CARRY.

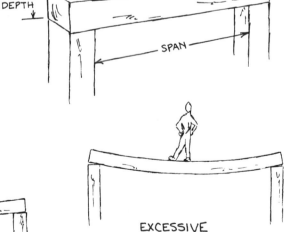

SHEAR FAILURE

FIBER FAILURE

EXCESSIVE BENDING AND DEFLECTION

CONT....

STRUCTURAL CHARACTERISTICS of TIMBERS....cont.
HOW TIMBERS REACT TO A LOAD

WE CAN INCREASE THE LOAD A BEAM CAN CARRY BY INCREASING THE WIDTH AND DEPTH OF THE BEAM. IT WILL BE SHOWN LATER THAT AN INCREASE IN A BEAM'S DEPTH IS MORE EFFECTIVE THAN AN INCREASE IN ITS WIDTH.

THIS SHORT REVIEW OF HOW TIMBERS REACT TO LOADS ILLUSTRATES THE COMPLEXITY OF BEAM DESIGN. FORTUNATELY, COMPUTERS CAN SAVE US FROM THE MATHEMATICAL GRIND THAT WOULD HAVE BEEN REQUIRED TEN YEARS AGO. COMPUTER-GENERATED DESIGN TABLES THAT HAVE TAKEN ALL OF THE ABOVE FACTORS INTO ACCOUNT WILL BE SHORTLY PRESENTED. THE MATHEMATICAL METHOD IS GIVEN IN APPENDIX I AND II.

TENONS: CHECKING FOR SHEAR

THERE IS A COMMON MISCONCEPTION THAT THE STRENGTH OF A BEAM IS REDUCED TO THE STRENGTH OF THE END TENONS. THIS IS NOT TRUE WITH PROPERLY DESIGNED JOINTS. THE MIDDLE OF THE BEAM MUST BE OF SUFFICIENT SIZE TO RESIST SHEAR, FIBER STRESS FROM BENDING, AND EXCESSIVE DEFLECTION. THE ENDS ONLY NEED TO RESIST SHEAR STRESS AND THUS CAN OFTEN BE CONSIDERABLY SMALLER IN CROSS-SECTION. WE THEREFORE NEED TO CHECK THE SIZE OF END TENONS ONLY FOR SHEAR STRENGTH.

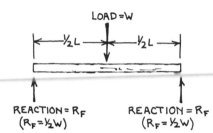

LOAD = W

½L   ½L

REACTION = R_F REACTION = R_F
($R_F = \frac{1}{2}W$)   ($R_F = \frac{1}{2}W$)

BEAM CENTRALLY LOADED

EXAMPLE HERE ILLUSTRATES SHEAR THAT IS CONTINUOUS ALONG A BEAM BUT FIBER STRESS THAT IS AT ITS MAXIMUM AT MIDSPAN.

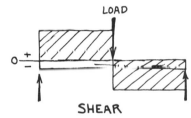

SHEAR

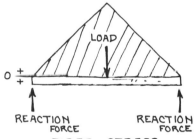

FIBER STRESS

BEAMS THAT ARE FULLY HOUSED OR SHOULDERED (BELOW) NEED NOT BE CHECKED, SINCE THE CROSS-SECTION HAS NOT BEEN REDUCED AT THE JOINT.

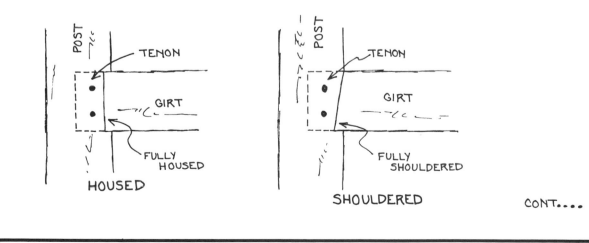

HOUSED

SHOULDERED

CONT....

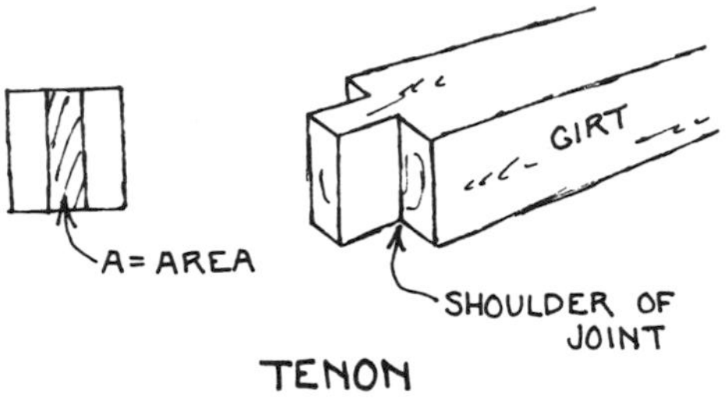

METHOD

— DETERMINE CROSS-SECTIONAL AREA (A) OF BEAM ENTERING THE JOINT.

— CALCULATE REACTION FORCE (R_F) AT END. APPENDIX I GIVES R_F VALUES FOR TYPICAL CASES.

— CALCULATE HORIZONTAL SHEAR (H).

$$H = \left(\frac{3}{2}\right) \times \left(\frac{R_F}{A}\right)$$

— COMPARE HORIZONTAL SHEAR (H) WITH MAXIMUM ALLOWABLE VALUE (h) FROM TABLE 6-1. IF H IS LESS THAN h, TENON IS OK. IF NOT, EITHER INCREASE THE SIZE OF THE TENON OR REDESIGN THE JOINT.

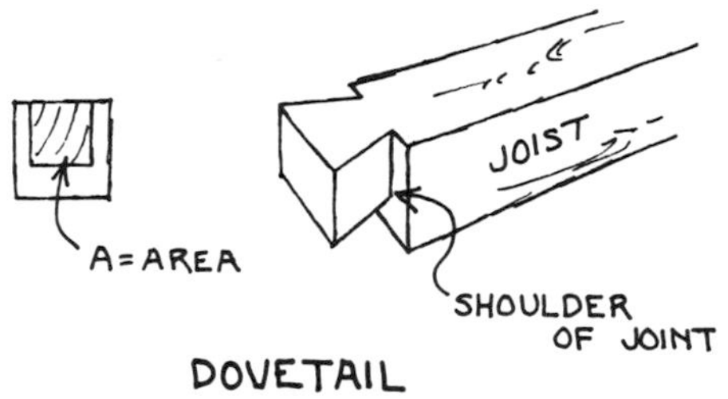

A = AREA

TENON

SHOULDER OF JOINT

GIRT

A = AREA

DOVETAIL

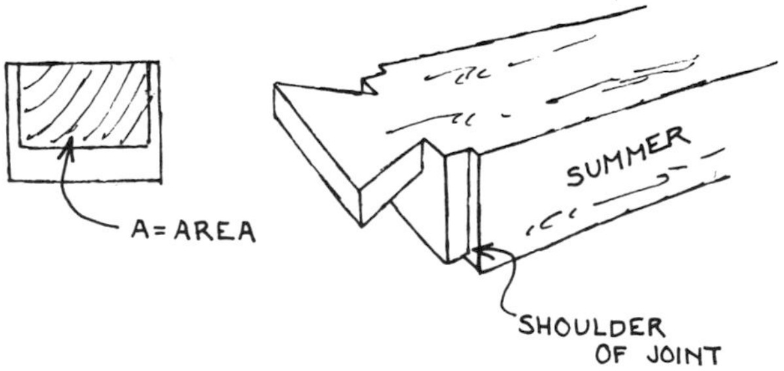

JOIST

SHOULDER OF JOINT

A = AREA

HOUSED DOVETAIL

SUMMER

SHOULDER OF JOINT

AN ADDITIONAL NOTE

TIMBERS WITH TENONS CUT FROM THE UPPER HALF, SUCH AS THE JOIST DOVETAIL (SHOWN ABOVE), ARE MORE LIKELY TO DEVELOP SPLITTING OR CHECKING BELOW THE TENON IF THE TIMBER IS HEAVILY LOADED. METHODS FOR MINIMIZING THIS PROBLEM ARE SUGGESTED IN CHAPTER 3, "DOVETAIL AND HALF LAP FOR JOISTS AND PURLINS." DESIGN CONSERVATIVELY FOR SHEAR, ALLOWING AN EXTRA MARGIN OF SAFETY.

CALCULATING LOADS on TIMBERS

WE HAVE REVIEWED THE PHYSICS OF FORCES AND HAVE GIVEN TABLE 6-1 DEPICTING THE INHERENT CHARACTERISTICS OF WOODS. NOW WE ARE READY TO SIZE TIMBERS.

THE FIRST STEP IS TO DETERMINE THE SIZE OF THE LOAD ACTING ON THE TIMBER. ON FLOORS, THE LOAD IS THE DEAD LOAD PLUS THE LIVE LOAD. ON ROOFS, IT IS THE DEAD LOAD PLUS THE SNOW LOAD (SEE TABLE 6-2).

CALCULATE THE SQUARE FOOTAGE OF FLOOR OR ROOF AREA THAT IS SUPPORTED BY THE BEAM. DETERMINE THE LOAD PER SQUARE FOOT FROM TABLE 6-2 AND MULTIPLY IT TIMES THE SQUARE FOOTAGE. THIS TOTAL LOAD (W) WILL EITHER BE EVENLY DISTRIBUTED ALONG THE TIMBER OR CONCENTRATED AT ONE OR MORE POINTS.

EXAMPLE I: CALCULATING LOAD ON A SUMMER BEAM

THE SUMMER BEAM ILLUSTRATED BELOW SUPPORTS HALF THE LOAD OF A SERIES OF JOISTS (SHADED AREA). THE LOAD CAN BE APPROXIMATED AS BEING UNIFORMLY DISTRIBUTED (SEE "DESIGNING BEAMS BY USING TABLES, CASE I, LOADING").

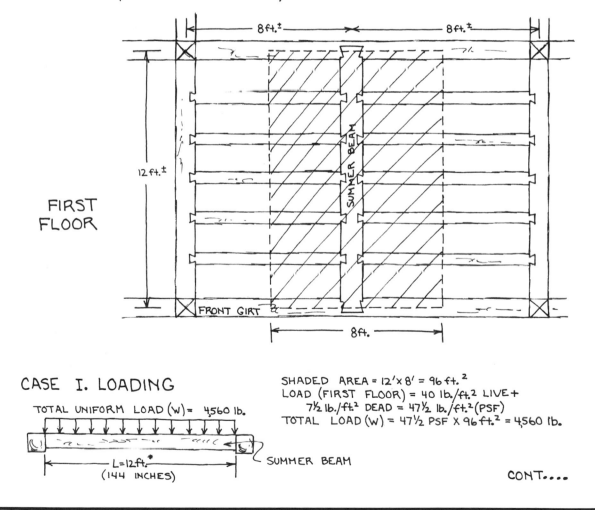

FIRST FLOOR

FRONT GIRT

CASE I. LOADING

TOTAL UNIFORM LOAD (W)= 4560 lb.

L=12ft.±
(144 INCHES)

SUMMER BEAM

SHADED AREA = 12' x 8' = 96 ft.²
LOAD (FIRST FLOOR) = 40 lb./ft.² LIVE +
  7½ lb./ft.² DEAD = 47½ lb./ft.² (PSF)
TOTAL LOAD (W) = 47½ PSF x 96 ft.² = 4560 lb.

CONT....

EXAMPLE II: CALCULATING LOAD ON A GIRT

A SIMILAR CALCULATION IS DONE FOR THE FRONT GIRT. SINCE NEARLY ALL OF THE LOAD IS APPLIED BY THE SUMMER BEAM, THIS CAN BE APPROXIMATED AS A CONCENTRATED POINT LOAD (SEE "DESIGNING BEAMS BY USING TABLES, CASE III").

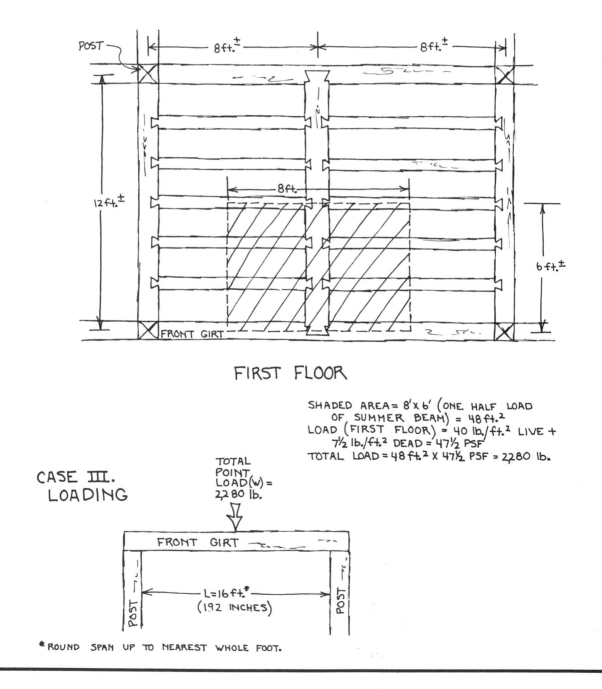

FIRST FLOOR

SHADED AREA = 8' x 6' (ONE HALF LOAD
OF SUMMER BEAM) = 48 ft.^{2}
LOAD (FIRST FLOOR) = 40 lb./ft.^{2} LIVE +
7½ lb./ft.^{2} DEAD = 47½ PSF
TOTAL LOAD = 48 ft.^{2} × 47½ PSF = 2280 lb.

CASE III.
LOADING

TOTAL POINT LOAD(w) = 2280 lb.

FRONT GIRT

L = 16 ft.*
(192 INCHES)

POST / POST

*ROUND SPAN UP TO NEAREST WHOLE FOOT.

DESIGNING BEAMS BY USING TABLES

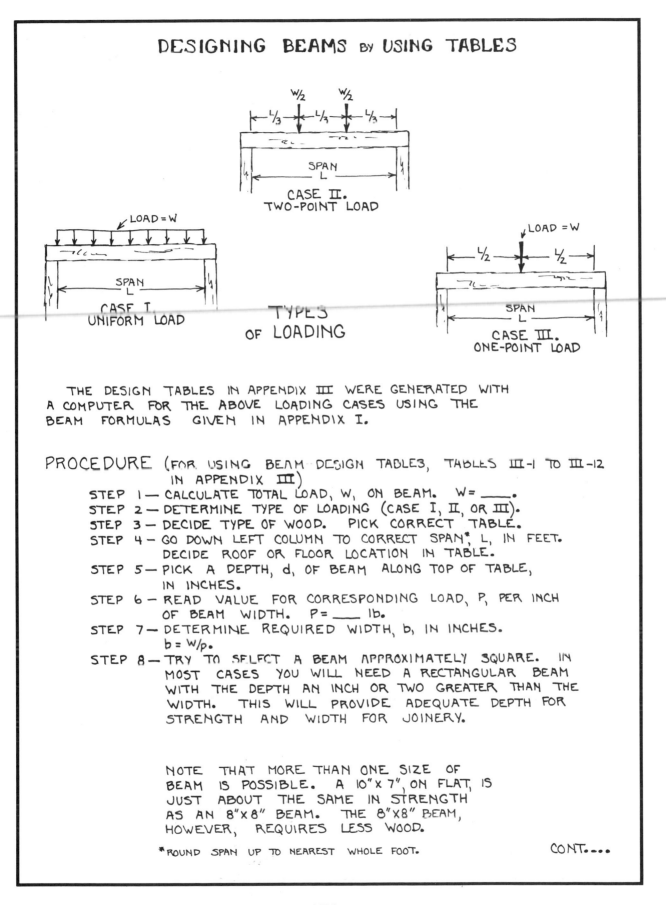

CASE II.
TWO-POINT LOAD

CASE I.
UNIFORM LOAD

CASE III.
ONE-POINT LOAD

TYPES
OF LOADING

THE DESIGN TABLES IN APPENDIX III WERE GENERATED WITH A COMPUTER FOR THE ABOVE LOADING CASES USING THE BEAM FORMULAS GIVEN IN APPENDIX I.

PROCEDURE (FOR USING BEAM DESIGN TABLES, TABLES III-1 TO III-12 IN APPENDIX III)

STEP 1 — CALCULATE TOTAL LOAD, W, ON BEAM. W = ____.
STEP 2 — DETERMINE TYPE OF LOADING (CASE I, II, OR III).
STEP 3 — DECIDE TYPE OF WOOD. PICK CORRECT TABLE.
STEP 4 — GO DOWN LEFT COLUMN TO CORRECT SPAN*, L, IN FEET. DECIDE ROOF OR FLOOR LOCATION IN TABLE.
STEP 5 — PICK A DEPTH, d, OF BEAM ALONG TOP OF TABLE, IN INCHES.
STEP 6 — READ VALUE FOR CORRESPONDING LOAD, P, PER INCH OF BEAM WIDTH. P = ____ lb.
STEP 7 — DETERMINE REQUIRED WIDTH, b, IN INCHES. b = W/P.
STEP 8 — TRY TO SELECT A BEAM APPROXIMATELY SQUARE. IN MOST CASES YOU WILL NEED A RECTANGULAR BEAM WITH THE DEPTH AN INCH OR TWO GREATER THAN THE WIDTH. THIS WILL PROVIDE ADEQUATE DEPTH FOR STRENGTH AND WIDTH FOR JOINERY.

NOTE THAT MORE THAN ONE SIZE OF BEAM IS POSSIBLE. A 10"x 7", ON FLAT, IS JUST ABOUT THE SAME IN STRENGTH AS AN 8"x8" BEAM. THE 8"x8" BEAM, HOWEVER, REQUIRES LESS WOOD.

*ROUND SPAN UP TO NEAREST WHOLE FOOT.

CONT.....

EXAMPLE I: CONTINUING EXAMPLE I "CALCULATING LOADS ON TIMBERS"

CASE I. LOADING

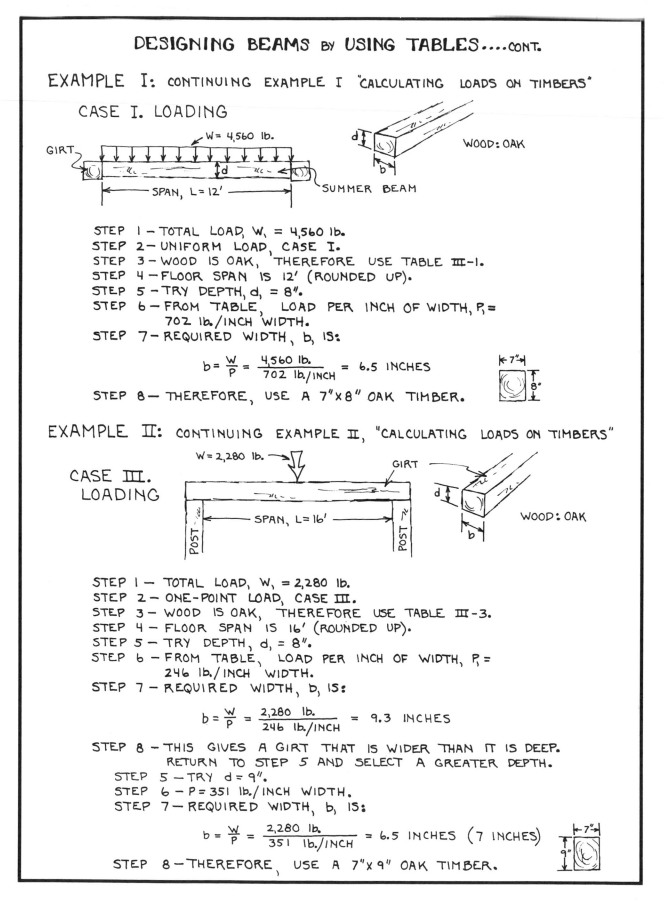

STEP 1 — TOTAL LOAD, W_1 = 4,560 lb.
STEP 2 — UNIFORM LOAD, CASE I.
STEP 3 — WOOD IS OAK, THEREFORE USE TABLE III-1.
STEP 4 — FLOOR SPAN IS 12' (ROUNDED UP).
STEP 5 — TRY DEPTH, d, = 8".
STEP 6 — FROM TABLE, LOAD PER INCH OF WIDTH, P_1 = 702 lb./INCH WIDTH.
STEP 7 — REQUIRED WIDTH, b, IS:

$$b = \frac{W}{P} = \frac{4,560 \text{ lb.}}{702 \text{ lb./INCH}} = 6.5 \text{ INCHES}$$

STEP 8 — THEREFORE, USE A 7"x8" OAK TIMBER.

EXAMPLE II: CONTINUING EXAMPLE II, "CALCULATING LOADS ON TIMBERS"

CASE III. LOADING

STEP 1 — TOTAL LOAD, W_1 = 2,280 lb.
STEP 2 — ONE-POINT LOAD, CASE III.
STEP 3 — WOOD IS OAK, THEREFORE USE TABLE III-3.
STEP 4 — FLOOR SPAN IS 16' (ROUNDED UP).
STEP 5 — TRY DEPTH, d, = 8".
STEP 6 — FROM TABLE, LOAD PER INCH OF WIDTH, P_1 = 246 lb./INCH WIDTH.
STEP 7 — REQUIRED WIDTH, b, IS:

$$b = \frac{W}{P} = \frac{2,280 \text{ lb.}}{246 \text{ lb./INCH}} = 9.3 \text{ INCHES}$$

STEP 8 — THIS GIVES A GIRT THAT IS WIDER THAN IT IS DEEP. RETURN TO STEP 5 AND SELECT A GREATER DEPTH.
   STEP 5 — TRY d = 9".
   STEP 6 — P = 351 lb./INCH WIDTH.
   STEP 7 — REQUIRED WIDTH, b, IS:

$$b = \frac{W}{P} = \frac{2,280 \text{ lb.}}{351 \text{ lb./INCH}} = 6.5 \text{ INCHES (7 INCHES)}$$

   STEP 8 — THEREFORE, USE A 7"x9" OAK TIMBER.

CHAPTER SEVEN
BUILDING FOR TODAY
DESIGN CONSIDERATIONS

Courtesy of David Bryant

It cost me much labour and many days, before these things were brought to perfection . . .

—Daniel Defoe: *Robinson Crusoe*

BROKEN down into its various aspects, building a house is a relatively simple matter. The fundamental recipe for house construction might read: "Raise frame on sound foundation. Attach insulated walls and protective roof to frame along with windows and doors. Install interior partitions where necessary and embellish to please. Add to this some water (in and out in equal proportions), provisions for heating and cooling and a few other odd items (a pinch of this, a dash of that), and cook on the fires of your energy until well done."

The reason it may not seem this simple is that for every ingredient that goes into the house, large or small, there must be a decision. And for every ingredient, you can believe there are a dizzying number of opinions and recommendations, all different. The type of foundation, the brand of insulation, the roofing material, and even the kind of nail suggested will depend on which book or article you just read. One wants foundations to be wooden poles; another says concrete slabs are best. This guy says no insulation is necessary in walls; that one tells you you can't get

enough. Here's a book that prescribes houses to be like caves in the ground; there's one urging you to sway in the wind, clutching the walls of your brand-new tree house.

As for us, we like timber frames. Since a frame is not a house, and since this type of structure has features and requires treatment different from other types of construction, we won't be able to avoid at least a minor contribution to the morass of opinion. As you read this, and as you sift through the mountain of information available on home construction, don't be intimidated. Building a house is really like baking a cake. So put together your best recipe, cling to common sense, use good ingredients, and keep stirring.

DESIGN

Before there are designs, there are people who have personal needs in their shelter and their living space. The site plan, the house style, the floor plan, and the choice of building materials should all spring from the concept of supporting the needs and ennobling the lives of these people. Some requirements of the plan are universal, others very personal. Universally, there is a need for every house to maintain heating and cooling requirements with the minimum consumption of fossil fuels. There is also a universal need for a judicious use of building materials. The number of rooms, their sizes, and arrangement are primarily personal decisions, dependent on how many people will be occupying the house and how each person uses the various living spaces. Many of the design parameters will be drawn by another personal consideration—budget. Through careful planning, all of these problems and many more can be wrestled with and solved while still only lines on paper.

There are many books with good advice on site plan considerations. *The Owner Built Home*, by Ken Kern, and *From the Ground Up*, by Charles Wing and John Cole, are both highly recommended. Remember that the idea here is to do with your house design the same kinds of things you would want to do if you were standing alone on the site without the house. If it were too hot, you'd search for shade; too cold, you would yearn to catch the rays of the sun; too windy, we'd find you huddled with your back to the wind. These are simple, uncomplicated responses, and, like a knee-jerk reaction, it doesn't take a college degree—it comes naturally. It also doesn't take a great deal of technical expertise to consider designing the shape of the house and its position on the site so that the building itself responds naturally to the environment.

If the house design begins in this manner, then it has begun under the important notion that form follows function. In other words, the house is not designed for the people who are driving thirty-five miles per hour down the street, but for those who spend so much of their time at the end of that driveway. So the size of the house should be determined by the needs of the occupants, and by the extended need that we all have to conserve energy and materials. These are two challenges of equal scope. One is physical, the other philosophical. As you write in the measurements that describe the dimensions of the house, you will have stated your opinion on both matters. My personal feeling is that if we are going to speak also to the quality of life, then energy efficiency has got to mean more than just small. Space for privacy is a require-

Skylights can provide light and ventilation. *Courtesy of Tafi Brown*

ment for a balanced and dignified life. At the same time, wasted space—that which is seldom or never used—should be eliminated. Some of the first candidates for removal might be these:

FULL BASEMENTS Your Engineered House, by Rex Roberts, is a good source for some wise and nasty comments about basements. They are expensive, dark, damp, and are generally only used as a very large utility room. Unless it receives enough light to serve a primary function, the basement area could be an early candidate for the wrath of the eraser.

FORMAL DINING ROOM Many homes have an eating area near or as part of their kitchen and then another room, also for eating, reserved for "special" occasions. This formal dining room can be easily eliminated

174

A gambrel house frame. *Courtesy of Tom Goldschmid*

without compromise. A single dining area, only separated from the kitchen by the massive timbers, can be comfortable enough to be informal, and dignified enough to be formal when the occasion arises. For daily use, a dining room should be as close as possible to the food and the tools of the kitchen. For formal dinners, the timbers can give a feeling of separation and provide a setting suitable for the finest china and the most elegant candelabra.

HALLWAYS Bad traffic patterns and partitions create the need for large areas to move traffic from one room to another. It's not unusual to see two hundred to two hundred fifty square feet consumed by halls (or enough square footage for two bedrooms). Reduced partitioning and the central utility hall, common to timber-framed houses, help to reduce this waste.

ATTICS The only apparent function for this part of the house is to store things that are no longer used. This area could be better utilized as a studio, office, playroom, or guest room. Better yet, the roofline might be dropped to accommodate the rooms of the second floor between the rafters. Skylights or "roof windows" are sophisticated enough today to provide light and ventilation effi-

ciently. What is the point of saving heaps of useless relics and old clothes whose best service is providing nesting areas for squirrels and whose worst is providing the material for your most combustible firetrap? Have a good yard sale instead, and spend the money earned for the skylights that will make this area interesting and livable.

SELDOM-USED SECONDARY LIVING AREAS Analyze your needs carefully to see if such spaces as family rooms, TV rooms, and special utility rooms might be incorporated into one of the primary areas. You might easily rationalize that thirty-five to forty dollars per square foot is too much to pay for the luxury of these rooms. Scaling down the size of the house by eliminating rarely used areas is consistent with the integrity of the fine workmanship common to timber frames. The labor effort of moving, jointing, and fitting the timbers, as well as the beauty of the wood itself, makes wasted space more than just a poor design feature. There is an element here that is very alive, very human, and it doesn't want to get lost in the dead spaces of the house.

If you have tried to get your building to respond to the conditions on the site, and if

Left: Saltbox with framed overhang. *Courtesy of Tafi Brown*

Below: Traditional cape. *Courtesy of David Bryant*

you have worked to conserve materials and space, then the shape of the building will automatically tend to be simple, natural, and pleasing. Most likely, it will also be a shape that is easily framed with timbers. Steeply pitched roofs are the best for solar collection, ideal for gaining living space under the slope of the roof, and are the traditional favorite in timber construction. Simple shapes of houses, like the simple shapes of timbers, complement practical timber joinery. It is also this functional kind of architecture that encloses a good deal of living space with the best conservation of time and materials. This is not to suggest that working with timbers presents extreme geometric limitations. It doesn't. The round Shaker barn and the vaulted ceilings often seen in European churches demonstrate ample limberness of form. But there isn't a great need for this kind of extravagance. My feeling is that we have just begun to explore the design possibilities existing within the simple lines and shapes that have given shelter to both peasants and kings for many centuries.

Basic architectural shapes also have the attributes of a chameleon. A change of the skin can completely alter the look and the feel of the building. Depending on the trim, the siding, and the windows, a house of exactly the same shape can appear to be a colonial reproduction or a contemporary.

Here's a traditional cape. . . .

Now, let's change the windows and the door. . . .

This time, we'll add a little more flair to the windows, change the trim and the siding, and add some solar panels. . . .

176

If this were a timber frame (and if you had a lot of money), you could have made those changes without tampering at all with the structure of the building.

When you have settled upon a building style and shape that fills your requirements and seems comfortable on the site, then you will need to draw a bent plan suitable for the house. If the house includes jogs or ells, more than one bent pattern may be needed. By working closely with the joinery layouts detailed in Chapter Three and the engineering principles outlined in Chapter Six, you will be able to put together a bent plan that is structurally sound. Here, and with the design of the rest of the frame, my best advice is to be conservative. Avoid the temptations of eliminating bracing, compromising joinery, or reducing the size of the timbers. Many buildings meet their end before they have a chance to escape from the drafting table.

The bent is the keystone of timber-frame construction. It is critical to the shape and to the strength of the building, and will now be a major factor in the design of the floor plan. The arrangement of the bents has the effect of dividing the house into separate parts, or "bays." In order to achieve a simple and direct definition of interior spaces, it is best to align the rooms so that their perimeters are outlined by major timbers. When the partitions are built, they will simply fill in the space between timbers and act only as nonsupporting, insulating curtains. Both the timbers in the bent and the beams that connect bents—such as summer beams, joists, and girts—can be used to define the rooms in this manner.

Although the bay arrangement presents design restrictions, it is balanced by constructive advantages. The rooms must compensate for the structure, but the structure is thus given the opportunity to serve double-duty: to support the room and also to embellish it. This restriction isn't severe because the distance between the bents and the location of summer beams and joists all can be adjusted somewhat to complement the room layout. But the overall design of spaces in the house is still partially limited by the bold lines of division caused by the bents. They may well seem like obstructions to the imagination. Obstructions, though, can also define the path. Where there are no paths, there are pioneers climbing over rocks and hills only to discover that the trail is through

It is best to align the rooms so that their perimeter is outlined by major timbers. Here Mary Gerakaris relaxes in her living room. *Photo by Richard Starr*

the valley. There is excitement and adventure enough in trying to put together a floor plan that is simple, practical, and economical. If an occasional bump against a bent steers you into this course, its effect will have been beneficial.

Your personal decision about the shape, proportion, and interior design of the house will no doubt be a battle waged between the ideal physical design requirements and gut-level reactions, such as: "It's too pointy" or, "Looks like a chicken coop" or even, "That window arrangement looks like a distorted face." Since house design is personal and emotional, you will emerge from the conflict bloodied by compromise, but happier and wiser for having marched into the fracas on your own behalf.

Your pencil now draws lines that are steady and resolute; it is pushed by the hand that has felt the direction of the wind, and guided by the eye that has followed closely the path of the sun. You have been forced to take a look at yourself—every line that is drawn is part of a revealing self-portrait. Decisions have been made about how you like to eat, sleep, socialize, and bathe; about areas of relaxation and areas for work; about how or whether you will find solitude and about how or whether you will house guests. And when you have come this far, you will have begun to realize—perhaps for the first time—that shelter is much more than roofs and walls; it also describes the spirit of what we are and houses our hopes, dreams, and fears.

Contemporary design to a traditional shape.

The "feel" of a house is a personal design consideration. This house was designed by its owner, architect Bill D'Antonio. *Photo by Robert Gere*

PLANS: AN EXAMPLE

THIS HOUSE WAS DESIGNED BY ROBERT AND BARBARA CHARTIER OF ALSTEAD, N.H., TO SUIT THEIR NEEDS. THIS EXAMPLE DEMONSTRATES WORKING DRAWINGS FOR THE FRAME AND ILLUSTRATES HOW CLOSELY RELATED THE FRAME IS TO THE FLOOR PLAN.

1 ↗ RAISING THE 3RD BENT.

2 ↙ PLACING CONNECTING GIRT.

3 ↙ ASSEMBLING RAFTER TRUSS.

CONT....

179

EAST ELEVATION

SOUTH ELEVATION

SCALE

0   4 ft.

CONT....

PLANS: AN EXAMPLE....CONT.

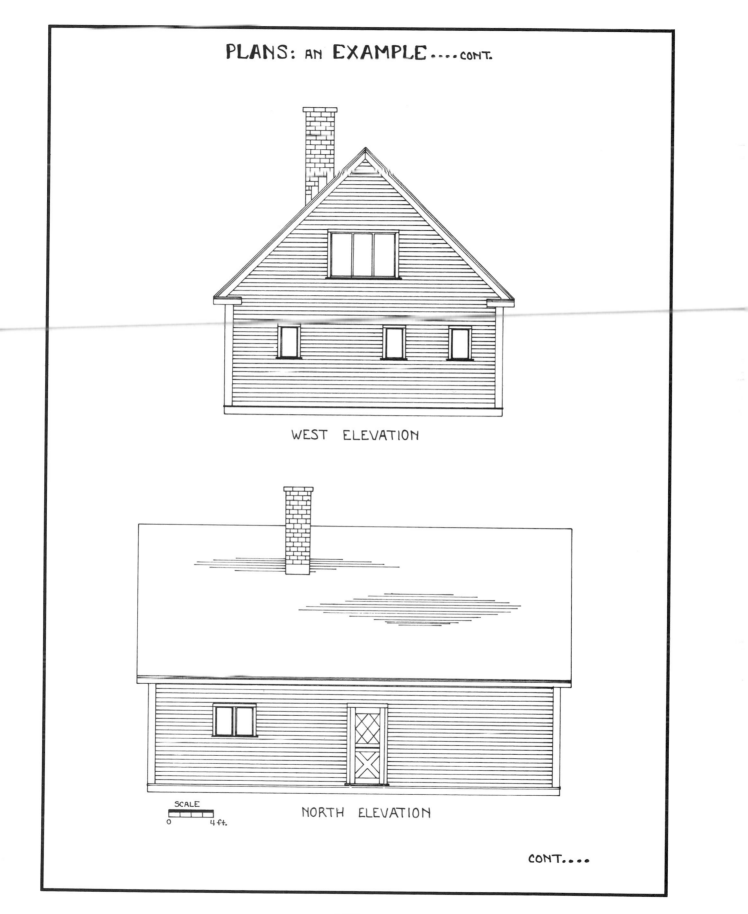

WEST ELEVATION

NORTH ELEVATION

SCALE
0   4 ft.

CONT....

PLANS: AN EXAMPLE....CONT.

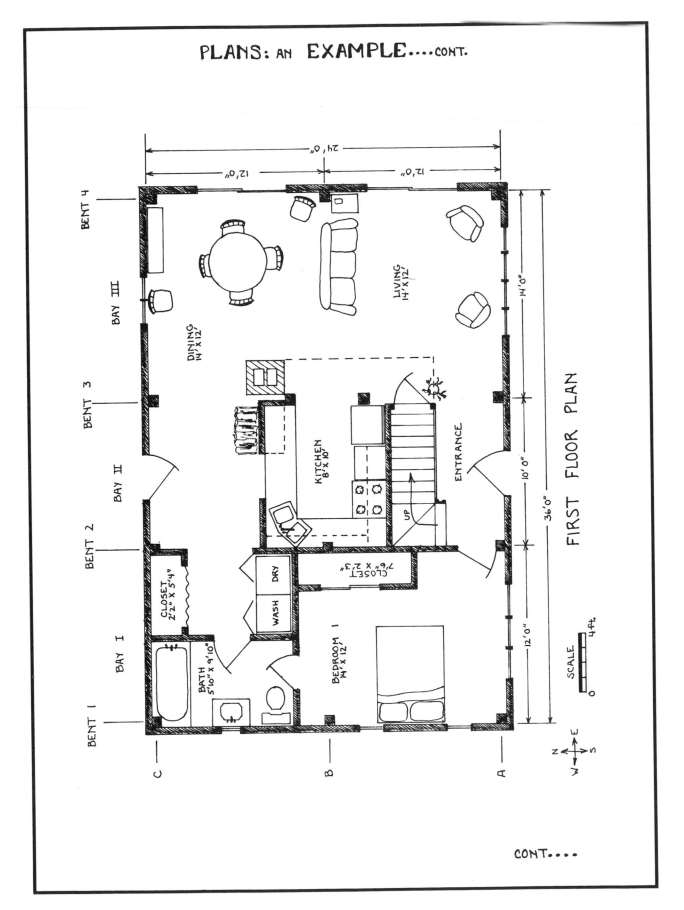

FIRST FLOOR PLAN

CONT....

182

PLANS: AN EXAMPLE....CONT.

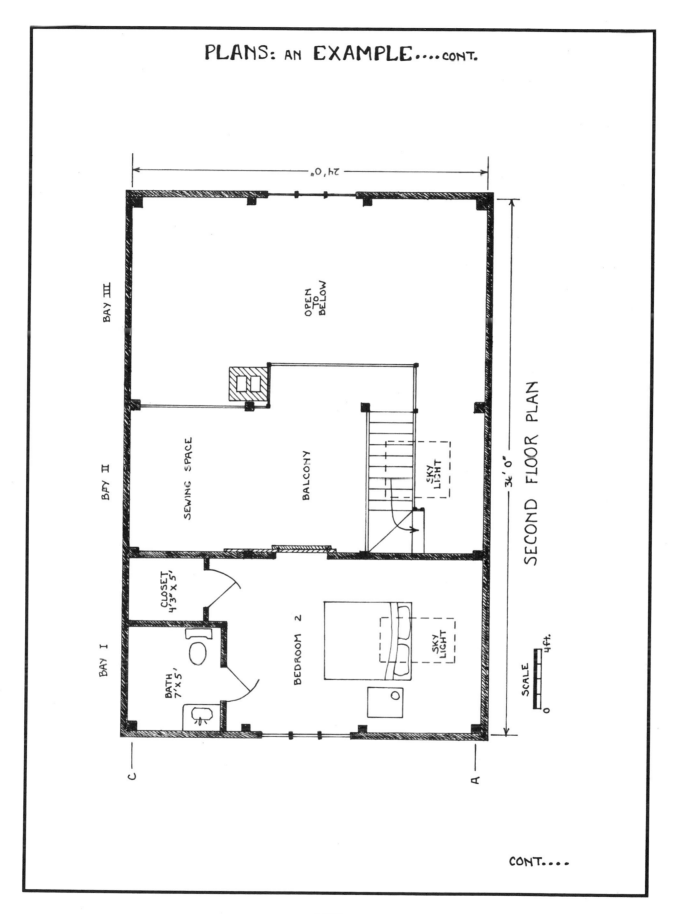

SECOND FLOOR PLAN

CONT....

183

PLANS: AN EXAMPLE....CONT.

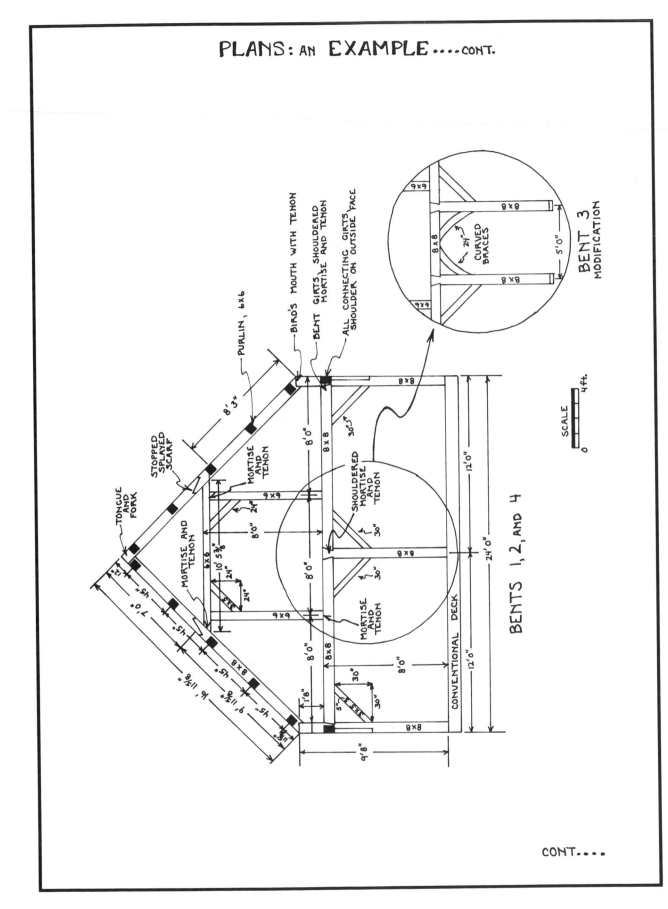

BENT 3
MODIFICATION

CURVED BRACES

9×9

8×8

24"

8×8

5'0"

SCALE

0   4 ft.

PURLIN, 6×6

BIRD'S MOUTH WITH TENON

BENT GIRTS SHOULDERED MORTISE AND TENON

ALL CONNECTING GIRTS SHOULDER ON OUTSIDE FACE

STOPPED SPLAYED SCARF

TONGUE AND FORK

MORTISE AND TENON

MORTISE AND TENON

SHOULDERED MORTISE AND TENON

MORTISE AND TENON

8×8

8'0"

9×9

6×6

8'0"

10' 5⅞"

24"

24"

8'0"

8×8

8'0"

9×9

8'0"

8×8

8'0"

30"

30"

30"

30"

1'8"

5"

BENTS 1, 2, AND 4

8×8

8×8

8×8

8×8

CONVENTIONAL DECK

12'0"

24'0"

12'0"

8'0"

8'0"

9'8"

8'3"

CONT....

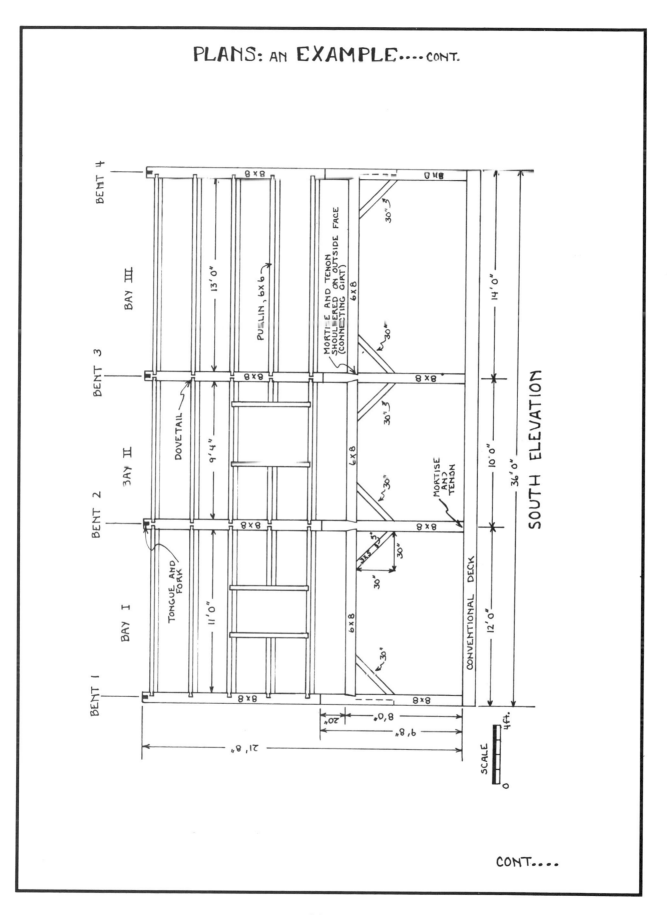

SOUTH ELEVATION

CONT....

185

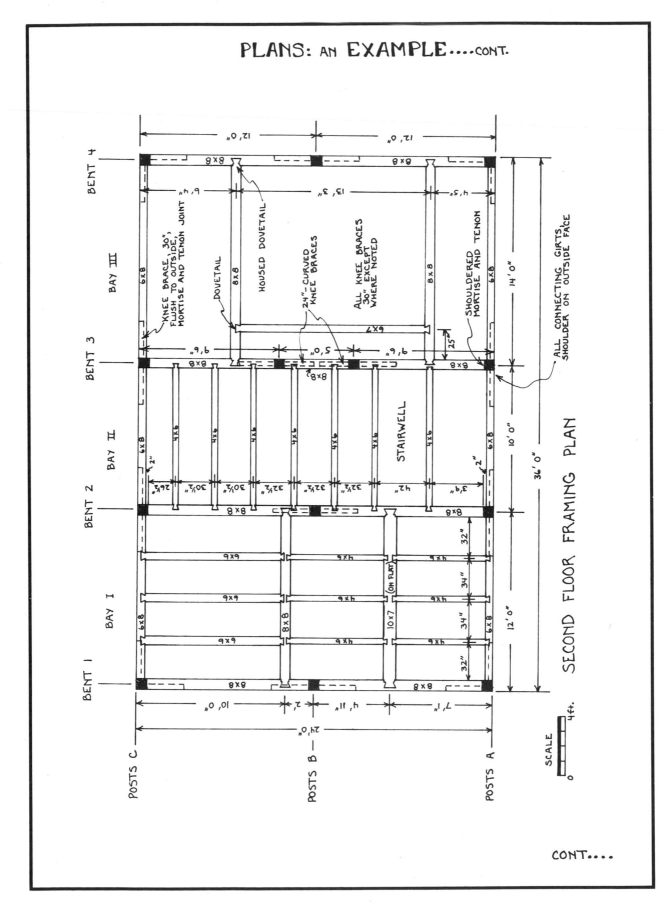

SECOND FLOOR FRAMING PLAN

CONT....

186

PLANS: AN EXAMPLE.... CONT.

4 →
LIVING-DINING
AREA.

← 5
LOOKING INTO
KITCHEN.

6 →
VIEW FROM
LOFT.

FOUNDATIONS

A simple rule for the foundation is that it should be as strong and as permanent as the structure it supports. When the building is framed with timbers, this represents a significant challenge. One of the major problems with early timber-framed buildings is that they were often placed on inadequate foundations. This was especially true during the early years of this country because the colonists were unprepared for the extreme weather changes and the deep penetration of frost. Despite this, most timber buildings demonstrated a resilience, a double-jointed kind of flexibility, which allowed them to bend and shift like a rubber raft in the changing tides. But the promise that we hold with today's improved foundation systems is that we can bring even longer life to this venerable building method.

For cold climates, a continuous perimeter foundation is best. It gives the support that is needed, helps to keep the house tight, and has a solid surface upon which insulation can be applied. Those who argue that the floor can be adequately insulated over an open foundation will have to talk fast; I write this with my feet well above a very cold floor that is insulated both above and below.

PERIMETER WALL The wall should sit on a footing that was poured down to well below frost line. I recommend a three-thousand-pound mix for the concrete and insist on reinforcing bar (also known as "re-bar"). When placed at the top and bottom of the wall, these bars tremendously improve its

strength by creating a rib effect that turns the wall into a large I beam. If you want a full basement, this wall can, of course, be eight feet tall.

SLAB AND WALL By pouring the slab simultaneously with the perimeter wall (frost wall), the wall will achieve additional strength from the surface area of the floor. Properly insulated, the slab can be the floor of the house and provide a built-in thermal mass for passive solar heat storage. The disadvantage is that there is no space below the house for pipes and wires.

In warm climates, other options are open. This does not mean that the foundation can be less strong, only that it can be adjusted to the conditions. Try to use three thousand pounds of concrete mix and plenty of reinforcing.

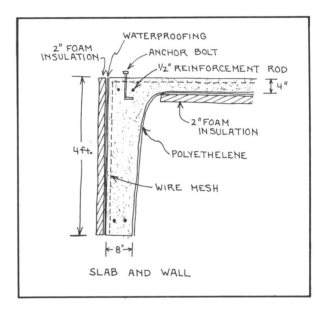

SLAB AND WALL

PERIMETER WALL The wall need not penetrate as deeply in warm climates, although a footing with a keyway is still a good idea. If it is going to be raised above the ground more than four feet, put another three to four feet below the surface for more strength.

FLOATING SLAB Shaped like an upside-down plate, this system is almost the same as the slab and wall, with much less depth around the edges. It derives much of its strength from the wire mesh and re-bar. Be sure they are included.

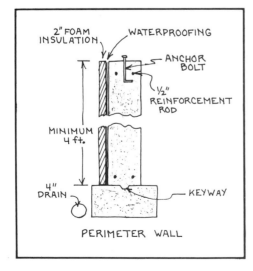

PERIMETER WALL

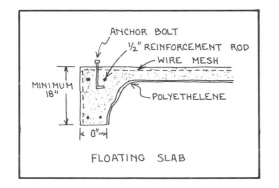

ANCHOR BOLT
½" REINFORCEMENT ROD
WIRE MESH
POLYETHELENE
MINIMUM 18"
0"
FLOATING SLAB

SONO-TUBES For an open foundation, this is the best method. Creosoted poles are popular, but they have a life of only eighty to one hundred years. Your timber frame would be just a babe at this age. Remember that the sono-tube, a cylinder of concrete, has very little resistance to horizontal forces, so put in several one-half inch re-bars to add cohesion. Use ten- to twelve-inch tubes and don't raise them more than three feet off the ground.

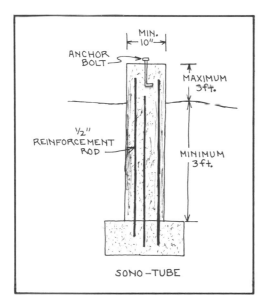

MIN. 10"
ANCHOR BOLT
MAXIMUM 3 ft.
½" REINFORCEMENT ROD
MINIMUM 3 ft.
SONO-TUBE

SHEATHING AND INSULATION

Timber frames have a long history of being able to respond to the conditions of the environment and the technology of the era. To make their buildings weather-tight, the Scandinavians often filled between the framing members with vertical staves or horizontal logs. In English frames, clay or brick was used to fill the spaces. American colonists studded between the timbers and then covered the whole building with clapboards.

All of these methods were more or less appropriate; they solved a particular problem with available materials. But none were ideal. It's hard to understand why some of these frames haven't rotted to the core because of exposure to the weather. And we can only speculate about the chilly days and nights spent trying to find refuge from the cold wind that must have wiggled through the walls. The frame was their *coup de maître*, a twenty-first-century concept (modern steel and concrete structures are born of the same concept), but the weather-protection systems would clearly mark the limitations of those cultures.

We are in no less of a predicament today. We fling the sleek products of our technology at the stars and plunge its mighty tools deep into the earth. But between heaven and earth, working and living in our buildings, we suffer for the lack of scientific solutions, mired in construction practices that march to the beat of production speed and fall out when the demand is for performance. To maintain comfort standards we consider up to date, we burn our precious fuels with the ferocity of Neanderthals. The extent to which we have allowed our buildings to become earth's parasitic leeches is an international shame.

Part of the reason we have allowed this waste to continue is that we tend to view economy through a tunnel and see only dollars and cents. A ravenously hungry world consumes energy at an alarming rate because it is "economical" to do so. Many people argue that too much insulation and solar energy are not worth the price; in the long run, we are told, the fuel is cheaper. This argument is doubly wrong. First, the "long run" usually refers to the length of the mortgage —up to twenty-five years—which reads as nothing at all on the tape measure of time. Second, the real cost of the fuel is much more than the seventy-five cents to one dollar per gallon that we pay for it; when it makes its last course through the copper lines and ignites in the furnace, it is gone—forever. Therefore, it shouldn't matter whether the price of the fuel is one cent or ten dollars per gallon. If we truly understood the real cost of using irreplaceable fuels, we would find ways to conserve energy because of the terrible waste, not because the price went up another ten cents.

Maximum energy conservation in our

buildings should be an immediate priority. It will mean bringing the best that the modern age has to offer to the simple concept of preventing heat from passing through the walls of buildings. Solar energy holds no hope if the heat gained is quickly lost through poorly insulated walls. Even in the hottest climates, air conditioning could be reduced to simple air circulation if the roof and walls effectively rejected the blazing heat. As a matter of fact, all the alternative heating and cooling concepts have in common the need for tighter, better insulated buildings. Poorly insulated buildings are the weakest connection in a train of progress that could be moving very fast.

To understand what heat loss is like in the average house today, it will be helpful to take a look at the furnace. It is said that a forced-air furnace should be rated to generate forty to fifty BTUs per hour, per square foot of living space, or a one-hundred-thousand-BTU-capacity furnace for a two-thousand-square-foot building. This same unit is designed with a blower large enough to turn over the total volume of air in the house three to four times per hour. Even with this capacity, these furnaces are often underrated and must work constantly to keep the house warm. This suggests that buildings often lose enough heat to keep the entire space warm at the rate of several times per hour!

The reason this is happening has to do with the way buildings are commonly framed and the material that is commonly used for insulation. The conventional stud-frame wall presents an absurd barrier to good energy conservation: there is a break every sixteen inches in the insulation. The result is frequent areas of rapid heat loss and inevitable air leaks. If the heat can't sneak through the insulation itself, it need only find one of the framing members for easy passage. To compensate for this, we must surely hope that the insulation is superb.

Remembering that the best insulators trap pockets of dead air, consider this: face-mask filters, cigarette filters, and filters for furnaces all have one thing in common—fiberglass. Why? Because air passes through it so easily—like a monkey through the jungle. Now, what the filter people sell for air movement, the insulation people sell for trapping air. If this seems confusing, blow through a couple of inches of fiberglass and you'll see why furnaces aren't choked, people breathe

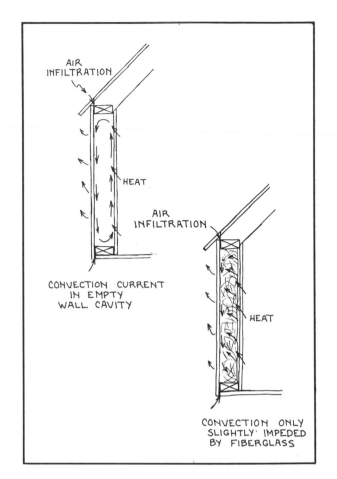

quite nicely through face masks, and cigarettes still cause cancer. (As a builder who has applied fiberglass to a number of buildings, the implications here cause me embarrassment and anger.) Each of the cavities between the stud-framing members, insulated with fiberglass, is like a little chimney. Wood, nails, and men don't make for completely airtight boxes, so there is first of all inevitable air infiltration. Add to this the turbulence caused by convection and the ease of air movement through fiberglass, and it should be no surprise that heat is leaving our houses on a dead run.

Using a timber frame, we can eliminate the problems common to stud construction. Because there is no need to compensate for a frame that is already rigid, and because we are not inclined to hide timbers that beg to be seen, *we* impose the limitations to good insulation, not the structure. Our attempts to develop twentieth-century solutions for enclosing a timber frame have proven that it is still responsive to the needs of the era. There have been some mistakes, but they are short-lived, because the most efficient and practi-

Sheetrock or plaster can be an excellent contrast with the timbers.
Photo by Richard Starr

cal procedures for putting finished walls and insulation onto a timber frame also happen to be the most economical and the best for energy conservation. If you follow a couple of rules and use good materials, the building will be uncommonly well insulated with relatively little effort.

The first rule is that the interior finish wall, insulation, and exterior wall all should be applied to the outside of the frame. Any other method turns the frame into an albatross. For example, if the interior finish is on the inside, it must be scribed and fitted to the timbers. Later the timbers will shrink and spoil the effort. On the other hand, nailed to the outside, it goes up quickly and shrinkage won't affect the fit. If the insulation were between the timbers instead of over them, it would be interrupted by the large framing members, tight seals would be impossible, and condensation would occur inside the building. The reason we would think to stud and insulate between the posts is probably rooted in tradition, but it represents a lot of extra work for less satisfactory results.

I was saddened to read in a recent book on home building that one of the authors had built a timber frame and then found himself studding between the posts in order to apply sheathing. His conclusion was that timber framing makes no sense. He had it backward. It was what he did to the frame that lacked wisdom.

The second rule for insulating timber frames is to use rigid foam panels. There are many different types, but in general they are

191

BUILT-UP WALL

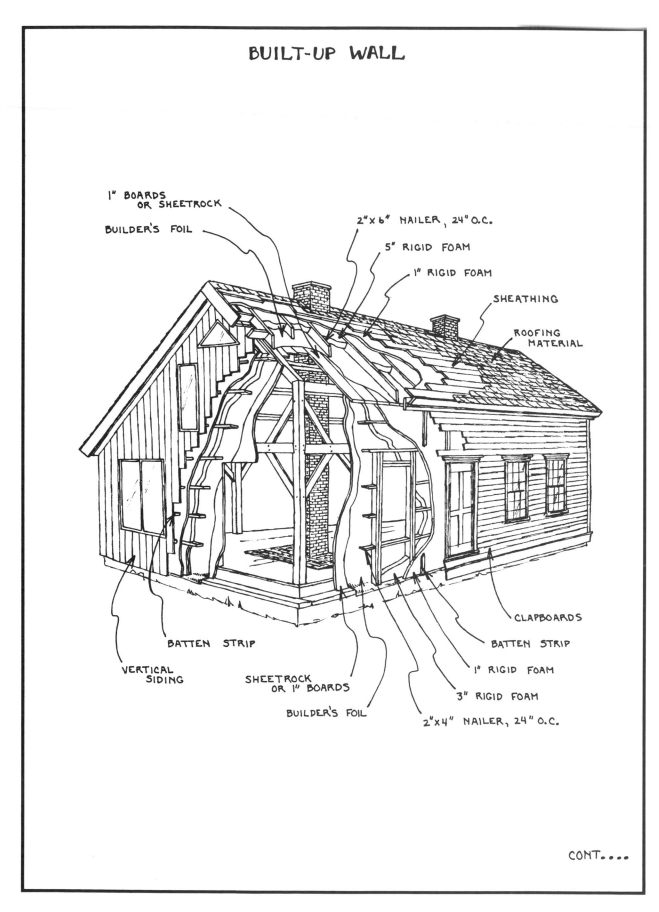

1" BOARDS OR SHEETROCK

BUILDER'S FOIL

2" x 6" NAILER, 24" O.C.

5" RIGID FOAM

1" RIGID FOAM

SHEATHING

ROOFING MATERIAL

CLAPBOARDS

BATTEN STRIP

1" RIGID FOAM

3" RIGID FOAM

2" x 4" NAILER, 24" O.C.

BUILDER'S FOIL

SHEETROCK OR 1" BOARDS

VERTICAL SIDING

BATTEN STRIP

CONT. . . . .

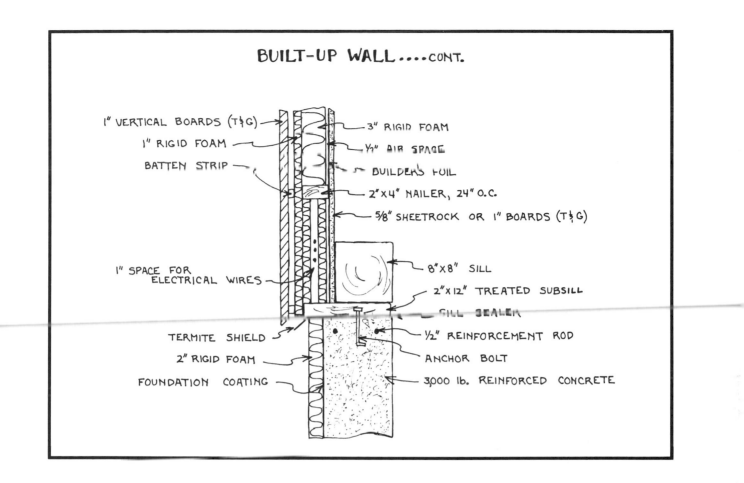

1" VERTICAL BOARDS (T&G)

1" RIGID FOAM

BATTEN STRIP

1" SPACE FOR ELECTRICAL WIRES

TERMITE SHIELD

2" RIGID FOAM

FOUNDATION COATING

3" RIGID FOAM

½" AIR SPACE

BUILDER'S FOIL

2"x4" NAILER, 24" O.C.

⅝" SHEETROCK OR 1" BOARDS (T&G)

8"x8" SILL

2"x12" TREATED SUBSILL

SILL SEALER

½" REINFORCEMENT ROD

ANCHOR BOLT

3,000 lb. REINFORCED CONCRETE

the state of the art. Since the air is trapped in a honeycomb of locked cells, its heat-resistant value will not be dependent on air movement, as it is with fiberglass. Except for beadboard, foam panels are also highly resistant to moisture penetration. The most frequent argument against the use of rigid plastic foams is that they are fire hazards with potentially dangerous fumes. Besides the fact that recent developments have reduced the flammability, I think they are relatively safe. Sealed between layers of sheathing and isolated from the movement of air, they wouldn't support a fire nearly as well as the drafty chimneys that are framed by studs. And in a fire, the toxic fumes that would be released from your nylon jacket, foam pillow, and polyester suit pose a more immediate danger than the insulation in the wall cavity on the outside of the building.

The most obvious way to apply the insulating skin to the building is piece by piece on the site. The primary advantage of this method is that it is less expensive, especially if you are building for yourself. Its major problem is the need for wood as a stiffener and a nailer. The additional wood seems like a major compromise, but the method is quick and the result displays some good insulating qualities. To decrease the heat conduction at the nailers, put an additional inch of foam over the whole network. Horizontal nailers are the easiest to install and are the best for fire safety, although you may want to run them vertically if the exterior siding is horizontal.

The choice of interior finish is purely a matter of taste. Many people choose boards for low maintenance and the warmth of wood. Sheetrock is also easily installed and provides an excellent background to the timber.

A less obvious and much better way to enclose the frame is to apply a composite skin that has both inner and outer sheathing skins, and contains totally uninterrupted,

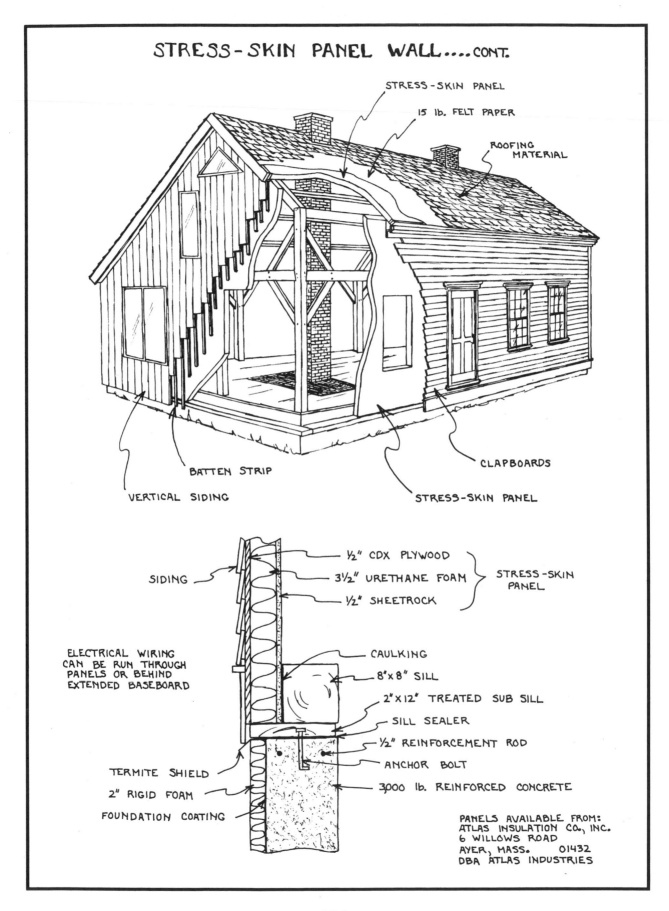

STRESS-SKIN PANEL WALL....CONT.

STRESS-SKIN PANEL

15 lb. FELT PAPER

ROOFING MATERIAL

BATTEN STRIP

VERTICAL SIDING

CLAPBOARDS

STRESS-SKIN PANEL

SIDING

½" CDX PLYWOOD

3½" URETHANE FOAM   STRESS-SKIN PANEL

½" SHEETROCK

ELECTRICAL WIRING CAN BE RUN THROUGH PANELS OR BEHIND EXTENDED BASEBOARD

CAULKING

8"x 8" SILL

2"x 12" TREATED SUB SILL

SILL SEALER

½" REINFORCEMENT ROD

ANCHOR BOLT

3000 lb. REINFORCED CONCRETE

TERMITE SHIELD

2" RIGID FOAM

FOUNDATION COATING

PANELS AVAILABLE FROM:
ATLAS INSULATION CO., INC.
6 WILLOWS ROAD
AYER, MASS.   01432
DBA ATLAS INDUSTRIES

194

Courtesy of Tafi Brown

high-value insulation. The stress-skin panel presents attributes of heat resistance never before seen in home construction and is a perfect match to timber frames. Those industries that understand the potential of the concept of enclosing something in an uninterrupted blanket of insulation make thermos bottles that will keep coffee hot for twelve hours, walk-in coolers that don't guzzle energy, and shipping crates to get California's iceberg lettuce, still fresh, into Japanese hamburgers. Stress-skin is not an entirely new idea. Fundamentally, the cardboard in boxes and hollow-core doors is born of this concept. Insulating stress-skins are used somewhat in commercial construction, although the application is limited because it must be attached to a rigid structure. Framing with timbers presents an opportunity for the application and development of this product in home construction.

To insulate as well as we can and to make houses as tight as we can present new challenges to the building industry. Houses will no longer naturally ventilate, because of our inability to get them tight. We can lock them up like thermos bottles if we like. To bring new air into the house, we'll have to design ventilation systems into the plans. With heat loss cut to the bones, we'll have to design natural and mechanical recirculation to keep the temperature even and the air fresh. In this kind of environment, the heat from appliances, lights, and even body heat will contribute significant proportions to the small heating requirements. In houses built this way, energy from the sun, wind, or water could easily replace fuel-fired power sources.

Energy conservation is the hope of the future. In conscience, we must mark the end of the era of substandard housing that is cheap to build but expensive and wasteful to maintain. In conscience, we should begin a time when houses contain energy-autonomous environments that consume no fossil fuels and are built to last centuries.

195

APPENDIX I
BEAM—DESIGN FORMULAS (FOR RECTANGULAR BEAMS)

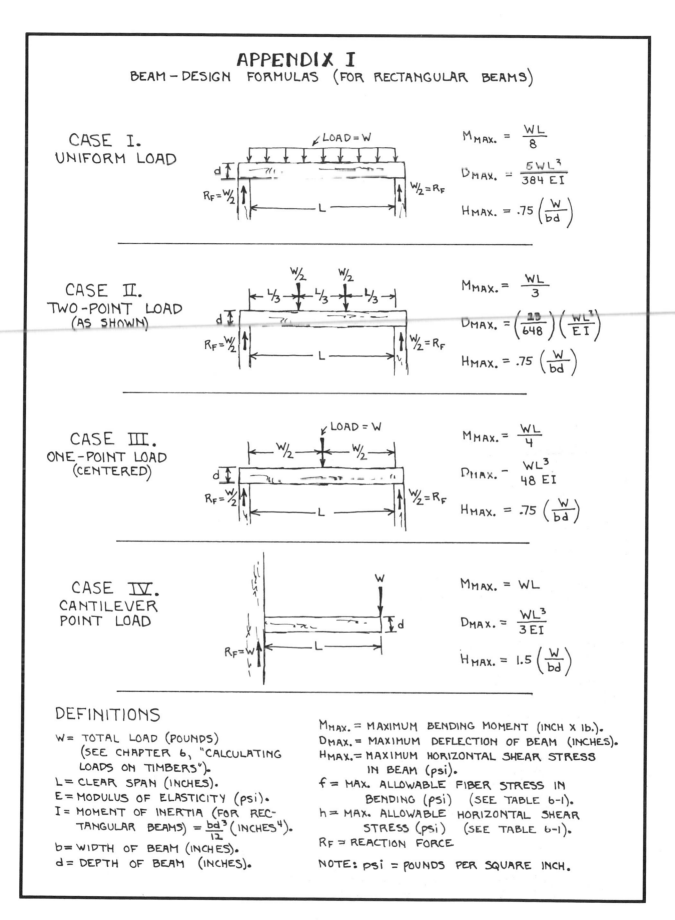

CASE I.
UNIFORM LOAD

$M_{MAX.} = \dfrac{WL}{8}$

$D_{MAX.} = \dfrac{5WL^3}{384\,EI}$

$H_{MAX.} = .75\left(\dfrac{W}{bd}\right)$

CASE II.
TWO-POINT LOAD
(AS SHOWN)

$M_{MAX.} = \dfrac{WL}{3}$

$D_{MAX.} = \left(\dfrac{23}{648}\right)\left(\dfrac{WL^3}{EI}\right)$

$H_{MAX.} = .75\left(\dfrac{W}{bd}\right)$

CASE III.
ONE-POINT LOAD
(CENTERED)

$M_{MAX.} = \dfrac{WL}{4}$

$D_{MAX.} = \dfrac{WL^3}{48\,EI}$

$H_{MAX.} = .75\left(\dfrac{W}{bd}\right)$

CASE IV.
CANTILEVER
POINT LOAD

$M_{MAX.} = WL$

$D_{MAX.} = \dfrac{WL^3}{3\,EI}$

$H_{MAX.} = 1.5\left(\dfrac{W}{bd}\right)$

DEFINITIONS

W = TOTAL LOAD (POUNDS)
(SEE CHAPTER 6, "CALCULATING LOADS ON TIMBERS").
L = CLEAR SPAN (INCHES).
E = MODULUS OF ELASTICITY (psi).
I = MOMENT OF INERTIA (FOR RECTANGULAR BEAMS) = $\dfrac{bd^3}{12}$ (INCHES^4).
b = WIDTH OF BEAM (INCHES).
d = DEPTH OF BEAM (INCHES).

$M_{MAX.}$ = MAXIMUM BENDING MOMENT (INCH X lb.).
$D_{MAX.}$ = MAXIMUM DEFLECTION OF BEAM (INCHES).
$H_{MAX.}$ = MAXIMUM HORIZONTAL SHEAR STRESS IN BEAM (psi).
f = MAX. ALLOWABLE FIBER STRESS IN BENDING (psi) (SEE TABLE 6-1).
h = MAX. ALLOWABLE HORIZONTAL SHEAR STRESS (psi) (SEE TABLE 6-1).
R_F = REACTION FORCE

NOTE: psi = POUNDS PER SQUARE INCH.

APPENDIX II
DESIGNING BEAMS BY USING FORMULAS
(FOR RECTANGULAR BEAMS)

PROCEDURE (FOR USING FORMULAS)

STEP 1 – PICK TYPE OF WOOD, TABLE 6-1.
$f =$ ___ psi
$E =$ ___ psi
$h =$ ___ psi

STEP 2 – DETERMINE TOTAL LOAD, W, AND TYPE OF LOAD DISTRIBUTION (CASE I, II, III, OR IV, APPENDIX I).

$W =$ ___ lb.

STEP 3 – DEFINE CLEAR SPAN L.

$L =$ ___ INCHES

STEP 4 – CALCULATE BENDING MOMENT, $M_{MAX.}$, FROM APPENDIX I.

$M_{MAX.} =$ ___ INCH POUNDS

STEP 5 – $\left(\dfrac{bd^2f}{6}\right) = M_{MAX.}$ FOR RECTANGULAR BEAMS. SUBSTITUTE, IN THE EQUATION BELOW, THE VALUE f, THE VALUE $M_{MAX.}$ FROM STEP 4, AND THE ASSUMED DEPTH, d, AND SOLVE FOR WIDTH, b.

$$b = \frac{6 M_{MAX.}}{d^2 f}$$

RECALCULATE IF NECESSARY TO GIVE BEAM APPROXIMATELY SQUARE SHAPE.

STEP 6 – CALCULATE $D_{MAX.}$ FROM APPENDIX I. FIRST CALCULATE MOMENT OF INERTIA, I, IN TABLE. THEN SUBSTITUTE VALUE TO CALCULATE $D_{MAX.}$

STEP 7 – CALCULATE $\dfrac{D_{MAX.}}{L}$. THIS MUST BE LESS THAN $1/360$ FOR FLOORS AND LESS THAN $1/240$ FOR ROOFS. IF NOT, INCREASE WIDTH, b, OR DEPTH, d, OF BEAM AND RECALCULATE $D_{MAX.}$

STEP 8 – CHECK SHEAR, $H_{MAX.}$, IN APPENDIX I. IS $H_{MAX.}$ LESS THAN ALLOWABLE SHEAR, h? IF YES, BEAM IS OK. OTHERWISE, INCREASE BEAM WIDTH OR DEPTH AND RECHECK SHEAR.

CONT....

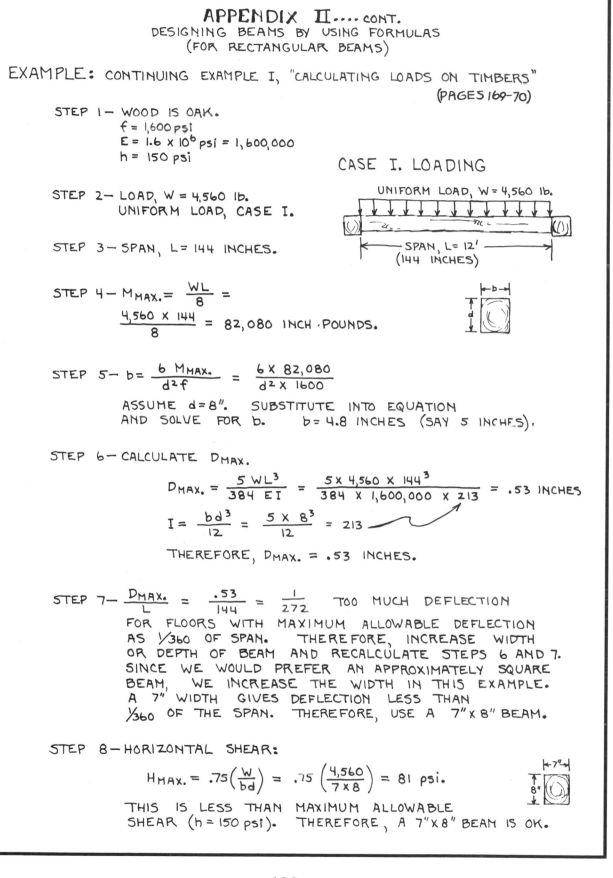

APPENDIX II.... CONT.
DESIGNING BEAMS BY USING FORMULAS
(FOR RECTANGULAR BEAMS)

EXAMPLE: CONTINUING EXAMPLE I, "CALCULATING LOADS ON TIMBERS"
(PAGES 169-70)

STEP 1 — WOOD IS OAK.
$f = 1,600$ psi
$E = 1.6 \times 10^6$ psi $= 1,600,000$
$h = 150$ psi

STEP 2 — LOAD, $W = 4,560$ lb.
UNIFORM LOAD, CASE I.

CASE I. LOADING

UNIFORM LOAD, $W = 4,560$ lb.

SPAN, $L = 12'$
(144 INCHES)

STEP 3 — SPAN, $L = 144$ INCHES.

STEP 4 — $M_{MAX.} = \dfrac{WL}{8} =$
$\dfrac{4,560 \times 144}{8} = 82,080$ INCH·POUNDS.

STEP 5 — $b = \dfrac{6 \, M_{MAX.}}{d^2 f} = \dfrac{6 \times 82,080}{d^2 \times 1600}$

ASSUME $d = 8''$. SUBSTITUTE INTO EQUATION
AND SOLVE FOR b. $b = 4.8$ INCHES (SAY 5 INCHES).

STEP 6 — CALCULATE $D_{MAX.}$

$$D_{MAX.} = \frac{5 \, WL^3}{384 \, EI} = \frac{5 \times 4,560 \times 144^3}{384 \times 1,600,000 \times 213} = .53 \text{ INCHES}$$

$$I = \frac{bd^3}{12} = \frac{5 \times 8^3}{12} = 213$$

THEREFORE, $D_{MAX.} = .53$ INCHES.

STEP 7 — $\dfrac{D_{MAX.}}{L} = \dfrac{.53}{144} = \dfrac{1}{272}$ TOO MUCH DEFLECTION
FOR FLOORS WITH MAXIMUM ALLOWABLE DEFLECTION
AS $\frac{1}{360}$ OF SPAN.   THEREFORE, INCREASE WIDTH
OR DEPTH OF BEAM AND RECALCULATE STEPS 6 AND 7.
SINCE WE WOULD PREFER AN APPROXIMATELY SQUARE
BEAM, WE INCREASE THE WIDTH IN THIS EXAMPLE.
A 7" WIDTH GIVES DEFLECTION LESS THAN
$\frac{1}{360}$ OF THE SPAN.   THEREFORE, USE A 7" x 8" BEAM.

STEP 8 — HORIZONTAL SHEAR:

$$H_{MAX.} = .75\left(\frac{W}{bd}\right) = .75\left(\frac{4,560}{7 \times 8}\right) = 81 \text{ psi.}$$

THIS IS LESS THAN MAXIMUM ALLOWABLE
SHEAR ($h = 150$ psi).   THEREFORE, A 7" x 8" BEAM IS OK.

TABLE III-1

BEAM DESIGN LOADS
(POUNDS PER INCH OF BEAM WIDTH)

OAK CASE I, UNIFORM LOAD

Design Values: Table 6-1
Allowable Deflection:
  Floor: 1/360
  Roof: 1/240

CASE I
UNIFORM LOAD

SPAN OF TIMBER (L) (feet)		DEPTH OF TIMBER (d)* (inches)							
		6	7	8	9	10	12	14	16
6	Floor	1066	1399	1500	1799	1999	2399	2799	3199
	Roof	1066	1399	1599	1799	1999	2399	2799	3199
7	Floor	870	1244	1599	1799	1999	2399	2799	3199
	Roof	914	1244	1599	1799	1999	2399	2799	3199
8	Floor	666	1058	1422	1799	1999	2399	2799	3199
	Roof	799	1088	1422	1799	1999	2399	2799	3199
9	Floor	526	836	1248	1599	1975	2399	2799	3199
	Roof	711	967	1264	1599	1975	2399	2799	3199
10	Floor	426	677	1011	1439	1777	2399	2799	3199
	Roof	639	871	1137	1439	1777	2399	2799	3199
11	Floor	352	559	835	1190	1616	2327	2799	3199
	Roof	528	791	1034	1309	1616	2327	2799	3199
12	Floor	296	470	702	999	1371	2133	2799	3199
	Roof	444	705	948	1199	1481	2133	2799	3199
13	Floor	252	400	598	852	1168	1969	2680	3199
	Roof	378	601	875	1107	1367	1969	2680	3199
14	Floor	217	345	515	734	1007	1741	2488	3199
	Roof	326	518	773	1028	1269	1828	2488	3199
15	Floor	189	301	449	639	877	1517	2322	3034
	Roof	284	451	674	959	1185	1706	2322	3034
16	Floor	166	264	395	562	771	1333	2117	2844
	Roof	249	396	592	843	1111	1599	2177	2844
17	Floor	147	234	349	498	683	1181	1875	2677
	Roof	221	351	524	747	1025	1505	2049	2677
18	Floor	131	209	312	444	609	1053	1672	2497
	Roof	197	313	468	666	914	1422	1935	2528

TABLE III-2

BEAM DESIGN LOADS
(POUNDS PER INCH OF BEAM WIDTH)

OAK CASE II, TWO POINT LOAD

Design Values: Table 6-1
Allowable Deflection:
  Floor: 1/360
  Roof: 1/240

CASE II
TWO POINTS LOAD

SPAN OF TIMBER (L) (feet)		DEPTH OF TIMBER (d)* (inches)							
		6	7	8	9	10	12	14	16
6	Floor	800	1088	1422	1799	1999	2399	2799	3199
	Roof	800	1088	1422	1799	1999	2399	2799	3199
7	Floor	638	933	1219	1542	1904	2399	2799	3199
	Roof	685	933	1219	1542	1904	2399	2799	3199
8	Floor	489	776	1066	1350	1666	2399	2799	3199
	Roof	600	816	1066	1350	1666	2399	2799	3199
9	Floor	386	613	916	1200	1481	2133	2799	3199
	Roof	533	725	948	1200	1481	2133	2799	3199
10	Floor	313	497	742	1056	1333	1920	2613	3199
	Roof	469	653	853	1080	1333	1920	2613	3199
11	Floor	258	410	613	873	1197	1745	2375	3103
	Roof	388	593	775	981	1212	1745	2375	3103
12	Floor	217	345	515	733	1006	1600	2177	2844
	Roof	326	517	711	900	1111	1600	2177	2844
13	Floor	185	294	439	625	857	1476	2010	2625
	Roof	277	441	656	830	1025	1476	2010	2625
14	Floor	159	253	378	539	739	1277	1866	2438
	Roof	239	380	567	771	952	1371	1866	2438
15	Floor	139	220	329	469	644	1113	1742	2275
	Roof	208	331	494	704	888	1280	1742	2275
16	Floor	122	194	289	412	566	978	1553	2133
	Roof	183	291	434	619	833	1200	1633	2133
17	Floor	108	172	256	365	501	866	1376	2007
	Roof	162	258	385	548	752	1129	1537	2007
18	Floor	96	153	229	326	447	772	1227	1832
	Roof	144	230	343	489	670	1066	1451	1896

Actual Size, Not Nominal Size

TABLE III-3

BEAM DESIGN LOADS
(POUNDS PER INCH
OF BEAM WIDTH)

OAK CASE III, ONE POINT LOAD

Design Values: Table 6-1
Allowable Deflection:
Floor: 1/360
Roof: 1/240

SPAN OF TIMBER (L) (feet)		DEPTH OF TIMBER (d)* (inches)							
		6	7	8	9	10	12	14	16
6	Floor	533	725	948	1199	1481	2133	2799	3199
	Roof	533	725	948	1199	1481	2133	2799	3199
7	Floor	457	622	812	1028	1269	1828	2488	3199
	Roof	457	622	812	1028	1269	1828	2488	3199
8	Floor	399	544	711	899	1111	1599	2177	2844
	Roof	399	544	711	899	1111	1599	2177	2844
9	Floor	329	483	632	799	987	1422	1935	2528
	Roof	355	483	632	799	987	1422	1935	2528
10	Floor	266	423	568	719	888	1279	1742	2275
	Roof	319	435	568	719	888	1279	1742	2275
11	Floor	220	349	517	654	808	1163	1583	2068
	Roof	290	395	517	654	808	1163	1583	2068
12	Floor	185	294	438	599	740	1066	1451	1896
	Roof	266	362	474	599	740	1066	1451	1896
13	Floor	157	250	374	532	683	984	1340	1750
	Roof	236	335	437	553	683	984	1340	1750
14	Floor	136	216	322	459	625	914	1244	1625
	Roof	204	311	406	514	634	914	1244	1625
15	Floor	118	188	280	399	548	853	1161	1517
	Roof	177	282	379	479	592	853	1161	1517
16	Floor	104	165	246	351	482	799	1088	1422
	Roof	156	248	355	449	555	799	1088	1422
17	Floor	92	146	218	311	427	738	1024	1338
	Roof	138	219	328	423	522	752	1024	1338
18	Floor	82	130	195	277	381	658	967	1264
	Roof	123	196	292	399	493	711	967	1264

TABLE III-4

BEAM DESIGN LOADS
(POUNDS PER INCH
OF BEAM WIDTH)

DOUGLAS FIR CASE I, CONTINUOUS LOAD

Design Values: Table 6-1
Allowable Deflection:
Floor: 1/360
Roof: 1/240

SPAN OF TIMBER (L) (feet)		6	7	8	9	10	12	14	16
6	Floor	959	1119	1279	1439	1599	1919	2239	2559
	Roof	959	1119	1279	1439	1599	1919	2239	2559
7	Floor	857	1119	1279	1439	1599	1919	2239	2559
	Roof	857	1119	1279	1439	1599	1919	2239	2559
8	Floor	666	1020	1279	1439	1599	1919	2239	2559
	Roof	749	1020	1279	1439	1599	1919	2239	2559
9	Floor	526	836	1185	1439	1599	1919	2239	2559
	Roof	666	907	1185	1439	1599	1919	2239	2559
10	Floor	426	677	1011	1349	1599	1919	2239	2559
	Roof	599	816	1066	1349	1599	1919	2239	2559
11	Floor	352	559	835	1190	1515	1919	2239	2559
	Roof	528	742	969	1227	1515	1919	2239	2559
12	Floor	296	470	702	999	1371	1919	2239	2559
	Roof	444	680	888	1124	1388	1919	2239	2559
13	Floor	252	400	598	852	1168	1846	2239	2559
	Roof	378	601	820	1038	1282	1846	2239	2559
14	Floor	217	345	515	734	1007	1714	2239	2559
	Roof	326	518	761	964	1190	1714	2239	2559
15	Floor	189	301	449	639	877	1517	2177	2559
	Roof	284	451	674	899	1111	1599	2177	2559
16	Floor	166	264	395	562	771	1333	2041	2559
	Roof	249	396	592	843	1041	1499	2041	2559
17	Floor	147	234	349	498	683	1181	1875	2509
	Roof	221	351	524	747	980	1411	1921	2509
18	Floor	131	209	312	444	609	1053	1672	2370
	Roof	197	313	468	666	914	1333	1814	2370

Actual Size, Not Nominal Size

TABLE III-5

BEAM DESIGN LOADS
(POUNDS PER INCH OF BEAM WIDTH)

DOUGLAS FIR CASE II, TWO POINT LOAD

Design Values: Table 6-1
Allowable Deflection:
  Floor: 1/360
  Roof: 1/240

CASE II
TWO POINTS LOAD

TABLE III-6

BEAM DESIGN LOADS
(POUNDS PER INCH OF BEAM WIDTH)

DOUGLAS FIR CASE III, ONE POINT LOAD

Design Values: Table 6-1
Allowable Deflection:
  Floor: 1/360
  Roof: 1/240

CASE III
ONE POINT LOAD

TABLE III-5 (Douglas Fir Case II, Two Point Load)

SPAN OF TIMBER (L) (feet)		DEPTH OF TIMBER (d)* (inches)							
		6	7	8	9	10	12	14	16
6	Floor	750	1020	1279	1439	1599	1919	2239	2559
	Roof	750	1020	1279	1439	1599	1919	2239	2559
7	Floor	638	875	1142	1439	1599	1919	2239	2559
	Roof	642	875	1142	1439	1599	1919	2239	2559
8	Floor	489	765	1000	1265	1562	1919	2239	2559
	Roof	562	765	1000	1265	1562	1919	2239	2559
9	Floor	386	613	888	1125	1388	1919	2239	2559
	Roof	500	680	888	1125	1388	1919	2239	2599
10	Floor	313	497	742	1012	1250	1800	2239	2559
	Roof	450	612	800	1012	1250	1800	2239	2559
11	Floor	258	410	613	873	1136	1636	2227	2559
	Roof	388	556	727	920	1136	1636	2227	2559
12	Floor	217	345	515	733	1006	1500	2041	2559
	Roof	326	510	666	843	1041	1500	2041	2559
13	Floor	185	294	439	625	857	1384	1884	2461
	Roof	277	441	615	778	961	1384	1884	2461
14	Floor	159	253	378	539	739	1277	1750	2285
	Roof	239	380	567	723	892	1285	1750	2285
15	Floor	139	220	329	469	644	1113	1633	2133
	Roof	208	331	494	675	833	1200	1633	2133
16	Floor	122	194	289	412	566	978	1531	2000
	Roof	183	291	434	619	781	1125	1531	2000
17	Floor	108	172	256	365	501	866	1376	1882
	Roof	162	258	385	548	735	1058	1441	1882
18	Floor	96	153	229	326	447	772	1227	1777
	Roof	144	230	343	489	670	1000	1361	1777

TABLE III-6 (Douglas Fir Case III, One Point Load)

SPAN OF TIMBER (L) (feet)		DEPTH OF TIMBER (d)* (inches)							
		6	7	8	9	10	12	14	16
6	Floor	499	680	888	1124	1388	1919	2239	2559
	Roof	499	680	888	1124	1388	1919	2239	2559
7	Floor	428	583	761	964	1190	1714	2239	2559
	Roof	428	583	761	964	1190	1714	2239	2559
8	Floor	374	510	666	843	1041	1499	2041	2559
	Roof	374	510	666	843	1041	1499	2041	2559
9	Floor	329	453	592	749	925	1333	1814	2370
	Roof	333	453	592	749	925	1333	1814	2370
10	Floor	266	408	533	674	833	1199	1633	2133
	Roof	299	408	533	674	833	1199	1633	2133
11	Floor	220	349	484	613	757	1090	1484	1939
	Roof	272	371	484	613	757	1090	1484	1939
12	Floor	185	294	438	562	694	999	1361	1777
	Roof	249	340	444	562	694	999	1361	1777
13	Floor	157	250	374	519	641	923	1256	1641
	Roof	230	314	410	519	641	923	1256	1641
14	Floor	136	216	322	459	595	857	1166	1523
	Roof	204	291	380	482	595	857	1166	1523
15	Floor	118	188	280	399	548	799	1088	1422
	Roof	177	272	355	449	555	799	1088	1422
16	Floor	104	165	246	351	482	749	1020	1333
	Roof	156	248	333	421	520	749	1020	1333
17	Floor	92	146	218	311	427	705	960	1254
	Roof	138	219	313	397	490	705	960	1254
18	Floor	82	130	195	277	381	658	907	1185
	Roof	123	196	292	374	462	666	907	1185

*Actual Size, Not Nominal Size

TABLE III-7

BEAM DESIGN LOADS
(POUNDS PER INCH OF BEAM WIDTH)

SPRUCE CASE I, UNIFORM LOAD

Design Values: Table 6-1
Allowable Deflection:
  Floor: 1/360
  Roof: 1/240

CASE I
UNIFORM LOAD

SPAN OF TIMBER (L) (feet)		DEPTH OF TIMBER (d)* (inches)							
		6	7	8	9	10	12	14	16
6	Floor	799	933	1066	1199	1333	1599	1866	2133
	Roof	799	933	1066	1199	1333	1599	1866	2133
7	Floor	653	933	1066	1199	1333	1599	1866	2133
	Roof	685	933	1066	1199	1333	1599	1866	2133
8	Floor	499	793	1066	1199	1333	1599	1800	2133
	Roof	599	816	1066	1199	1333	1599	1866	2133
9	Floor	395	627	936	1199	1333	1599	1866	2133
	Roof	533	725	948	1199	1333	1599	1866	2133
10	Floor	319	508	750	1079	1333	1599	1866	2133
	Roof	479	653	853	1079	1333	1599	1866	2133
11	Floor	264	419	626	892	1212	1599	1866	2133
	Roof	396	593	775	981	1212	1599	1866	2133
12	Floor	222	352	526	749	1028	1599	1866	2133
	Roof	333	529	711	899	1111	1599	1866	2133
13	Floor	189	300	448	639	876	1476	1866	2133
	Roof	284	451	656	830	1025	1476	1866	2133
14	Floor	163	259	386	551	755	1306	1866	2133
	Roof	244	388	580	771	952	1371	1866	2133
15	Floor	142	225	337	479	658	1137	1742	2133
	Roof	213	338	505	719	888	1279	1742	2133
16	Floor	124	198	296	421	578	999	1587	2133
	Roof	187	297	444	632	833	1199	1633	2133
17	Floor	110	175	262	373	512	885	1406	2007
	Roof	166	263	393	560	768	1129	1537	2007
18	Floor	98	156	234	333	457	790	1254	1872
	Roof	148	235	351	499	685	1066	1451	1896

TABLE III-8

BEAM DESIGN LOADS
(POUNDS PER INCH OF BEAM WIDTH)

SPRUCE CASE II, TWO POINT LOAD

Design Values: Table 6-1
Allowable Deflection:
  Floor: 1/360
  Roof: 1/240

CASE II
TWO POINTS LOAD

SPAN OF TIMBER (L) (feet)		DEPTH OF TIMBER (d)* (inches)							
		6	7	8	9	10	12	14	16
6	Floor	600	816	1066	1199	1333	1599	1866	2133
	Roof	600	816	1066	1199	1333	1599	1866	2133
7	Floor	479	700	914	1157	1333	1599	1866	2133
	Roof	514	700	914	1157	1333	1599	1866	2133
8	Floor	366	582	800	1012	1250	1599	1866	2133
	Roof	450	612	800	1012	1250	1599	1866	2133
9	Floor	289	460	687	900	1111	1599	1866	2133
	Roof	400	544	711	900	1111	1599	1866	2133
10	Floor	234	372	556	792	1000	1440	1866	2133
	Roof	352	490	640	810	1000	1440	1866	2133
11	Floor	194	308	459	654	898	1309	1781	2133
	Roof	291	445	581	736	909	1309	1781	2133
12	Floor	163	258	386	550	754	1200	1633	2133
	Roof	244	388	533	675	833	1200	1633	2133
13	Floor	138	220	329	468	643	1107	1507	1969
	Roof	208	330	492	623	769	1107	1507	1969
14	Floor	119	190	283	404	554	958	1400	1828
	Roof	179	285	425	578	714	1028	1400	1828
15	Floor	104	165	247	352	483	834	1306	1706
	Roof	156	248	371	528	666	960	1306	1706
16	Floor	91	145	217	309	424	733	1165	1600
	Roof	137	218	326	464	625	900	1225	1600
17	Floor	81	129	192	274	376	649	1032	1505
	Roof	121	193	288	411	564	847	1152	1505
18	Floor	72	115	171	244	335	579	920	1374
	Roof	108	172	257	366	503	800	1088	1422

*Actual Size, Not Nominal Size

TABLE III-9

BEAM DESIGN LOADS
(POUNDS PER INCH OF BEAM WIDTH)

SPRUCE CASE III, ONE POINT LOAD

Design Values: Table 6 1
Allowable Deflection:
Floor: 1/360
Roof: 1/240

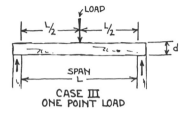

CASE III
ONE POINT LOAD

SPAN OF TIMBER (L) (feet)		DEPTH OF TIMBER (d)* (inches)							
		6	7	8	9	10	12	14	16
6	Floor	399	544	711	899	1111	1599	1866	2133
	Roof	399	544	711	899	1111	1599	1866	2133
7	Floor	342	466	609	771	952	1371	1866	2133
	Roof	342	466	609	771	952	1371	1866	2133
8	Floor	299	408	533	674	833	1199	1633	2133
	Roof	299	408	533	674	833	1199	1633	2133
9	Floor	246	362	474	599	740	1066	1451	1896
	Roof	266	362	474	599	740	1066	1451	1896
10	Floor	199	317	426	539	666	959	1306	1706
	Roof	239	326	426	539	666	959	1306	1706
11	Floor	165	262	387	490	606	872	1187	1551
	Roof	218	296	387	490	606	872	1187	1551
12	Floor	138	220	329	449	555	799	1088	1422
	Roof	199	272	355	449	555	799	1088	1422
13	Floor	118	187	280	399	512	738	1005	1312
	Roof	177	251	328	415	512	738	1005	1312
14	Floor	102	162	241	344	472	685	933	1219
	Roof	153	233	304	385	476	685	933	1219
15	Floor	88	141	210	299	411	639	871	1137
	Roof	133	211	284	359	444	639	871	1137
16	Floor	78	124	185	263	361	599	816	1066
	Roof	117	186	266	337	416	599	816	1066
17	Floor	69	109	164	233	320	553	768	1003
	Roof	103	164	246	317	392	564	768	1003
18	Floor	61	98	146	208	285	493	725	948
	Roof	92	147	219	299	370	533	725	948

TABLE III-10

BEAM DESIGN LOADS
(POUNDS PER INCH OF BEAM WIDTH)

PINE CASE I, UNIFORM LOAD

Design Values: Table 6-1
Allowable Deflection:
Floor: 1/360
Roof: 1/240

CASE I
UNIFORM LOAD

SPAN OF TIMBER (L) (feet)		DEPTH OF TIMBER (d)* (inches)							
		6	7	8	9	10	12	14	16
6	Floor	599	746	853	959	1066	1279	1493	1706
	Roof	599	746	853	959	1066	1279	1493	1706
7	Floor	514	699	853	959	1066	1279	1493	1706
	Roof	514	699	853	959	1066	1279	1493	1706
8	Floor	416	612	799	959	1066	1279	1493	1706
	Roof	449	612	799	959	1066	1279	1493	1706
9	Floor	329	522	711	899	1066	1279	1493	1706
	Roof	399	544	711	899	1066	1279	1493	1706
10	Floor	266	423	632	809	999	1279	1493	1706
	Roof	359	489	639	809	999	1279	1493	1706
11	Floor	220	349	522	736	909	1279	1493	1706
	Roof	327	445	581	736	909	1279	1493	1706
12	Floor	185	294	438	624	833	1199	1493	1706
	Roof	277	408	533	674	833	1199	1493	1706
13	Floor	157	250	374	532	730	1107	1493	1706
	Roof	236	375	492	623	769	1107	1493	1706
14	Floor	136	216	322	459	629	1028	1399	1706
	Roof	204	324	457	578	714	1028	1399	1706
15	Floor	118	188	280	399	548	948	1306	1706
	Roof	177	282	421	539	666	959	1306	1706
16	Floor	104	165	246	351	482	833	1224	1599
	Roof	156	248	370	506	624	899	1224	1599
17	Floor	92	146	218	311	427	738	1152	1505
	Roof	138	219	328	467	588	847	1152	1505
18	Floor	82	130	195	277	381	658	1045	1422
	Roof	123	196	292	416	555	799	1088	1422

*Actual Size, Not Nominal Size

TABLE III-11

BEAM DESIGN LOADS
(POUNDS PER INCH OF BEAM WIDTH)

PINE CASE II, TWO POINT LOAD

Design Values: Table 6-1
Allowable Deflection:
Floor: 1/360
Roof: 1/240

SPAN OF TIMBER (L) (feet)		DEPTH OF TIMBER (d)* (inches)							
		6	7	8	9	10	12	14	16
6	Floor	450	612	800	959	1066	1279	1493	1706
	Roof	450	612	800	959	1066	1279	1493	1706
7	Floor	385	525	685	867	1066	1279	1493	1706
	Roof	385	525	685	867	1066	1279	1493	1706
8	Floor	305	459	600	759	937	1279	1493	1706
	Roof	337	459	600	759	937	1279	1493	1706
9	Floor	241	383	533	675	833	1200	1493	1706
	Roof	300	408	533	675	833	1200	1493	1706
10	Floor	195	310	463	607	750	1080	1470	1706
	Roof	270	367	480	607	750	1080	1470	1706
11	Floor	161	256	383	545	681	981	1336	1706
	Roof	242	334	436	552	681	981	1336	1706
12	Floor	135	215	322	458	625	900	1225	1600
	Roof	203	306	400	506	625	900	1225	1600
13	Floor	115	183	274	390	535	830	1130	1476
	Roof	173	275	369	467	576	830	1130	1476
14	Floor	99	158	236	336	462	771	1050	1371
	Roof	145	237	342	433	535	771	1050	1371
15	Floor	86	138	206	293	402	695	980	1280
	Roof	130	207	309	405	500	720	980	1280
16	Floor	76	121	181	257	353	611	918	1200
	Roof	114	182	271	379	468	675	918	1200
17	Floor	67	107	160	228	313	541	860	1129
	Roof	101	161	240	342	441	635	864	1129
18	Floor	60	95	143	203	279	483	767	1066
	Roof	90	143	214	305	416	600	816	1066

TABLE III-12

BEAM DESIGN LOADS
(POUNDS PER INCH OF BEAM WIDTH)

PINE CASE III, ONE POINT LOAD

Design Values: Table 6-1
Allowable Deflection:
Floor: 1/360
Roof: 1/240

SPAN (L) (feet)		6	7	8	9	10	12	14	16
6	Floor	299	408	533	674	833	1199	1493	1706
	Roof	299	408	533	674	833	1199	1493	1706
7	Floor	257	349	457	578	714	1028	1399	1706
	Roof	257	349	457	578	714	1028	1399	1706
8	Floor	224	306	399	506	624	899	1224	1599
	Roof	224	306	399	506	624	899	1224	1599
9	Floor	199	272	355	449	555	799	1088	1422
	Roof	199	272	355	449	555	799	1088	1422
10	Floor	166	244	319	404	499	719	979	1279
	Roof	179	244	319	404	499	719	979	1279
11	Floor	137	218	290	368	454	654	890	1163
	Roof	163	222	290	368	454	654	890	1163
12	Floor	115	183	266	337	416	599	816	1066
	Roof	149	204	266	337	416	599	816	1066
13	Floor	98	156	233	311	384	553	753	984
	Roof	138	188	246	311	384	553	753	984
14	Floor	85	135	201	286	357	514	699	914
	Roof	127	174	228	289	357	514	699	914
15	Floor	74	117	175	249	333	479	653	853
	Roof	111	163	213	269	333	479	653	853
16	Floor	65	103	154	219	301	449	612	799
	Roof	97	153	199	253	312	449	612	799
17	Floor	57	91	136	194	266	423	576	752
	Roof	86	137	188	238	294	423	576	752
18	Floor	51	81	121	173	238	399	544	711
	Roof	77	122	177	224	277	399	544	711

*Actual Size, Not Nominal Size

205

GLOSSARY

ADZE. An axelike tool with its blade at right angles to its handle, used to shape or dress timbers.

ANCHOR BEAM. Major tying beam. Joined to post with shouldered through-tenon, wedged from the opposite side.

ANCHOR BOLT. A bolt protruding from the top of the foundation onto which the sill plate is fastened with a nut.

AUGER. A tool for boring holes in wood.

BACKFILLING. Replacing excavated soil around a foundation.

BAY. Space between two bents.

BEAM. A main horizontal member in a building's frame.

BEETLE. A large wooden mallet typically weighing fifteen to twenty pounds. A maul.

BENT. Structural network of timbers or a truss that makes up one cross-sectional piece of the frame.

BIRD'S MOUTH. A V-shaped notch that resembles a bird's open beak. It is cut into the base of a rafter and received by the plate.

BORING MACHINE. A hand-operated device with gears that drive an auger bit for boring large holes.

BRACED FRAME. Timber frame.

BRESSUMER. English term for a beam supporting an upper wall of timber framing.

BROADAXE. A type of axe that has an unusually wide blade beveled only on one side, with an offset handle. Used to hew timbers from logs. A side axe.

BUCKLING. Bending of a timber as a result of a compressive force along its axis.

CANTILEVER BEAM. A projecting timber that supports an overhang.

CARRYING STICKS. Sticks placed under a timber to provide an easy hand hold for carrying. Typically, two carrying sticks and four people are needed to carry a timber in this way.

CHAMFER. A simple bevel done for embellishment of a timber.

CHECKS. Separation of wood fibers following the direction of the rays. Caused by the tension of uneven drying.

CIRCULAR SAW. Power saw with circular saw blade.

COLLAR PURLIN. Horizontal longitudinal beam supporting collar ties.

COLLAR TIE. Horizontal connector between a pair of rafters used to reduce sagging or spreading of rafters.

COMBINATION SQUARE. A tool that can be used to lay out 45-degree or 90-degree angles. The stop is adjustable along the blade for use as a depth gauge.

COME-ALONG. A hand-operated ratchet winch. Used for pulling joints together, as a safety tie when raising a bent, and for pulling the frame together during the raising.

COMMON RAFTERS. Closely and regularly spaced inclined timbers that support the roof covering. Independent of bent system (see principal rafters).

COMPRESSION. Caused by a pressing or crushing type of force.

CONDUCTION. A movement of heat through a material.

CONVECTION. The transference of heat by circulation or movement.

CORNER CHISEL. A heavy-duty L-shaped chisel struck with a mallet. Used for cleaning out corners of a mortise.

CROSSCUT SAW. Saw designed to cut across the grain.

CROWN OF TIMBER. Convex side of timber.

CROWN POST. Central vertical post of a roof truss that connects the bent plate or girt to the collar tie or collar purlin.

CRUCK. Primitive truss formed by two main timbers, usually curved, set up as an arch or inverted V. Each half of the cruck is called a blade, and a pair is often cut from the same tree.

CRUSHING. A compressive failure. Permanent deformation resulting from compression.

DEAD LOAD. Weight of building (roof, floors, walls, etc.).

DEPTH. The vertical thickness of a beam.

DIAGONAL GRAIN. Grain that is other than parallel to the length of a timber. This will greatly reduce the strength of a timber.

DIMENSIONAL LUMBER. Planed lumber that is sold according to its nominal size.

DISC SANDER. Circular-action power sander.

DOVETAIL. A tenon that is shaped like a dove's spread tail to fit into a corresponding mortise.

DRAW KNIFE. A knife blade with handles on both ends so that the knife can be pulled by both hands toward the user.

DRIFT HOOK. Drift pin.

DRIFT PIN. Used to pin joints temporarily when test-assembling a frame.

DROP. Ornamental pendant. The tear-shaped termination to the lower ends of the second-story post of a framed overhang. Also known as a pendill.

EXCESSIVE BENDING AND DEFLECTION. Values of allowable bending of timbers within a frame that have been established by building codes. Anything greater than these values is considered excessive.

FIBER FAILURE. Failure from tension in the lower fibers of a timber.

FRAMING CHISEL. A heavy-duty chisel typically with one-and-one-half- to two-inch-wide blade. Designed to be used with a mallet.

FRAMING SQUARE. Also called a steel square. L-shaped metal tool used for laying out joinery. It has a body twenty-four inches long and two inches in width, and a tongue sixteen inches by one and one-half inches.

GABLE ROOF. A double-sloping roof that forms an A-shape.

GAMBREL ROOF. A double-pitched roof with the lower slope steeper than the upper slope.

GIRDER. Major timber that spans between sills.

GIRT. Major horizontal timber that connects posts.

GREEN WOOD. Wood freshly cut that is not dried or seasoned.

GUNSTOCK POST. A post wider at the top than the bottom. The wider portion provides more wood for intersecting joinery.

HALF DOVETAIL. A dovetail tapered only on one side.

HALF LAP. A joint in which the two timbers are lapped or let-in to each other.

HALF-TIMBERED FRAME. An ancient building system in which the space between the timbers is filled with brick, plaster, or wattle and daub, so that the timbers are revealed to the exterior and to the interior of the building. The wattle was a framework of woven withes covered by layers of daub consisting of clay, lime, horsehair, and cow dung.

HALVING. The removal of half the depth of two timbers in order that they may cross each other. A half lap.

HAMMER BEAM. A roof bracket projecting from the top of the wall that supports a roof truss. The design creates a large roof span with relatively short timbers.

HARDWOOD. Wood of certain deciduous trees, e.g., oak, maple, ash, etc.

HOOK PIN. Drift pin.

HOUSING. The shallow mortise or cavity for receiving the major part of a timber end. Usually coupled with a smaller deep mortise to receive a tenon for tying the joint.

JOINERY. The art or craft of connecting timbers using woodworking joints.

JOINT. The connection of two or more timbers.

JOISTS. Small, parallel timbers that complete the floor frame.

KERFING. Either a series of cuts with a circular saw set at a desired depth to remove a section of wood or the hand-sawing along the shoulder of an assembled joint to improve the fit of the joint.

KEYWAY. A joint between the footing and foundation wall.

KING POST. A central, vertical post extending from the bent plate or girt to the junction of the rafters.

KNEE BRACE. A small timber that is framed diagonally between a post and a beam.

LAYOUT. The drawing of a joint on a timber before it is cut.

LEAN-TO. A shed section of a building that is framed into the main frame.

LIVE LOAD. Weight due to occupancy of building (people, furnishings, etc.).

LOAD. Weight.

MALLET. A hardwood hammer weighing from one and one-half to two and one-half pounds. Used for driving a chisel.

MAUL. Beetle.

MAXIMUM ALLOWABLE FIBER STRESS IN BENDING. Safe design standard for fiber stress.

MAXIMUM ALLOWABLE HORIZONTAL SHEAR STRESS. Safe design standard for shear stress.

MODULUS OF ELASTICITY. A measure of rigidity of a material. The ratio of stress (force per area) to strain (deformation).

MOMENT. The product of force times distance from which it acts. This causes a beam to bend.

MOMENT OF INERTIA. A property that reflects the strength of a timber dependent upon the size and shape of its cross section.

MORTISE. A groove or slot into which or through which a tenon is inserted.

MORTISE-AND-TENON JOINT. Any joint in which a projection on one end of a timber is inserted into a groove or slot in another timber.

NOMINAL SIZE. Undressed dimension of lumber. For example, lumber with a nominal size of two inches by four inches will have an actual size of about one and one-half inches by three and one-half inches.

OVERALL LENGTH. Total length of timber including length of tenons on either end.

OVERHANG. Projection of second story beyond the first.

PEG. A wooden dowel one to one and one-half inches in diameter, usually of oak or locust.

PIKE POLE. A long pole pointed with a sharpened spike used for raising frames. These tools were known as early as the fifteenth century, when they were called "butters."

PIN. Small peg.

PLATES. Major horizontal timbers that support the base of the rafters.

PLUMB. Vertical.

POST. Vertical or upright timber.

POST-AND-BEAM FRAME. Timber frame.

POWER HAND PLANER. A hand-held planer with rotating cutting blades. Used for finishing surfaces of rough-sawn timbers.

PRINCIPAL RAFTERS. A pair of inclined timbers that are framed into a bent.

PURLINS. Horizontal timbers that connect rafter trusses.

PYTHAGOREAN THEOREM. For a right triangle, the sum of the squares of the sides is equal to the square of the hypotenuse.
$$a^2 + b^2 = c^2$$
Used in calculating rafter and knee-brace lengths.

QUEEN POST. A pair of vertical posts of a roof truss standing on the bent plate or girt and supporting the rafters or collar tie.

RACK. The action of straining or winching a frame to bring it into square or plumb.

RAFTER FEET. The lower ends of the rafters that are framed into the plate.

RAFTER PEAK. The point where the tops of the rafters meet.

RAISING THE FRAME. Erecting the bents and roof trusses and joining and pegging the other timbers to the frame.

REACTION. A force pushing up in response to a load.

REARING THE FRAME. English term. Equivalent to "raising the frame."

RIDGEPOLE. A horizontal timber at the peak of the roof to which the rafters are attached.

RIP SAW. Saw designed to cut parallel to grain.

ROOF PITCH. Inches of rise per foot of run. For example, a 45-degree roof has twelve inches of rise for each foot of run and is therefore called a "twelve pitch" roof.

ROOF TRUSS. A structural network of timbers that form a rigid structure to support the roof.

ROUTER. A power tool with rotating cutting blades used in timber framing for rounding or embellishing edges of timbers.

SCARF. A joint for splicing two timbers, end to end.

SCRIBE. To mark a timber by scratching a line with a sharp instrument; also to cut or shape a timber so that it fits the somewhat irregular surface of another.

SEASONED WOOD. Dried wood.

SHAKES. Separation of wood fibers that follow the curvature of the growth rings. Normally occurs during growth of the tree.

SHEAR FAILURE. Failure from shearing along the fibers of a timber.

SHEARING. A force causing slippage between layers.

SHEATHING. The covering of boards or of waterproof material on the outside wall of a house or on a roof.

SHED ROOF. A roof sloping in one direction.

SHIM. Thin tapered pieces of material such as a shingle. Used for leveling sill timbers.

SHOULDER OF TIMBER. Point of intersection at the joint of two assembled timbers. Refers to timber with tenon.

SHOULDER-TO-SHOULDER LENGTH. Length of timber between the shoulders of the two end joints. (The overall length minus length of end tenons.)

SILL TIMBERS. Horizontal timbers that rest upon the foundation.

SLICK. A chisel with a blade two and one-half or more inches in width. It is pushed by the hands instead of being struck with a mallet.

SOFFIT. The underside part of a building such as under a roof overhang.

SOFTWOOD. Wood primarily of a conifer or evergreen, e.g., pine, spruce, Douglas fir, etc.

SPAN. The shoulder-to-shoulder distance.

SPLITS. Complete separation of wood fibers.

SQUARING OFF. The process of drawing and cutting off one end of a timber so that the cut gives a plane surface perpendicular to the timber's length.

STICKERS. Spacers used between timbers or boards when stacking to provide air circulation. Also used to separate stacked bents for ease of working clamps, ropes, and come-alongs.

STRESS-SKIN PANEL. A sandwich of materials, containing two skins, one inside and one outside, and a core of insulation.

STRUT. A short timber placed in a structure either diagonally or vertically, designed to act in compression along the direction of its length.

STUB TENON. Tenon that stops within the timber it joins.

SUMMER BEAM. Major timber that spans between girts or plates.

TEMPLATE. A full-size pattern of thin material for laying out and checking joints.

TEMPORARY BRACING. Method of temporarily adding rigidity to a frame during the raising.

TENON. The projecting end of a timber that is inserted into a mortise.

TENSION. A force causing the tendency of extension. In timber framing, captured tension adds rigidity and strength.

THROUGH TENON. A tenon that passes through the timber it joins. It may extend past the mortise and be wedged from the opposite side.

TIMBER. A large squared or dressed piece of wood ready for fashioning as one member of a structure.

TIMBER FRAME. A frame of large timbers, joined and pegged together, supporting small timbers to which roof, walls, and floors are fastened. Same as braced frame.

TONGUE AND FORK. A type of joint in which one timber has the shape of a two-prong fork and the other a central tongue that fits between the prongs.

TRANSIT. A telescope set on a tripod used for leveling foundation or sill timbers.

TRUNNEL OR TREENAIL. A peg. Sometimes refers to an extra-large peg.

TRUSS. Assemblage of timbers forming a rigid framework. Example: A bent.

WALKING BEAMS. Two parallel beams laid on the ground used to assist moving timbers with a pivoting action.

WATER LEVEL. A flexible tube with glass ends, filled with water. Used for leveling foundation or sill timbers. A substitute for a transit.

WIDTH. The horizontal thickness of a beam, or thickness of a post.

WIND BRACE. English term. Equivalent to knee brace.

REFERENCES

Arthur, Eric and Dudley, Whitney. *The Barn*. Greenwich, Conn.: New York Graphic Society Publishers, Ltd., 1972.

Bronowski, Jacob. *The Ascent of Man*. London: British Broadcasting Corp., 1973.

Brown, Percy. *Indian Architecture*. Bombay: D. B. Taraporevala Sons and Co., 1942.

Bunker, B. *Cruck Buildings*. N. Sheffield, England: B. Bunker, 1970.

Burroughs, John. *In the Catskills*. Cambridge, Mass.: Houghton Mifflin, 1911.

———. *The Birds of John Burroughs: Keeping a Sharp Lookout*. New York: Hawthorn, 1976.

Clark, Kenneth. *Civilization*. New York: Harper & Row, 1969.

Cole, John and Wing, Charles. *From the Ground Up*. Boston: Little, Brown and Company, 1976.

Cummings, Abbott Lowell. *The Framed Houses of Massachusetts Bay, 1625–1725*. Cambridge: Harvard University Press, 1979.

Early Trades and Crafts Society. *Barn Builder's Words*. New York: Early Trades and Crafts Society, 1971.

Eccli, Eugene. *Low-Cost, Energy-Efficient Shelter*. Emmaus, Pa.: Rodale Press, Inc., 1975.

Fitch, James Marston. *American Building*. New York: Schocken, 1966.

Fitchen, J. *The New World Dutch Barn*. New York: Syracuse University Press, 1968.

Gardiner, Rena. *The Guildhall Lavenham, Suffolk*. Norwich, England: The National Trust, 1975.

Garner, T. and Stratton, A. *The Domestic Architecture of England During the Tudor Period*. London: B. T. Batsford Ltd., 1910.

Hansen, Hans Jurgen. *Architecture in Wood*. New York: Viking Press, Inc., 1971.

Hewett, Cecil Alec. *The Development of Carpentry 1200-1700, An Essex Study*. New Abbot, England: David and Charles Ltd., 1969.

Kellogg, Elijah. *The Ark*. Boston: Lee and Shepard, 1869.

———. *The Bay Farmers*. Boston: Lee and Shepard, 1869.

Kelly, Frederick J. *Early Domestic Architecture of Connecticut*. New York: Dover Publications, Inc., 1963.

Kern, Ken. *The Owner Built Home*. New York: Charles Scribner's Sons, 1972.

Oberg, Fred R. *Heavy Timber Construction*. Chicago: American Technical Society, 1972.

Ramsey, Charles and Sleeper, Harold. *Architectural Graphic Standards*. New York: John Wiley and Sons, Inc., 1956, 1970.

Reader's Digest Association. *Complete Do-It-Yourself Manual*. Pleasantville, N.Y.: Reader's Digest Association, Inc., 1973.

Roberts, Rex. *Your Engineered House*. New York: Evans and Co., Inc., 1964.

Ryder, G. H. *Strength of Materials*. London: MacMillan and Co. Ltd., 1969.

Seike, Kiyosi. *The Art of Japanese Joinery*. New York and Tokyo: John Weatherhill, Inc., 1977.

Siegele, H. H. *Roof Framing*. New York: Drake Publishers Inc., 1971.

Silvester, Frederick D. *Timber, Its Mechanical Properties and Factors Affecting Its Structural Use*. Oxford, England: Pergamon Press, 1967.

Sneller, Anne Gertrude. *A Vanished World*. Syracuse, N.Y.: Syracuse University Press, 1964.

Spencer, Harold. *Readings in Art History*. New York: Charles Scribner's Sons, 1976.

Sprague, Marshall. *Money Mountain*. Boston: Little, Brown, 1953.

Stein, Richard G. *Architecture and Energy*. New York and Garden City: Anchor Press, 1977.

U.S. Forest Products Laboratory. *Wood Handbook: Wood as an Engineering Material*. Washington, D.C.: U.S. Department of Agriculture, 1974.

Watson, Aldren A. *Country Furniture*. New York: Thomas Y. Crowell Co., 1974.

Williams, Henry L. and Williams, Ottalie K. *Old American Houses, 1700–1850*. New York: Bonanza Books, 1967.

Wigginton, Brooks Eliot. *The Foxfire Book*. Garden City, N.Y.: Anchor Press/Doubleday, 1972.

Wood, Margaret. *The English Mediaeval House*. London: Phoenix House, 1965.

Yarwood, D. *The English Home*. London: B. T. Batsford Ltd., 1956.

LIST OF PLATES